Alexander

# CIA

*a history*

# CIA

*a history*

John Ranelagh

BBC BOOKS

**To Richard Price**

Published by BBC Books,
a division of BBC Enterprises Limited,
Woodlands, 80 Wood Lane, London W12 0TT
First published 1992

ISBN 0 563 36250 2

Designed by David Robinson
Set in Garamond
Printed and bound in Great Britain by Butler & Tanner Ltd, Frome
Jacket printed by Lawrence Allen Ltd, Weston-super-Mare

**PICTURE CREDITS**
Camera Press 104, 135–139, 177; Courtesy CIA 2, 13; Hulton Picture Company 14, 21, 43, 76,
106–109, 129, 165, 181, 205; Popperfoto 32, 35, 46, 52, 81, 93, 97, 101, 114/115, 132, 210, 223,
224; Rex Features 60/61, 85, 151, 172/173, 203, 214–221, 229, 235; © 1992 Roger Ressmeyer-
Starlight 8, 158, 244; Sovfoto 64; TRH Pictures 94, 155; Wide World Photos 121, 153,
188–200, 232.

# Contents

# Acknowledgements

In writing this book I am enormously indebted to my old friend, Deirdre McMahon, who was a mine of ideas and helpfulness. Timothy Dickinson read and commented on my text, as always with generosity and great benefit to the author. My wife, Elizabeth, responded with gentleness to the roars and rants that came from behind the word processor. Michael Shaw at Curtis Brown was a constant support. Sue Howes juggled with the manuscript, retyping with nitroglycerine speed. To Hilary Lawson I owe gratitude for encouraging me to propose a television history of the agency, and pointing me towards BBC Bristol.

In Bristol, John Shearer, head of television, and then Daniel Wolf, head of television features, took up my proposal that we should make a documentary series on the CIA, and gave the idea their full support. Peter Salmon, who succeeded Daniel, adopted the project as his own, showing a paternal budgetary care. Bjørn Nilsen at NRK was instrumental in making the series happen: he telephoned me in September 1987 to say that he would join the effort, thus making the necessary coproduction possible. NRK was, throughout, steadfast. Nick Devatzes at Arts & Entertainment was strong in backing the project when other US broadcasters shied away, fearful of controversy. My friend, Richard Price, at Primetime threw his energy and enthusiasm behind the project and its writer from the outset, and every day since. Bob Shay at Primetime USA was an invaluable *consigliere*. Without these people, the series would not have happened.

I owe a great deal of my understanding to the friendships and conversations I have had over the years with John Bross, Lawrence Houston, Walter Pforzheimer, Samuel Halpern, Carleton Swift. The production team that helped to translate a story of the CIA to the television screen provided stimulus and great fun: Judy Andrews, Hannelore Brenner, George Carey, Carlos Carrasco, Marie Coyne, Toby Farrell, Tamara Holbol, Simon Holland, William Treharne Jones, Tim Jordan, John Kelly, Ian Kennedy, Roger Long, Peter Lunde, Julie Martingell, Bjørn Nilsen, Lawrence Simanowitz, Linda Stephens, Bjørn Tonnesen, Sandy Wadeson, James Walker, Kevin Waters, Andrew Weir. David Thaxton and Kevin Green contributed their superb knowledge of visual archive material, and history, to the project. My editors at BBC Books, Sheila Ableman and Martha Caute, were generous and wonderfully supportive. David Cottingham and David Robinson contributed their visual expertise. But while it is convention to say it, it is also no less a fact that the opinions and any inaccuracies in the following pages are mine alone.

John Ranelagh, Grantchester, May 1992

# Abbreviations

| | |
|---|---|
| AFL-CIO | American Federation of Labor-Congress of Industrial Organizations |
| ARVN | Army of the Republic of Vietnam |
| BfV | Bundesamt für Verfassungsschutz (Federal Office for the Protection of the Constitution) |
| BND | Bundesnachrichtendienst (West German foreign intelligence service) |
| CI | Counterintelligence |
| CIO | Congress of Industrial Organizations |
| COI | Coordinator of Information |
| CORDS | Civil Operations & Rural Development Support |
| DCI | Director of Central Intelligence |
| DDA | Deputy Director of Administration |
| DDI | Deputy Director of Intelligence |
| DDO | Deputy Director of Operations |
| DDP | Deputy Director of Plans |
| DDS&T | Deputy Director of Science & Technology |
| DIA | Defense Intelligence Agency |
| FBI | Federal Bureau of Investigation |
| G-2 | (Army Intelligence) |
| GRU | (Soviet Military Intelligence) |
| ICBM | Intercontinental Ballistic Missile |
| ICEX | Intelligence Coordination & Exploitation Operation |
| JCS | Joint Chiefs of Staff |
| KGB | (Soviet Secret Police and Intelligence) |
| MACV | Military Assistance Command, Vietnam |
| NIO | National Intelligence Officer |
| NKVD | (Soviet Secret Police and Intelligence – precursor of KGB) |
| NSA | National Security Agency |
| NSC | National Security Council |
| ONE | Office of National Estimates |
| OPC | Office of Policy Coordination |
| OSO | Office of Special Operations |
| OSS | Office of Strategic Services |
| PFIAB | President's Foreign Intelligence Advisory Board |
| R&A | Research and Analysis |
| SIS | Secret Intelligence Service |
| SLBM | Submarine-launched Ballistic Missile |

Divided into geographical and subject sections in an open plan area, the CIA's Watch and Alert Center is constantly manned to stay abreast of events around the world, and to flash news and warnings to decision makers in the US government.

# INTRODUCTION

*D*uring the early years of the Central Intelligence Agency, its strength lay in its people and their contacts, rather than in the power of the organization. Its people were a self-confident élite and proud of it; certain of the part they would play in a great democracy which was at last beginning to take its international role seriously.

The mystique of the CIA had a magnetic attraction for potential recruits. Ray Cline, who like so many of the founders of the agency served in the Office of Strategic Services – the wartime precursor of the CIA – and was a senior CIA officer, recalled that there was a 'romantic atmosphere of adventure that no amount of disclaimer could deflate', although the reality was more prosaic:

> It made no difference: exceptionally bright men and women fresh from high school or college flocked to take jobs, no different from those in the Pentagon or other civil service organizations ... because the work often dealt with important events and glamorous faraway places.[1]

Clandestine operations were particularly attractive. William Colby, who also served in the OSS and became Director of Central Intelligence in the mid-1970s, evoked the peculiar atmosphere and dangers of that hermetic, secretive milieu, noting how easy it was for those involved in covert activities to drop out of the real world:

> [They formed] a sealed fraternity ... They ate together ... they partied almost only among themselves ... so their defenses did not always have to be up. In this way they increasingly separated themselves from the ordinary world and developed a rather skewed view of that world. Their own dedicated double life became the proper norm ... And out of this grew ...

an inbred, distorted élitist view of intelligence that held it to be above the normal processes of society.[2]

The first generation of senior CIA people came mainly from the prestigious Ivy League colleges and the east coast establishment. More junior staff members tended to come from such places as the City College of New York, New York University, Fordham, the University of Michigan, and the University of California's Los Angeles campus. As an institution recruiting among people who were keenly aware of the Depression, the agency could attract talent even at relatively low government pay levels. In 1950 the CIA had a staff of about 5000 who came from backgrounds that were broadly OSS, FBI and the military services and included lawyers, academics, public relations people and journalists.

Over the next five years there was a huge expansion of the agency in the aftermath of the Korean War (1950–3) and by 1955 it employed approximately 15,000 people. A report on the agency commissioned by Eisenhower in 1954 gave a revealing insight into agency recruitment. Men composed 58 per cent of CIA staff; the average age of a CIA officer was 34.2 years and two-thirds of the staff were in the 25–39 year age bracket. When it came to education, 68 per cent were high school graduates, 47 per cent had BA or equivalent degrees, and 24 per cent had done postgraduate work. In addition, 73 per cent had some foreign language training.

Since then, the CIA's full-time staff has remained between 15,000 and 20,000. There are others who are freelance contract workers. Recruitment came under closer scrutiny in 1967. By then the agency's people had shifted from the east coast to the mid-west universities and to the armed services, but there was a noticeable lack of blacks and women. Of 12,000 non-clerical CIA employees, there were fewer than twenty blacks in 1967 and efforts to recruit more proved unsuccessful.[3] Since then, the agency has been successful in recruiting blacks and women, but it has never had a large number of either at its senior levels. In 1981 the agency was sued by a woman staff member with thirty-six years' service who claimed that she and 500 other female staff had been consistently discriminated against.[4]

There is one category of recruit, however, which the CIA has been determined not to employ: homosexuals. In the 1950s the risks of blackmail were enormous and so the agency's reluctance was understandable. There was also the unsavoury aftertaste of the Burgess-Maclean-Philby affair – British traitors of the 1940s and early 1950s – in which homosexuality, alcohol, and treachery were inextricably linked. But even when sexual attitudes and the law became more permissive, the CIA would not relent. In 1983, when an aerospace worker was sacked after he disclosed his homosexuality in a routine security check, the CIA guidelines on sexual conduct appeared to suggest that homosexuality was a 'personality disorder'.[5]

In the late 1960s and 1970s, after the traumas of Vietnam and Watergate and the CIA scandals revealed by the Church Committee set up by Congress to investigate the agency in the mid-1970s, recruitment at American universities was often difficult, if not impossible. By 1985, however, as the careers officer at Stanford University noted, there had been a 'pretty dramatic change . . . Ten years ago the CIA wouldn't have been able to stay on the campus. There would have been a big demonstration against their presence.' In 1985 the agency launched a recruiting drive which attracted record numbers of applicants: 150,000. This figure was even more astonishing since it coincided with the 'yuppy' phenomenon and occurred at a time when government service seemed a less rewarding career choice than banking and the law. Another careers officer, this time at the University of Southern California, explained the resurgence in popularity of a CIA career: 'The CIA can offer graduates a fairly independent job with a high degree of responsibility – and they can become specialists within two or three years.'[6]

The agency stresses these qualities in its advertisements:

You're a bright, self-reliant, self-motivated person we need to help us gather information and put together a meaningful picture of what's happening in the world. One of an élite corps of men and women. You rely on your wits, your initiative and your skills. And, in return, enjoy recognition, positions of responsibility, life in foreign places, plus knowing that you belong to a small, very special group of people doing a vital, meaningful job in the face of challenges and possible hardship.

## WORKING FOR THE CIA

When recruits enter the agency today, they become career trainees for a two-year period. The first year consists of formal training in which the trainees are instructed in the importance of security, the organization of the agency and the wider intelligence community, and the policies of the agency and the government. Light weapons training and instruction in basic espionage techniques such as bugging, surveillance and interrogation, are also available. The second year of on-the-job training depends on which directorate the trainee is assigned to. Today there are four directorates: operations – DDO (which used to be called plans – DDP); intelligence – DDI; administration – DDA, and science and technology – DDS&T – which was set up in 1962.

Approximately half of the CIA's employees are engaged in clerical, secretarial and routine administrative duties. They can tell their friends for whom they work but they can't discuss the work they do. The CIA may be the world's most public secret intelligence service, but security is tight. For example, the agency's telephone book is kept deliberately incomplete so that no overall view of who works for the agency is possible; the book is also changed every six months. Personal notices on the bulletin board contain only names and telephone extension numbers.

The agency has a well-earned reputation for looking after its employees. It has its own credit union, home and car insurance services; there are well-organized extra-mural activities and opportunities for further education. The agency has its own health scheme with doctors and psychiatrists cleared by the agency. Given the stresses of the job, nervous breakdowns are not unusual and as a result do not carry the same stigma as may be the case elsewhere in government or business.

## LANGLEY

The headquarters of the agency is at Langley in Virginia, eight miles from the White House in Washington DC. It is a huge glass and concrete structure which for years has been a useful landmark for pilots flying into Washington's National Airport. It was built in 1961 and soon was bursting at the seams. In 1982 a $46 million extension was approved so that the agency could re-assemble on one site the various sections which had to be boarded out in nearby towns and suburbs.

The sprawling layout of Langley makes it a difficult place to work. It aggravates the problems of compartmentalization and coordination within the agency. It is not just bureaucratic rivalry which is involved, it is the sheer physical difficulties of contacting a particular office, of knowing the geography of the agency and of the corridors of Langley itself. The architects who designed the original headquarters building were never told the exact number of people they had to build for, and the consequence was a building which never suited the occupants. One particular CIA officer remembered that he had been working for four years

IN HONOR OF THOSE MEMBERS
OF THE CENTRAL INTELLIGENCE AGENCY
WHO GAVE THEIR LIVES IN THE SERVICE OF THEIR COUNTRY

In the main hall of the CIA's headquarters at Langley, Virginia, stars mark the deaths on active service of CIA officers since the founding of the agency in 1947.

at the agency before he ever set eyes on the legendary head of counterintelligence, James Jesus Angleton. It was a further fourteen years when, by then a division chief, he was actually introduced to him.

On the marble walls of the main lobby at Langley fifty small stars are carved, each one representing a CIA officer who has died in the service of the agency. The most recent belongs to William Buckley, the CIA station chief in Beirut, who was kidnapped and brutally tortured in the Lebanon in 1984. It is a chilling reminder that the CIA, for all its amenities and its leafy headquarters, its academics and researchers, is in the brutal world of secret intelligence. 'And ye shall know the truth, and the truth shall make you free', the words of the Gospel of St John, are also carved into the wall of the main lobby, reminding every one of the CIA people who stream in and out each day that a basic function of intelligence is to discern the truth.

Drydock No. 1 at Pearl Harbor immediately after the Japanese attack on 7 December 1941. In the foreground are the destroyers USS Downes (left) and USS Cassin (right). Behind, the battleship USS Pennsylvania, 33,100 ton flagship of the US Pacific Fleet, suffered relatively light damage.

# 1
# **CREATION**
## *1941*

*T*hey took off at dawn. Forty-three Japanese fighter planes climbed for height and turned east. One hundred bombers and dive bombers followed. The six aircraft carriers continued their course, immediately preparing for the return of the airplanes and for the counterattack which they had to expect. The *Kido Butai* task force was completing its mission. In Washington DC the time was 11.25 a.m. on Sunday, 7 December 1941.

The day before, the translators and codebreakers of US naval intelligence had deciphered a long message to the Japanese Ambassador in Washington from Tokyo. It was in Japan's most secret code, 'Purple', and concluded that:

> The Japanese Government regrets to have to notify hereby the American Government that in view of the attitude of the American Government it cannot but consider that it is impossible to reach an agreement through further negotiations.

'This means war,' said President Franklin D. Roosevelt when he read the message on Saturday night. What Roosevelt did not know was where, or when, war would start.

A second, very short message followed, which was deciphered early on Sunday morning. It instructed the ambassador to deliver the first message at 1.00 p.m. Washington time on 7 December. A navy lieutenant commander, responsible for the US codebreaking, ran through the streets of Washington to the State Department with the decrypt at 10.30 a.m., an hour before *Kido Butai* launched its airplanes. He had realized the significance of the two messages and he was trying to warn his government. He had also checked the map and times, knew that 1.00 p.m. Washington time was 7.30 a.m. in Hawaii and dawn in the Philippines – traditional times for launching attacks.

At 1.25 p.m. Washington time – 7.55 a.m. in Hawaii – the first wave of *Kido Butai* airplanes began attacking Battleship Row in Pearl Harbor. Within minutes, eighteen ships of the US Pacific Fleet – including seven battleships[1] – had been sunk or seriously damaged, 183 airplanes destroyed, and 2375 sailors and soldiers and 68 civilians killed. The United States was at war with Japan.

The Central Intelligence Agency was established six years later in 1947 to prevent the United States being caught unprepared again. American wealth, might, and technology had won World War II, but lack of coordination and centralized analysis lay behind the failure to alert Pearl Harbor to a possible Japanese attack. All the information about Japanese plans and intentions had been available in Washington, but no one was in a position to put it all together properly. Richard Helms, who served in the Office of Strategic Services, the wartime US intelligence group under General 'Wild Bill' Donovan, and who became a founding member of the CIA and was its head from 1966 to 1973, said:

> It had become crystal clear to most people in this country that Pearl Harbor was not only a disaster, but a disaster that could have been prevented, because the material was available to the government in various places, which if put together and properly analyzed would have indicated that the Japanese intended to attack, and that then we would have been forewarned and we wouldn't have lost that fleet at Pearl Harbor.[2]

The surprise at Pearl Harbor was total. On the mainland, Lockheeds, the California aircraft company, flew all the airplanes they had in stock out into the desert for protection but, in the ensuing panic, subsequently forgot where some of them were hidden. Once the dust had settled, the questions and the recriminations erupted. Why had America been caught napping? Whose responsibility should it be to see that such a disastrous failure in intelligence would never happen again?

## WILLIAM DONOVAN

Pearl Harbor was a potent symbol of the complacency of American isolationism: its 'island state psychology' which bred such a dangerous illusion of invulnerability. David Bruce, one of the founding fathers of the Office of Strategic Services, observed after the war that foreign affairs had seemed 'infinitely remote and rather ridiculous'. Thus the impact of Pearl Harbor was shattering: 'a gigantic dissonant firebell in the night of our false security', as Bruce strikingly described it.[3]

Bruce's view was also shared by the army. During the Senate hearings on the National Security Bill which established the CIA in 1947, Lieutenant General Hoyt Vandenberg did not mince his words about pre-war attitudes:

> Before Pearl Harbor we did not have an intelligence service in this country comparable to that of Great Britain, or France, or Russia, or Germany, or Japan. We did not have one because the people of the United States would not accept it... There was a feeling that all that was necessary to win a war – if there ever were to be another war – was an ability to shoot straight... All intelligence is not sinister, nor is it an invidious type of work.[4]

Only twelve years before Pearl Harbor, in 1929, the then Secretary of State, Henry Stimson, had declared that 'Gentlemen do not read each other's mail'. Stimson then dissolved the Black Chamber, the small but successful code-breaking unit set up during World War I. After Pearl Harbor, the country realized the price it had paid for his gentlemanly reticence.

The Central Intelligence Agency was the brainchild of William Donovan, a smart, energetic New York lawyer with a penchant for action. Donovan had a remarkable career, as remarkable as the man himself. His grandparents had been impoverished and uneducated Irish immigrants, but Donovan was one of the first 'modern' Irish-Americans, more concerned with the interests and ideals of the new country than with the age-long battles of the old. Though he was brought up and remained a Catholic, he was a staunch member of the New York Republican Party in a city where to be Irish was synonymous with being a Democrat. Also, and unusually for an Irish-American, he was a firm anglophile.

Donovan had a heroic military record in the First World War in which he won the Distinguished Service Cross, the Distinguished Service Medal and the Medal of Honor. He was the most highly decorated American officer of the war. He established a successful Wall Street law practice and with his legal and Republican connections he had the entrée to the most influential political circles in New York and Washington.

As early as 1935 Donovan sensed that another war was likely and that America, for all its much-vaunted isolationism, would be unlikely to escape it. 'In the age of bullies we cannot afford to be a sissy', he told the American Legion. Donovan made frequent trips to Europe in the later 1930s and his incisive reports to the War Department attracted considerable attention and praise. As a result of these trips, Donovan became convinced of the need for better intelligence, a conviction he did his best to impress on the Roosevelt administration.

After Stimson closed down the Black Chamber in 1929, US intelligence consisted almost entirely of code-breaking units run by the armed services and the State Department. Such intelligence provided excellent information about military and diplomatic activity, but it was not good at revealing politics, strategy, and intentions. As the situation in the Far East and Europe deteriorated during the 1930s, the lack of good political intelligence became critical. But it took the start of war in Europe to spur Roosevelt and his advisers to act. In June 1940, Donovan accepted an invitation from the White House to go to Britain to assess morale and military capabilities and to study British intelligence and counterintelligence methods. Donovan's month-long visit during the anxious summer of 1940 marked the beginning of a long and close relationship between the American and British intelligence services.

## WILLIAM STEPHENSON

The CIA calls the British Secret Intelligence Service 'The Friends', while SIS calls the CIA 'The Cousins'. With no tradition of secret operations in the American political system, the men who formed the nucleus of America's first secret service, the OSS, drew heavily on the expertise of the British. Over the following decades the balance of the relationship was to change dramatically but, despite periodic troughs of suspicion and distrust, the strength of the bonds forged in wartime – intellectual, political, diplomatic, historic – was to endure.

Donovan's June 1940 mission had been suggested by William Stephenson who was in charge of SIS liaison with the FBI. He had identified Donovan, who campaigned for US entry into the war on the side of Britain and for a US intelligence agency, as the man most likely to have influence in US intelligence matters when, and if, a US agency was created.

Stephenson, of Scots-Canadian background, had a colourful career that compared to Donovan's. He had been a champion boxer, a World War I flying ace and was a millionaire financier. Stephenson and Donovan, nicknamed 'Little Bill' and 'Big Bill', became close friends. Donovan's anglophilia led to the suspicion in some Washington quarters, which intensified after the war, that he was unduly influenced by Stephenson and the British. But he was very much his own man.

When Donovan arrived in England in 1940, Colonel Stewart Menzies, head of SIS, made sure that he was thoroughly briefed by the highest sources. The American ambassador in London, Joseph Kennedy, had taken a panicky view of Britain's chances in the war. The British knew this, and were anxious to convince Roosevelt that Kennedy was wrong. Donovan met Churchill and members of the war cabinet and was shown the latest top secret military inventions, including radar. He was also briefed on British propaganda and psychological warfare methods.

When he returned to Washington, Donovan told the President and leading members of Congress that the British were determined to fight to the end, and would eventually win, but that victory would come sooner if the United States helped them with military aid. It was an overly optimistic judgement: Britain might have remained unoccupied, but alone could not have liberated Europe. Donovan, however, wanted the United States to enter the war against Germany: he considered that US power was necessary to destroy the Nazi evil.

The scale of American aid increased dramatically over the next six months. Roosevelt gave the British fifty destroyers in return for American rights to British bases in the Western hemisphere. He also returned a number of war planes ordered by the Air Force to the factories so that they could be resold to Britain instead. In March 1941 the Lend-Lease Act was passed which empowered the President to lend billions of dollars' worth of goods to countries he considered vital to the defence of the United States. It was a virtual declaration of economic warfare against the Axis. Donovan's role in helping to bring this about was gratefully acknowledged by the British who suggested that Donovan's appointment as Ambassador to Britain would be welcomed in place of Kennedy.[5]

Donovan returned to Britain in December 1940, this time for a more extended visit of three months. Stephenson advised London that if they were 'completely frank' with him, Donovan 'would contribute very largely to our obtaining all that we want from the United States'. The British paid for his trip (an indication of how close Donovan was to them) and arranged for Donovan to tour various war zones in the Mediterranean.[6]

When he returned to the USA in March 1941, Donovan's reports of his travels made a considerable impression within the Roosevelt administration and his influence increased accordingly. Treasury Secretary Henry Morgenthau, Jr, said that Donovan 'is the first man I have talked to that I would be willing to really back ... I think he knows more about the situation than anybody I have talked to by about a thousand per cent. And he is not discouraged'.[7] When Donovan talked with the President on 18 March, the consequences of their meeting were to be even more momentous. He told Roosevelt that he was now more than ever convinced of the vital necessity for centralized intelligence. Roosevelt told him to present a plan.

By the time Donovan presented his proposals on 26 April, news that a super intelligence agency was being planned had begun to circulate around the Washington bureaucracy. A battle began over the powers of the agency and who would control it: this was also to be a consistent thread in the history of the CIA.

## BATTLE FOR CENTRAL INTELLIGENCE

During his visit to Britain and to the British war zones in the Mediterranean, Donovan had been particularly impressed by the way the British had combined military special operations work with research, collection and analysis of intelligence information. The British were also dealing with areas that either they or their allies knew intimately whereas the US government, as Donovan was only too aware, was dismally unimaginative about the rest of the world after its long period of isolation.

The aspect of British intelligence organization which particularly impressed itself on Donovan was that it was responsible to the Prime Minister, not to Parliament. When he returned to America he was determined that if an American centralized intelligence agency was to be effective, it would have to be under the President's direct control. This would give it better protection from the machinations of other government departments, notably State, War and Navy.

Donovan was right to foresee opposition to his plans. The groundwork for some kind of centralized intelligence agency had already been prepared. In 1939, as war approached in Europe, an intelligence coordinating committee consisting of the FBI, the Office of Naval Intelligence and G-2 (Army intelligence) was set up to work out programmes for investigating foreign espionage and sabotage in the USA. This was a serious question: in 1915–17, during US neutrality in World War I, German agents had blown up American factories and munitions installations, and sought to sabotage ships and docks. By mid-1940 these agencies realized the necessity for coordinating undercover intelligence activities. Because of Washington rivalries, however, a centralized agency was not set up. Instead, Roosevelt divided the fields of espionage and counterespionage abroad: the FBI had the western hemisphere; the Navy had Asia and the Pacific rim; the Army

In 1941 William Donovan, America's first spymaster, visited neutral Ireland's Prime Minister, Eamon de Valera, in Dublin. It was one of many stops on a tour of Europe which Donovan undertook as President Roosevelt's personal representative. On his return, Donovan told Roosevelt that the United States should help Britain.

was responsible for Europe, Africa and the Panama Canal Zone. Hawaii was a joint Army-Navy area. In November 1940 the State Department set up a division of foreign activity correlation which concentrated on information about foreign visitors and political leaders.

The bureaucratic and political rivalries in Washington were – and are – the underpinning to the story of US intelligence. The US constitution, as a matter of policy, establishes three power groupings within the government: the presidency – the executive; Congress – the legislature; and the Federal judiciary – the judicial branch. Each one was devised so that it had to argue and joust with the other two for position and influence. The intention of the founding fathers of the United States in making these arrangements was to prevent any one element of the government becoming too powerful and able to suppress people's rights.

A second element in the Washington rivalries was the power of the military. Before Pearl Harbor, the United States military was very small, and did not have much clout in Congress. Americans saw themselves as a peace-loving nation, uninterested in military matters, isolated from the troubles of the world. So, in early 1941, the military was not able to generate powerful opposition to Donovan and Roosevelt over a centralized civilian intelligence agency. They tried to, because they considered that intelligence needed to be geared to military requirements, particularly in wartime. Donovan, in fact, accepted the justice of the military view and tried hard to show that he was not attempting to usurp their rights. But at all times he clung to the idea that US central intelligence should be civilian, as befitted a democracy, and for the practical reason that military types are not best suited to analysing foreign politics especially if an ideological conflict is involved.

A third element in the rivalries was the nature of President Roosevelt himself. He was a man of great courage, great charm, and great ruthlessness. As a matter of policy he constantly set people and institutions against each other. He did not like experts, and so disliked the idea of a professional intelligence corps. He created new organizations and posts all the time – a central intelligence agency would be just another in a long line – so as to provide more competition within the bureaucracy, and more patronage and choice for himself. In 1941, Donovan was one of three or four individuals who each thought they had the President's support for 'their' intelligence plans. Today, we speak of Donovan as the father of modern US intelligence because he had the vision and the stamina to see his plans through to success.

The division of intelligence responsibilities between the FBI, State, the Army and the Navy did not provide a solution to the problem of how to coordinate intelligence. The agencies appreciated this, but they also reacted with predictable hostility to the idea of any super-agency trespassing on their respective bailiwicks. Apart from the fact that each one felt it should be the predominant agency, the Army and the Navy especially resented any hint of civilian interference in military affairs. When the news of Donovan's plan began to circulate, Brigadier General Sherman Miles warned the Army Chief of Staff, General George Marshall, that from the standpoint of the War Department, such a move 'would appear to be very disadvantageous, if not calamitous'.[8]

Donovan's proposals, when finally presented on 26 April 1941, showed a wily appreciation of Washington power politics and manoeuvrings. Although Donovan wanted the new agency to be controlled by the President, who would also have discretion over its funds which should remain secret, he said that he did not envisage the new agency encroaching on the territory of the FBI, the Army or the Navy. He did not need to press for their territory: he knew it would come to him naturally once his agency began to operate.

The FBI and the military were quite right to fear that Donovan was seeking dominance in intelligence, and so they kept information from him. He did not know, for example, the extent to which naval intelligence had cracked Japanese codes. However, he was insistent that his agency should have responsibility for overseas intelligence work and that it should coordinate, classify and interpret for the President information from all sources. The agency would be involved in the interception and inspection of mail and cables; the interception of radio communication; the use of propaganda behind enemy lines, and the organization of active subversive operations in enemy countries. The final section of Donovan's report described the modus operandi of the British SIS, with its linking of foreign and domestic intelligence through the Prime Minister's private office, and used this as a model for how US intelligence should operate.[9]

Part of Donovan's report had been drafted by William Stephenson who wanted him to head the new agency. Donovan was initially reluctant as he still hoped to renew his military career in the event of war. Roosevelt pre-empted him. On 11 July he met Donovan in the Oval Office and appointed him Coordinator of Information. His instructions were to implement the proposals he had put forward. He was to act as the President's chief intelligence officer and was to coordinate the analysis and collection of information.

## COORDINATOR OF INFORMATION

The creation of the office of Coordinator of Information (COI) was a landmark in American government. It was the first peacetime, civilian, centralized intelligence agency and it was the result of an executive order. Although Congress could, through its financial powers and with sufficient majorities, effectively circumscribe the activities of the President and the agency – something which became commonplace in the 1970s – it was much more difficult to do this in the 1940s when the mystique of the presidency was much greater, and when there was a broad consensus in foreign policy. In any event, with war spreading in Europe and Asia, Congress did not object to the creation of the COI.

In 1941 the establishment of the COI was a sign of the enormous expansion of presidential power which took place during the war, and which Arthur Schlesinger, Jr, has described as 'the imperial presidency'. But more important still was its psychological significance: it was a retreat by the Roosevelt administration from the complacency of isolation. America First, which opposed intervention in the war, was at the height of its popular support. In May 1941, only 21 per cent of Americans questioned supported participation in the war. It was a measure of public opinion that the terms of the executive order setting up the COI were not released to the press at the time, as the White House wanted to avoid awkward questions about the President's intentions and expectations, and his use of his powers, although the United States was still not at war.

While Donovan had won the first round of the battle for centralized intelligence, this did nothing to dispel the distrust of the military and the FBI for an intelligence establishment that might not have limits. J. Edgar Hoover cherished particular animosity towards Donovan who in 1924, when he was Assistant Attorney General, had opposed Hoover's appointment as Director of the FBI. Hoover referred to the COI contemptuously as 'Roosevelt's folly' and made sure that it did not intrude on the FBI's South American area of operation (which at the time was seen as the United States' one long-term intelligence preoccupation). Military intelligence was more accommodating and gave the COI access to their undercover foreign intelligence agents and activities, not least because this took attention away from their real secret: codebreaking success.

Donovan devoted the first few months to laying the groundwork of administration and staffing. The military may have handed over their undercover operations but this magnanimous gesture was no more than academic. In July 1941, the United States was very sophisticated in the realm of private intelligence (banks; investment houses; law firms; international companies), but in the US government there were very few people who had even rudimentary espionage skills. Donovan turned to his Wall Street contacts, and to Stephenson and the British for advice. The British set up a training school in Canada for COI recruits and sent SIS officers on secondment to the COI. Donovan said later that Stephenson taught the COI everything it knew about foreign intelligence.

The relationship between British and American intelligence inevitably changed with the creation of the COI. The British were anxious not to upset Hoover and the FBI with whom they had strong connections; Donovan and the COI were naturally concerned to establish their independence and integrity, and did not wish to be seen as the tail on a British dog.

The basic problem for the British was that US institutions were improvised and did not mesh with the long-term nature of their British counterparts. The British needed the COI to be on their side, and powerful in Washington; the COI had to establish itself in Washington. In order to help establish the COI, the British gave Donovan secrets and intelligence opportunities, taking the risk that their sources and methods might be exposed. In trade-offs with the United States, the British always paid heavily. As soon as the COI and later the OSS began to find their feet, there were secrets which they were reluctant to divulge to their British allies. The debt to the British was deeply felt, but David Bruce, Donovan's liaison officer in London later in the war, emphasized that the COI/OSS were not subservient clones of British intelligence:

As our armies, air forces and fleets began to fight abroad, our operational intelligence developed rapidly and successfully. American Army and Navy officers, the majority of whom were not professionals, aided by civilian specialists, adapted British operational intelligence techniques to their own requirements, frequently improving on them.[10]

In assembling his staff it was natural that Donovan should turn to friends and acquaintances in New York and Washington. For example, Herschel Williams, a neighbour of Donovan's in New York, was offered the job as head of operations in Morocco. James Murphy, Donovan's former law clerk, joined the COI as his executive assistant. The men he recruited in 1941 were typical of the men who were to dominate the CIA for the next forty years. Williams thought that Donovan recruited 'a lot of people out of the social class he looked up to. The result was that he hired a lot of jerks!'[11] Murphy demurred:

Socially, financially, we had quite a gathering of Ivy League Wall Street people. Most of them whom I had contact with were very able people and made important contributions whenever they were called upon – Henry Morgan and Junius Morgan and Bill Vanderbilt. They worked hard. They came down to Washington and they kept regular hours and they paid their own expenses. Most of them didn't draw any salaries.[12]

From the first Donovan paid special attention to research and analysis and he assembled a formidable team of academics and specialists headed by the poet and critic, Archibald MacLeish, who was also librarian of Congress. For advice on propaganda films, Donovan consulted two top Hollywood directors, John Ford, who had recently won an Oscar for *The Grapes of Wrath*, and Merian C. Cooper, the producer of *King Kong*.

Donovan personally developed a methodology for American intelligence in the event of war which was called the 'wave theory'. There were three waves, Donovan argued. The first was the collection and analysis of information; the second was commando action to test the enemy; the third was the invasion force. Intelligence played an essential role in each wave. For the first wave information had to be gathered and propaganda designed; for the second wave accurate intelligence would be needed for successful guerrilla combat. The third wave would be based on the accumulated knowledge and experience of the first two. This blueprint was to become the basis for Donovan's efforts during the war, and for CIA covert actions in the 1950s.

As the Japanese airplanes attacked Pearl Harbor, Donovan had his organization, his staff and his blueprint. But it was too new and inexperienced, still finding its feet in Washington, to be effective. And despite his title of 'coordinator', Donovan found that most of the information about Japanese activities in the run-up to Pearl Harbor had remained in the State, War and Navy Departments, and had not been given to him.

# 2
# LEGACY
## 1942–1947

*D*onovan himself only learned of the attack on Pearl Harbor several hours after it had taken place, when James Roosevelt, the President's son, telephoned him from the White House. The attack was a lightning bolt for American intelligence. 'We were betrayed by the complete failure of our intelligence services,' wrote David Bruce later, 'any intelligence service worthy of the name should have foretold this event.'[1] His view was shared by the President, by Donovan, by Congress, by the press, and by the military. Intelligence was so far down the appreciation index that even though accurate judgements had been made, it could not effect appropriate action at the highest level. This situation was a legacy of US isolation. Now there was a genuine determination that there should be an effective intelligence organization set up so that the United States should not be caught by surprise again.

Accordingly, the outbreak of war immediately created problems for the COI in that it sparked off another round of bureaucratic wrangling about intelligence. The State Department pressed for control of propaganda, while the military urged Roosevelt to allocate the various components of COI among the military services. Yet it was with the military that Donovan decided to seek a tactical alliance during the war, arguing that COI should be retained as a complete organization under the control of the newly created Joint Chiefs of Staff.

Donovan's decision had far-reaching consequences for the agency. During the war, Donovan had reasoned, intelligence would necessarily be geared towards military interests and he had no doubt that the military would come to see it as a vital part of their operations. After the war, the support of the military, strengthened politically by numbers and victory (he had no doubt that the United States would win the war), would be valuable in ensuring the post-war survival of centralized intelligence.[2]

Seeking an alliance with the military in order to ensure the future of the agency was due in part to Donovan's awareness that his relationship with Roosevelt had changed. Eleanor Roosevelt once said of her husband that he used those who suited his purposes; when they no longer fulfilled that purpose they were ruthlessly discarded, however close the previous relationship. Nobody was indispensable. This was the cold manipulative side of the famous Roosevelt charm.[3]

The first pay-off for siding with the military came in the new allocation of intelligence responsibilities. The COI lost its foreign information service (collecting news from around the world) – it was a small sacrifice: it could now concentrate on intelligence – but Roosevelt made clear to Hoover and the State Department that he was against any further break-up of COI functions, and he endorsed its amalgamation with the military. On 13 June 1942 he signed a presidential order establishing the Office of Strategic Services under the jurisdiction of the Joint Chiefs of Staff. The OSS replaced the COI. Donovan was director with the rank of major general.

## OFFICE OF STRATEGIC SERVICES

The functions of the OSS were the same as those of the COI, with the exception of the foreign information service which was transferred to the Office of War Information. Temperamentally, Donovan much preferred the excitement of commando and guerrilla operations, and being part of the military enabled him to give vent to this element. He put the emphasis on improvisation and a can-do, try-anything outlook which strongly influenced the OSS and later the CIA. And while being part of the US military, with uniforms and ranks, Donovan saw to it that the OSS remained civilian-minded at all times: for him, the long-term battle was to ensure that the US would have a peacetime, civilian, centralized agency. In Yugoslavia an OSS lieutenant in the American mission to Tito was asked by a US army colonel in the same mission to encode a message. The lieutenant said it could wait for a day. 'I'll admit it's not much fun coding,' said the colonel, gently making his point, 'but that's true of lots of things in the Army. Orders, after all, are orders in the Army.' 'Army?' the lieutenant asked. 'Did you say Army? Hell, man, we're not in the Army. We're in the OSS.'[4]

A constant stream of ideas poured from Donovan's hospitable imagination. Some were brilliant, some doubtful, others half-baked. For example, working on the (unproven) theory that the Japanese were terrified of bats, he and Roosevelt once concocted an elaborate scheme to parachute hundreds of bats onto the Japanese mainland. Unfortunately, the bats froze to death at high altitudes and the experiment had to be abandoned.[5]

Donovan was also stimulated by the intellectual problems of research and analysis and it was in this field that he was to bequeath one of his most signal achievements to the post-war CIA. His assistant, James Murphy, said that in Donovan's opinion 'if you used your talents and research facilities properly, you could outsmart the enemy simply by the use of brainpower'.[6] He thought that too much emphasis on secret intelligence gathering, such as signals and code-breaking, produced lazy analysis. Collection should never be an end in itself, argued Donovan, it was less than useless without proper analysis. It was his 'unique selling proposition' as they say in marketing, and was, by inference, suggesting that the OSS would outdo military intelligence. This argument became an article of faith for the CIA.

The importance which Donovan attached to tying in the backroom work of research and analysis (R&A) to operations was entirely justified. It proved to be one of the most successful and effective areas of OSS activity during the war, and was an American innovation in intelligence. The highly trained scholars and analysts of R&A were the first to appreciate the mass of valuable information which could be systematically extracted from ordinary academic books, journals, newspapers, magazines, and from the files of American companies on their overseas operations. Such sources enabled R&A to predict accurately that man-power and not food production would be the critical problem for the German war effort. R&A also accurately estimated German U-boat and battle casualties by scrutinizing casualty lists in German newspapers. It seemed so simple and so obvious, but to the military, who had not troubled to hide their scorn for the ivory-tower 'eggheads', the value of R&A's information was an eye-opener. After the war, the discovery by the strategic bombing survey team that Allied bombing had actually helped to increase German military production at the expense of civilian consumption, gave far more authority to the analytical side of intelligence. It showed that accurate and powerful imagination could have a central role in determining strategy.

To Donovan, intelligence research and analysis was not just about German war production or battle statistics; it concerned political, social and cultural affairs as well. This was the core of OSS strength, and Donovan made the most of it by appealing to the imagination of American élites. The links forged with academe by the OSS were strengthened considerably by the CIA, and this respect for scholarship was to give the agency a clear intellectual advantage over the KGB which persisted in regarding old-fashioned spying as the basis of intelligence. Ray Cline, who worked in R&A during the war and later became the CIA Deputy Director for Intelligence, was in no doubt on this point:

> The most valuable OSS legacy that ensued was Donovan's belief in the value of bringing able people from all walks of life into intelligence work. He lifted intelligence out of its military rut, where it had little prestige and little dynamism, and made it a career for adventurous, broad-minded civilians. This tradition carried down to the CIA, which regularly recruited some of the most able graduates from US universities to learn the intelligence business.[7]

## AT WAR

The operational functions of the OSS, as defined by the Joint Chiefs, were primarily sabotage, espionage, counterespionage, covert action and subversion. By the end of the war the OSS employed some 25,000 people. To many outside the organization, the OSS was undisciplined and badly organized – a bohemian quality was one of its defining characteristics, and also of the CIA, until the late 1960s.

Donovan enlisted an enormously cosmopolitan and disparate group of recruits who cemented the ranging nature of OSS activity. The strong Ivy League–Wall Street ethos established by him, with OSS officers coming from most of the great American families like Morgan, Mellon, Bruce and Vanderbilt, prompted the nickname 'Oh So Social'. But this was not the whole story. 'I'd put Stalin on the OSS payroll if I thought it would help us to defeat Hitler,' said Donovan. He recruited communists and members of the Abraham Lincoln Brigade (Americans, most of them communist or socialist, who had fought against Franco during the Spanish Civil War), prompting another nickname, 'Oh So Socialist'. An OSS Labor branch established contacts with trade unions in occupied Europe, contacts which were of inestimable value after the war.

Many of America's most distinguished public servants had their first government service in the COI and the OSS. Four future directors of the CIA were OSS officers: Allen Dulles; Richard Helms, who served in England, France and Germany; William Colby, who took part in parachute and guerrilla operations in France and Norway; and William Casey, who served in London. David Bruce, the OSS station chief in London, later served as ambassador to France, West Germany, Britain and NATO. Presidential advisers Walt Rostow, Arthur

Schlesinger, Jr, Douglass Cater, Arthur Goldberg, and Carl Kaysen were also former OSS men.

## ALLEN DULLES

Allen Dulles, who later became the fifth and longest serving director of the CIA, was one of the first people recruited by Donovan to the COI. Donovan offered to make him head of secret intelligence in Western Europe under David Bruce but Dulles declined, preferring to work on his own. Donovan then created a post for him in Switzerland as head of covert operations in Europe. In 1943 Dulles arrived in Berne with a $1 million letter of credit, a suitcase and two suits.

The Berne post made Dulles one of the best-placed OSS operatives and he paid special attention to establishing contacts in Germany, especially with disaffected members of the German Army, military intelligence and Foreign Ministry. There was Fritz Molden, son of a professor at the University of Vienna, who through his father's friends and colleagues had built up a network of informants in Austria, Hungary, Czechoslovakia and Yugoslavia. It was through Molden that Dulles first heard about the German V-1 and V-2 rocket project at Peenemunde (although the British already had hard intelligence on the subject).

Hans Bernd Gisevius, a German who worked with Dulles, was a friend of Admiral Wilhelm Canaris, head of the *Abwehr*, German military intelligence. Gisevius told Dulles that not only had the *Abwehr* broken some OSS and State Department codes, but also that there was a German agent, codenamed Cicero, in the British Embassy in Turkey. Gisevius gave Dulles much valuable information about the strength of the anti-Hitler opposition within the German Army. After the ignominious failure of the 20 July 1944 plot to kill Hitler, most of this opposition was arrested and liquidated, including Canaris. With Dulles' help Gisevius escaped and after the war was an important witness at the Nuremberg Trials.

Dulles' most important contact was Fritz Kolbe, a senior German Foreign Ministry official who, like Gisevius, was a member of the anti-Hitler opposition operating at the very heart of the German government. Kolbe's job entailed frequent visits to Switzerland where he had first approached the British but had been rejected by them as a possible double agent. Washington also thought that Kolbe was suspect but Dulles believed in him. Until July 1944, when Kolbe became frightened that his visits to Switzerland would attract suspicion because of the anti-Hitler plot, he provided Dulles with hundreds of copies of telegrams

Allen Welsh Dulles, longest-serving Director of Central Intelligence (1953–61), brother of John Foster Dulles, Eisenhower's Secretary of State, and the first professional American intelligence officer. His career ended with the public failure of the Bay of Pigs operation against Fidel Castro.

and letters between Berlin and German embassies abroad. Kolbe's documents suggested that the Soviet Union planned to impose communist rule in Central and Eastern Europe after the war, but since this was in line with German propaganda, it only increased the suspicion of him in Washington.

No one was more suspicious than the British. Kolbe's material, in the opinion of Sir Claude Dansey, deputy head of SIS, was obviously 'a plant' and Dulles, he said contemptuously, 'had fallen for it like a ton of bricks'.[8] Someone else in SIS had a vested interest in rubbishing Kolbe: Kim Philby, then chief of SIS's Iberian section and a Soviet spy inside SIS. The last thing the Russians wanted was a strong German underground opposition, in league with the Americans, that might provide a basis for democratic resistance to communist rule after the war.

Despite doubts in Washington and London, Molden, Gisevius and Kolbe were good informants. In the opinion of one of Dulles' officers they were:

> absolutely priceless agents . . . A real criticism of British intelligence during the war was that they were overtly suspicious of the motives of the people with whom they had to deal, and the consequence was that as far as I was concerned, the three best agents that Allen Dulles had were rejected by the British . . . The British had turned them all down, and it was Allen Dulles' wit that picked them up.[9]

The brutal reality was that Dulles was desperate for sources, having come late (1943) to the table. If the British had been in his shoes, they would probably have picked up the same people.

## COLD WAR

In the spring of 1944, the shape of Soviet intentions in Eastern and Central Europe was still unclear and at such a critical time in the war, it was generally considered impolitic to rock the boat with Stalin. In addition, Roosevelt was convinced that he would be able to reach a satisfactory post-war settlement with 'Uncle Joe', and so refused to sanction any intelligence operations designed to discover Soviet war aims. But Dulles, and as it happened Donovan, distrusted their Soviet ally and his motives. Tired out powers tend to trust allies; fresh and energetic powers do not.

After the German invasion of Russia in June 1941, when Stalin finally joined the Allies, Donovan made several attempts to establish some sort of intelligence cooperation with the Soviets. In December 1943 he visited Moscow and suggested joint sabotage missions behind enemy lines but, perhaps not surprisingly, the plan never materialized. If there were suspicions of the Russians in Washington, which there were in plenty, they paled beside the paranoia about the West rampaging in Moscow. Stalin was at best always a reluctant ally.

The reports reaching Donovan in 1944 led him to suggest to Roosevelt that the OSS should target the activities of the Red Army in occupied territory. Although Roosevelt refused, Donovan continued to keep an eye on the Russians, and the OSS was to take some of the first tentative steps in the Cold War. It was obvious that if Germany was to be broken as a power, then the question of Soviet power in Central Europe would automatically emerge. However, on the eve of the second front – the Allied invasion of Europe on D-Day, 6 June 1944 – neither Roosevelt nor Churchill wanted trouble with Stalin, and they both acted to allay Stalin's suspicions that they would sign a separate peace with Germany. Stalin took advantage of this. There was an escalation of communist activity in Eastern Europe and the Balkans, with attempts to control the various resistance movements in readiness for when the Germans moved out. In Bucharest in September 1944 an OSS agent, Robert Bishop, established contact with a top-secret unit of Romanian intelligence which had penetrated the Romanian communist party. For the next six months Bishop was kept informed about Soviet plans for Romania and the rest of Eastern Europe. He reported the intelligence to Donovan. Soviet plans were to create slave states which would be a buffer between Russia and Western Europe after the war. The operation was blown in March 1945, when the Romanian intelligence unit was captured by the Russians as they occupied Romania. They were never seen again.

Further corroboration of Soviet plans came in November 1944 when Finnish intelligence presented the OSS with a huge book of Soviet codes, including some intelligence codes, which they had captured. The Russians never realized their codes had been captured and continued to use them. When Roosevelt heard that the OSS had these codes, he ordered Donovan to return them, uncopied, to the Russians. Donovan did return them – but he also copied them secretly. Ironically, these codes later enabled the FBI to get on the trail of the Rosenberg spy ring and the British double-agent Donald Maclean.

## THE GEHLEN ORGANIZATION

Within weeks of the end of the war in Europe, a German general, Reinhard Gehlen, head of the German Army's Soviet intelligence section, was taken up by US Army intelligence. Gehlen was to have a long and profitable relationship with the CIA and was subsequently head of the West German Federal Intelligence Service, the *Bundesnachrichtendienst* (BND). Gehlen impressed his debriefers with his forecasts of Soviet policy in post-war Europe. According to Gehlen, Stalin was determined to keep Poland effectively occupied, with Czechoslovakia, Hungary, Romania, and Bulgaria all becoming Soviet satellite states. And unless the Western Allies made clear to Stalin that they were prepared to defend their zones of occupation in Germany, the Soviets intended to occupy the whole of Germany too. Gehlen also presented the US Army with a cache of documents, his 'Kremlin secrets' as he called them, which he had buried in the Bavarian Alps days before Germany's surrender. They included the names of OSS men whom Gehlen claimed were members of the Communist party, and the Soviet order of battle at the time of the German surrender.

Donovan and Allen Dulles (now head of OSS, Germany) were told about Gehlen and his information, and they recommended that he be taken on by the Army. When an attempt was made on Gehlen's life – the car he was

General Reinhard Gehlen who headed the *Bundesnachrichtendienst* (BND), West Germany's Federal Intelligence Service, from its formation under CIA auspices in 1950 until his retirement in 1968. During World War II, Gehlen headed the German Army's intelligence against the USSR, and handed his wartime records to the US Army shortly after the German surrender in 1945.

in was hit by a bullet – it was decided to spirit him away to Washington. He arrived there on 20 September 1945: the day that President Truman signed an executive order which gave Donovan just ten days to disband the OSS.

# OSS INTO CIA

Donovan was in Paris on 12 April when the news of Roosevelt's sudden death was announced. 'What will happen now to OSS?' asked his deputy, Ned Buxton. 'I'm afraid it's the end,' said Donovan gloomily.

With the end of the war in sight Donovan had stepped up the pressure for the survival of the OSS as a peacetime civilian intelligence agency, but this was also the signal for opponents of the idea to checkmate him. Many Americans simply wanted to go home at the end of the war, and not be involved in the world's troubles. The isolationist instinct was very strong, and was a political reality. In many quarters Donovan's intelligence agency was seen as being the thin end of a wedge that would force the United States to remain involved with the rest of the world.

In particular, Donovan and the OSS were portrayed as being British puppets. An anti-OSS campaign, connected at the time to J. Edgar Hoover, was raging in sections of the press. Newspaper headlines provide a taste of the hostility: 'OSS is branded British Agency to Legislators' and 'British Control of OSS Bared in Congress Probe'. The origins of the OSS, which owed so much to British intelligence, were now catching up with Donovan and bringing out a virulent strain of anglophobia. The gossip columns rehashed gibes about 'Oh So Social', 'Oh So Secret' and 'The Glamour Set'. Truman received a secret report which accused the OSS of corruption, inefficiency, neglect and orgies. This report had actually been commissioned by Roosevelt: another example of his method of playing people off against each other.

In presenting the case for the post-war survival of the OSS, Donovan was hamstrung. Who was the enemy? In the euphoric atmosphere of victory and with the sufferings of the Russians during the war still vivid in people's minds, public opinion would not take kindly to suggestions that one of America's wartime allies would soon be a peacetime enemy. So Donovan, although personally convinced of the Cold War intentions of the Soviets, had to fall back on historical and bureaucratic arguments for a post-war agency, and these were particularly unpersuasive at a time when there was a longing to return to peacetime normality and to be free of the fetters of war.

There were other reasons for the disbandment of the OSS. Truman was a direct, straightforward midwesterner. He disliked secret organizations and he particularly disliked the aura of secrecy which hung over the OSS. It was also a fact that he and Donovan were poles apart temperamentally. 'Donovan was a

Catholic Republican. Truman was a Democratic Baptist. They never saw eye to eye on anything', observed James Murphy. Donovan left the world of intelligence.

On 22 January 1946, exactly four months after he had disbanded the OSS, Truman issued a directive creating a Central Intelligence Group (CIG). The military had sought to maintain a central intelligence service by forming the Strategic Services' Unit, drawn from the OSS. This now became the nucleus of the CIG which was jointly funded and staffed by the Departments of State, War and Navy. Truman also ordered a thorough reappraisal of national security and this was to lead directly to the National Security Act of 1947 which established a unified Department of Defense and the civilian Central Intelligence Agency. His attitude towards intelligence was changed by his experience of Soviet expansionism in Europe and the activity of the Red Army and security forces: arresting and deporting to the Gulag non-communist politicians, academics, and journalists; refusing to hold democratic elections.

The birth of the CIA was accompanied by the same bitter wrangling which had accompanied those of the COI and the OSS: what it should be, who should have it and who should control it. In the end, the vitriolic feuding between the Departments of State, War and Navy did more than anything else to strengthen the case for a new independent civilian agency under presidential control. 'Central' in its title indicated that the CIA was to be the hub of the wheel of US intelligence, drawing information not only from its own sources, but also from all the other intelligence agencies in the government.

It was the combination of the developing Cold War in Europe and Truman's own changing perceptions of the Soviet Union which finally decided the future of central intelligence. In the face of flagrant breaches of the Yalta and Potsdam agreements of 1945, US public hostility towards the Soviets, as reflected in opinion polls, increased dramatically and Truman warned grimly: 'Unless Russia is faced with an iron fist and strong language another war is in the making.' The CIA was part of Truman's iron fist.

Because the CIA was a response to the Cold War, this was to create problems for the agency's development. The Cold War was neither war nor peace; no one thought it would last decades, and because it followed hard on the heels of the Second World War, there was a natural tendency to regard it as an extension of it. When the terms of the National Security Bill were being drafted in 1946–7, the legal operating position of the new agency came under close scrutiny. In wartime the President enjoyed extraordinary legal powers but in peacetime the position was different. What would be the position if the CIA killed someone? That question would not arise in war, but in peace it certainly would. What would be the role of the Congress in overseeing intelligence? These thorny problems were the backdrop to the new legislation.

## NATIONAL SECURITY ACT 1947

The National Security Bill was sent to Congress on 27 February 1947. It proposed unified control of the armed services (including, for the first time, a completely separate air force) in a new National Military Establishment, and a Central Intelligence Agency under the supervision of a National Security Council. The FBI, which was going to lose its control of intelligence activities in Latin America, organized a last ditch stand, but this time to no avail. Giving evidence to the Senate Armed Services Committee, General Vandenberg, Director of the Central Intelligence Group, declared:

> I feel that the people of this country, having experienced the disaster of Pearl Harbor and the appalling consequences of a global war, are now sufficiently informed in their approach to intelligence to understand that an organization such as [the CIA] or the intelligence divisions of the armed services, or the FBI, cannot expose certain of their activities to public gaze . . .[10]

The National Security Act came into force on 26 July 1947. The CIA was to be headed by a director who was a presidential appointee. The agency was responsible directly to the President through the National Security Council (NSC), which advised the President, who was its head. Initially, the primary purpose of the new agency was intelligence and not operations, and it was only later that it was to acquire a covert action capacity.

The functions of the CIA were to make recommendations about intelligence coordination; to correlate and evaluate intelligence, and to perform such services of common concern to the government's intelligence organizations as the NSC might determine.

## DIRECTOR OF CENTRAL INTELLIGENCE

The act also dealt with the position of the Director of Central Intelligence, a post first established by Truman when he created the CIG in 1946. Now the DCI's position, formally, was that he had three hats: he was overall head of all US intelligence; the President's principal intelligence officer; and head of the CIA. By making him head of the CIA, the centrality of the agency was expected to be enhanced.

It was – and is – a position strong on paper and weak to the point of ineffectiveness in practice. No DCI has ever been able to control the different intelligence agencies. The Director of the FBI, for example, is also a presidential appointee with the status to fight the DCI if necessary; the State Department's intelligence outfit could always appeal to the Secretary of State in a conflict with the DCI; the various military intelligence units could always look to the Secretary of Defense, and so on.

The DCI was also specifically charged with the protection of sources and methods of intelligence, a provision motivated by the Army's distrust of a civilian agency. In 1947 this clause seemed no more than academic, but for Richard Helms thirty years later, when faced with the choice of protecting his source or answering to Congress, it was not.

# 3
# DIRECTORS

*T*he first Director of Central Intelligence was Rear Admiral Sidney Souers. The second was Lieutenant General Hoyt Vandenberg. The third, and first head of the CIA, was Rear Admiral Roscoe Hillenkoetter, sworn in on 1 May 1947. During the war Hillenkoetter had been Admiral Nimitz's intelligence officer in the Pacific region. By appointing a military officer to run the CIA, Truman was placating military concern about giving intelligence secrets to civilians.

Hillenkoetter had a calm, quiet manner which led some to conclude that he was indecisive, but this was to underrate both him and the enormous problems he faced as director of the new agency. His main aim was to establish the primacy of the CIA in the intelligence bureaucracy. What made Hillenkoetter's position difficult was the lack of clear policy guidelines from the President and the National Security Council. This was to remain a persistent problem for the agency.

When the new NSC proposed that the new DCI be made its executive agent, thus giving him day-to-day superiority over the other intelligence agencies, there was such an uproar from the State Department and the military that Hillenkoetter had to back down. This was to have serious implications, for it meant that almost from its inception the DCI never had the dominating position within the intelligence community that had clearly been intended. This, in turn, affected the CIA's position which depended upon the relationship between the President and the DCI. In Truman, Hillenkoetter was dealing with a president who was never clear what to do with the agency and was never prepared to give it the support necessary to establish its priority. That situation changed under Eisenhower and his DCI, Allen Dulles, who had a very close relationship. In the 1960s Kennedy, and later Nixon, were to give presidential backing to their DCIs as the overall head of the intelligence community but they never developed the practical means to enforce it. In the 1980s, although Reagan gave William Casey cabinet rank, it was personal to Casey. It did not mean that the DCI had overall administrative control of intelligence.

During the first year Hillenkoetter had little respite from the CIA's bureaucratic rivals. There were bitter arguments with Army intelligence over control of overseas agents. The State Department fiercely resisted the CIA's use of diplomatic cover and communications systems, a row which went on for decades. The FBI, still smarting over the loss of its South American bailiwick, did everything to frustrate the agency when it came to take over FBI offices abroad. Files were burned and agents vanished with the explanation that the CIA was not sufficiently security conscious. J. Edgar Hoover's enmity was unrelenting and the relationship between the two organizations remained frosty until his death in 1972.

As the Cold War intensified, this bureaucratic bickering became less and less acceptable. In July 1948, a full year after the National Security Act, the *New York Times* described intelligence as 'one of the weakest links in our national security' and criticized the feuding and rivalry among the various intelligence organizations. It was a particularly sensitive time for these criticisms to be aired. Besides the very tense international situation in Europe and the Far East, a presidential election was in the offing and Truman's prospects were considered poor. In August 1948 the House Un-American Activities Committee heard sensational allegations about communist infiltration of the government, notably the State Department. Truman could not afford accusations of slack security and he appointed a three-man commission to conduct a thorough investigation of the working of the agency. It consisted of Allen Dulles, William Jackson (a future deputy DCI) and Mathias Correa, who had been assistant to Navy Secretary James Forrestal during the war. All three were New York lawyers. They presented their report to the NSC in January 1949. It became known as the Dulles report, and was the blueprint for the CIA's future administration.

## THE DULLES REPORT

The Dulles report called for the creation of five divisions to replace the multitude of ad hoc offices and sections in the CIA which aggravated a sense of disorganization. The proposed divisions were estimates, country surveys and other topics of importance; research and reports, which would provide the raw material for estimates and monitor current intelligence information requiring speedy analysis; operations, including covert action, espionage and counterintelligence; administration, which would look after day-to-day housekeeping; and coordination, which would link the CIA to other government intelligence agencies.

Coordination, Dulles stressed, was the key. The agency was not just another intelligence service, its job was to coordinate and synthesize intelligence information. Dulles criticized the failure to promote inter-agency cooperation and coordination, a failure, he said, which lay at the heart of the CIA's poor performance in centralizing and coordinating the work of the other intelligence agencies to date. He saw the agency as being at the heart of policymaking.

Dulles' report coincided with another which had been commissioned by the United States Intelligence Board – the President's oversight body for all the government intelligence agencies – composed of the good and the great. It recommended that the DCI be recognized by the other agencies as having responsibility for the coordination of all intelligence functions and activities. Lawrence Houston, the CIA's general counsel, described it as a 'devastating' blow to those who were trying to keep down the powers and authority of the CIA and the DCI, particularly officers in military intelligence. When Hillenkoetter read out the report, Houston recalled: 'There was a deathly hush around the room. General Chamberlain, the G-2, looked up and said, "Hilly, what's all this about? You're the boss." And the colonel down at the end of the table turned absolutely green.'[1]

## THE 1949 ACT

In the wake of the Dulles and USIB reports, a Central Intelligence Agency Act was passed in 1949 which became the legal and administrative linchpin for CIA operations. It also set out the authority of Congress to regulate the CIA, although this authority was left deliberately vague when it came to the CIA's clandestine activities. This, and the political consensus of the time that the CIA was necessary and was doing necessary – if unpleasant – work, gave the agency considerable flexibility and freedom. It never had to account for its expenditure of discretionary funds (except to the President) and it could hire as many people as it wanted.

At the height of the Cold War, it was tacitly accepted that Congress would not scrutinize the CIA too closely. When the Cold War generation of congressman and senators began to move off stage in the late 1960s and early 1970s, and as the Vietnam war and Watergate broke down political habits and fuelled popular suspicions of government and secrecy, the agency's mystique seemed less impressive to their successors. But at the start, and for the first twenty years, the agency led a charmed life when it came to congressional and public scrutiny.

From left to right: Georges Bidault, French Foreign Minister, Anthony Eden, British Foreign Secretary, and General Walter Bedell Smith, meeting near Geneva in May 1954. Smith was leading the US delegation to the Geneva Conference on Vietnam. He had been the fourth Director of Central Intelligence, 1950–3, and Eisenhower's wartime Chief of Staff.

## BEDELL SMITH

In October 1950 Hillenkoetter was appointed commander of the Navy Task Force in Korea. He was succeeded as DCI by General Walter Bedell Smith, US Ambassador in Moscow 1946–9, and formerly Eisenhower's wartime Chief of Staff. Smith was regarded by many in the CIA as perhaps the best director the agency ever had. Nicknamed 'Beetle', Smith was a magnetic, shrewd and determined man. He made things happen. He had a notorious temper, which was exacerbated by stomach ulcers. Ray Cline, one of the first CIA recruits, described him as a man 'with broad experience and absolutely no tolerance for fools... He had an intimidating personality and was a perfectionist.'[2] Largely self-educated, he had a photographic memory, an encyclopedic knowledge, and shrewd judgement about people and ideas. Another senior agency official recalled with relish how Bedell Smith, using all the prestige of his previous military career, demolished the CIA's erstwhile rivals in the military: 'He treated the generals and admirals ... as schoolboys. He'd make fun of them in front of all of us. It was embarrassing sometimes.'[3]

Smith's pugnacity was needed, for his appointment occurred at a critical time for the agency. On 25 June 1950 North Korea had invaded the South, thus precipitating the Korean war. The agency had failed to give any clear warning about the invasion and there were emotive references to Pearl Harbor, not just in an accusing press, but in the highest Washington circles. The assumption was that the CIA's job was to monitor the whole world, whether or not what was happening affected US interests. Bedell Smith determined upon the complete overhaul of the agency, in particular its estimating procedures.

Drawing heavily on the Dulles report, Smith fundamentally provided the framework for the way the agency works today. He created three new directorates, each run by a deputy director, each focused firmly on the targets set for the agency by the National Security Act and the directives of the National Security Council. Each directorate was known by the initials of the post of the deputy director responsible, thus the Directorate of Intelligence was DDI; the Directorate of Plans (i.e., operations, the covert action and espionage side of the house) was DDP; the Directorate of Administration was DDA, and so on.

## ESTIMATES AND ANALYSIS

Research and analysis had been one of the most successful areas of OSS activity during the war. As the post-war situation in Europe and the Far East deteriorated and the demand for detailed and accurate reports increased, estimates acquired a crucial importance within the CIA. (Estimates are reports pulling together all the available information – secret and public – on a subject.)

The Director of Central Intelligence is personally responsible for the estimates which were never intended to encompass all opinions. In a directive of September 1948, Hillenkoetter set out the bases for National Intelligence Estimates:

Departmental participation in the preparation of national intelligence reports and estimates is undertaken to ensure that authorized recipients (a) are presented with intelligence that comprises all the best available expert knowledge and opinion; (b) are aware, in the case of disputed points, of the views of the departments on substantive matters within their special fields of responsibility and interest… Dissent published in a national intelligence paper should present a distinct difference of opinion on which the CIA and the dissenting intelligence organization have found it impossible to agree.[4]

When Bedell Smith became DCI he had invited Professor William L. Langer, the distinguished historian who had been in charge of OSS research and analysis, to take a sabbatical from Harvard and return to revamp the estimates and the estimating procedure. Some surveys read like academic dissertations. One early report on Norway, for example, was forty-one pages long with six chapters and five appendices. For all the laborious effort, it produced a mouselike conclusion, dismissing the possibility that Norway was a threat to peace as 'extremely remote'.

Langer established a Board of Estimates as a judging panel of senior people, retired and serving, from academe and government service. The Board scrutinized draft estimates produced by the DDI and the research that lay behind them, and made recommendations and suggestions to the DDI. It also acted as a sounding board of senior people for the DCI, separate from the bureaucracy of the agency.

The success of the Smith-Langer partnership helped the agency to banish the aura of failure which had hung over it since the outbreak of the Korean war. The new estimates were sharp and concise and made a good impression on the President and his senior advisers.

William Bundy, who joined the agency as an analyst in 1951, recalled that Bedell Smith and Langer had a very clear idea of what was needed:

> I remember one occasion when Bedell Smith said 'Don't start that research paper on China by saying "China is a great land mass!"' People could always get that from someone else . . . He was no great stylist, but he went straight to the heart of the matter. He and Langer would not take junk by way of drafting.[5]

The work of drafting estimates took place in the DDI. Robert Amory, a Harvard Law School professor, left Boston to become DDI in 1952, staying in the job for the next ten years. He had responsibility for national estimates and current intelligence (the rapid analysis of information as it came in on a day-to-day basis), and produced a daily digest of intelligence for the President and his senior advisers. Within the DDI was the Office of Collection and Dissemination (later becoming the CIA's central reference service), a computerized library of intelligence that provided the research backbone, and the Office of National Estimates (ONE), by far the most important of the DDI's units. It consisted of two sections: the Board of Estimates (known as the 'college of cardinals'), and the estimates staff.

Once approved, the estimates were sent to the Intelligence Advisory Com-

Henry Cabot Lodge, US Ambassador to the United Nations, showing the UN Security Council the microphone that was hidden inside the carved wooden Great Seal of the United States that hung in the office of the US Ambassador in Moscow in the early 1950s. The seal had been given to the Ambassador as a gift by a group of Russians.

mittee which was composed of the heads of Military Intelligence, the FBI, the State Department's Office of Intelligence and Research, and the Atomic Energy Commission. The committee was a forum for bureaucratic rivalries to be cancelled out, rather than a committee instrumental in shaping estimates.

This system lasted for twenty-five years and, as the Church Committee investigating the CIA noted in 1976, was 'by far the best analytical organization for the production of finished intelligence within the government'.[6]

The other offices within the DDI (research and reports, geographical research, scientific intelligence and current intelligence) provided the driving force of analysis and conducted most of the basic research for ONE. The effectiveness of their work was ample testimony to Donovan's foresight in 1941 when he correctly believed that the best brains in the country could make an important contribution to national intelligence. When Langer returned to Harvard in 1952, he was succeeded at the Board of Estimates by his deputy, Sherman Kent, who held the job for sixteen years and was widely acknowledged as the *éminence grise* of CIA research and analysis.

Kent was a stickler for accuracy, and under him the estimates became the accepted forum in Washington for the collective wisdom of the US government on any subject. He sought to employ exact wording wherever possible, warning against the use of adjectives such as 'possibly' and 'probably', and giving certain words a numerical value. Thus if the word 'probably' had to be used, it meant that there was a 90 per cent chance of something happening; 'likely' would mean a 60 per cent chance; 'possibly' would mean a 30 per cent chance, and so on. He fought to keep the estimates unsullied by political or personal pressures, determined that they be as objective as possible, even if policymakers did not like the conclusions.

Kent's policy worked at first, not least because of the respect the CIA had within government. But as time went on the monopolistic estimating position of the CIA caused friction with other agencies and departments. In efforts to reach peaceful working arrangements within the Washington bureaucracy, and to keep its position, CIA estimates gradually became less punchy and more bland. Because of this, in the 1980s the system was changed.

## OPERATIONS

Covert operations and action, the province of the Directorate of Plans, was an area which, literally and metaphorically, had proved a minefield for the agency. Who was to control them? The answer to that question had been one of the most hotly fought issues between the CIA and its rivals.

At the beginning of 1949 the NSC created the blandly titled Office of Policy Coordination (OPC) to combat Soviet and communist activity generally. It was headed by Frank Wisner, a former OSS officer who had served in Germany in 1945. Wisner was a wealthy Wall Street lawyer from Mississippi and many of the people he recruited came from the same Ivy League-Wall Street-OSS background as he did. By temperament and background Wisner had a natural affinity for covert work, and the derring-do ethos of the OSS permeated his group. The OSO, by contrast, was more disciplined and career-oriented. Richard Bissell, who became DDP in 1958, described the differences:

> There were always two philosophies about clandestine operations . . . OSO had an emphasis on high professionalism, with very tight security and the maintenance of espionage and counterespionage. OPC placed a great deal more emphasis on covert action and was probably less professional and secure.[7]

By 1952 the relationship between the two offices was becoming untenable. There were major salary differences between the two – OPC people were paid more than OSO – which caused serious disagreement and, worst of all, they regularly found themselves competing for the same agents. Smith successfully used his influence and insisted that the OPC and OSO should merge within the CIA, arguing that since the agency was responsible for the OPC's 'quarters and rations' it should have responsibility for running OPC too. In July 1952, the OSO and OPC were merged in the DDP. Frank Wisner became DDP with Richard Helms of the OSO as his number two as chief of operations. The DDP absorbed about 60 per cent of the CIA's staff and 80 per cent of the CIA's budget.

## ADMINISTRATION

Supporting the Directorates of Intelligence and Plans was the Directorate of Administration (DDA), which looked after personnel, day-to-day housekeeping, agency communications, and logistical support for covert operations, as well as more routine tasks such as the audit section, the medical service and internal security and staff monitoring. Its job was a big one, occupying a substantial number of CIA staff, many of whom served abroad as part of CIA stations. In 1992 it had a staff of over 5000 people.

The DDA tried to institutionalize a freewheeling spirit in the agency career structure. Staff can choose the directorate they want to serve in, and systems are in place so that moves can be made from one directorate to another. But at the start, as one Deputy Director for Administration recalled in 1984, snobbery and élitism were significant obstacles to orderly arrangements:

> There was some animosity against the eastern establishment set. I can think of some people in pretty senior positions when I was serving through the years who felt their further advancement had been inhibited because they didn't go to this school or that school or they weren't invited to this party or that party or their words weren't given sufficient credence because they were not part of the inner set. There was some of that, but it disappeared as time went by because you don't have the same kind of people today that you had twenty years ago. You take a hard look at the leadership of the agency today and you will find little hint of the eastern establishment – it's gone.[8]

# 4
# FRIENDS?
## *1946–1956*

O
n 22 February 1946, George Kennan, a senior diplomat, sent an eight-thousand-word telegram from the US Embassy in Moscow to the State Department, warning Washington that the Soviet Union had a warlike view of relations with the West: capitalism and communism, said Stalin, could not peacefully coexist. The 'long telegram' is a celebrated document, one of the key texts of the Cold War. In it Kennan argued that the Soviets posed a serious, long-term threat all over the world but particularly in Europe. Stalin, he maintained, was taking every opportunity to weaken the West, using 'an underground operating directorate of world communism, a concealed comintern tightly coordinated and directed by Moscow to reach their goal of world domination'. It was thus vital, Kennan concluded, to resist communist attempts to subvert, discredit and overthrow Western institutions.[1]

In his memoirs Kennan recalled that he had been issuing such warnings for eighteen long months but that they had fallen on unreceptive ears. This time, however, the response was different. Just the week before Kennan sent his telegram, an extensive Soviet spy ring had been uncovered in Canada which had betrayed atomic secrets to Moscow. This brought home to Americans that sooner or later the Soviets would have the bomb too, and the bomb was, thus far, the factor which gave the United States an insurmountable advantage over the Soviets in any military confrontation.

The exposure of the Canadian network was followed by a whole series of spy scandals: Elizabeth Bentley, Klaus Fuchs, the Rosenbergs and, most sensational of all, the Burgess-Maclean-Philby affair.

The European scene was particularly disturbing to the Truman administration. Eastern Europe was firmly under Soviet control, and from Washington, Western Europe seemed on the verge of sliding under Soviet control as well. Within nine months of V-E Day, de Gaulle had resigned in France; in Britain, Churchill had been voted out of power by an electorate which was physically and emotionally drained by the war; there was a bitter communist-instigated civil war in Greece. Secret Soviet support was going to the Communist parties in France and Italy, and to communist-controlled trade unions and newspapers, fomenting strikes and political disruption.

In 1946 the United States was the only country capable of dealing with the Soviet threat. The British had been crippled financially by the war and the abrupt curtailment of lend-lease in August 1945 had left their economy on the verge of collapse. In July 1946 Truman authorized a $3.7 billion loan to Britain, and although this eased British problems temporarily, it was obvious that they were finding it difficult to meet military and occupation commitments to their allies around the world.

On 21 February 1947, the First Secretary at the British Embassy in Washington, H. M. Sichell, hurried to the State Department for an urgent meeting. He handed in two documents from his government. The first concerned Greece and stated that unless the Greek government received $200 million immediately, the communist guerrillas would win the civil war. The second document was no less bald and warned that a similar fate awaited Turkey.

Truman agonized over whether to give aid to Greece and Turkey. Isolationist pressure was still strong and he was distrustful of British motives. But in the end he concluded that the USA must intervene. He, George Marshall, the Secretary of State, and Dean Acheson, the Under Secretary of State, met senior Congressional leaders to secure their support. Acheson recalled:

> I knew we were met at Armageddon . . . These Congressmen had no conception of what challenged them: it was my task to bring it home . . . In the past eighteen months, I said, Soviet pressure on the Straits, on Iran and on northern Greece had brought the Balkans to the point where a highly possible Soviet breakthrough might open these continents to Soviet penetration. Like apples in a barrel infected by one rotten one, the corruption of Greece would infect Iran and all to the east. It would also carry infection to Africa through Asia Minor and Egypt, and to Europe through Italy and France, already threatened by the strongest domestic Communist parties in Western Europe. The Soviet Union was playing one of the greatest gambles in history at minimal cost . . . We and we alone were in a position to break up the play.[2]

Acheson's record provides a fascinating glimpse of the arrival in the USA of a global and long-distance perspective in foreign affairs. It was, as yet, unsophisticated. There is little evidence to show that contamination spread: Greece going communist was no guarantee that Turkey would follow. It was the start of the domino theory, the subtext of which was that Lenin had been right to think that there was a world revolution waiting to happen. In fact the failure of South East Asia to go communist after the fall of South Vietnam to communist forces in 1975 finally demonstrated Lenin's and the domino fallacy.

On 12 March Truman addressed a joint session of Congress, and set out what became known as the Truman Doctrine:

> We must assist free peoples to work out their own destinies in their own
> way ... Totalitarian regimes forced upon free peoples, by direct or indirect
> aggression, undermine the foundations of international peace and hence the
> security of the United States.

He asked for $400 million in military and economic assistance for Greece and Turkey. Congress – Democrats and Republicans – agreed. The money was used overtly in Greece and Turkey and additional covert action was undertaken by the CIA in France and Italy to help democratic political parties, trade unions and newspapers in the propaganda and political battle against the communists.

The Truman Doctrine was followed three months later by the Marshall Plan. With Europe suffering from the devastation of the war, Truman, Acheson and Marshall believed that support for the non-communist European economies was a vital part of the measures to defend democratic values in the West.

## PLAYING HARDBALL WITH THE COMMUNISTS

It was against this background of fear and urgency that the CIA began to engage with the Soviets. The Italian elections in April 1948 were the first big test for the agency. As in France, communists had played a leading role in the wartime resistance movement and used this as a base to bid for power. For almost two years after the end of the war, communists shared power in coalition governments in France, Belgium and Italy. In Italy, the Communist party, which was already receiving extensive support from the Soviets, won important victories in local elections and there were forebodings about the outcome of the general election set for the spring of 1948.

Italian voters and supporters in Cassino of Alcide de Gasperi, the Christian Democrat leader and Prime Minister, during the 1948 elections which his coalition won. The United States, through the CIA, gave financial help to De Gasperi's coalition. The Soviet Union was giving financial support to the Italian Communist party – the largest in Western Europe.

The CIA, through its Office of Special Operations, helped the non-communist democratic parties, notably Alcide de Gasperi's Christian Democrats. It paid the election expenses of various politicians; it met the printing costs of posters, leaflets and pamphlets. The anti-communist press also received financial aid. This was to be the pattern in other countries of CIA support, which was given not just to parties of the right and centre but also to the non-communist left.

De Gasperi was re-elected, but the following year the agency went into action again, this time in support of the non-communist trade unions in Italy, France and Germany. The unions, as Tom Braden recalled, were 'a particular target – that was one of the activities in which the communists spent the most money'.[3] In France and Italy the communists controlled large parts of the trade union movement. In France the communist-dominated unions were behind the waves of strikes which broke out in the winters of 1946–7 and 1947–8. In 1947 the non-communist unions led by Leon Jouhaux formed their own organization with help from the CIA. In Italy the trade union movement was dominated by the communists and by the marxist-socialists led by Pietro Nenni. In 1949, with CIA support, the non-communist unions seceded from the movement and founded a rival organization. In West Germany, financial support was given to unions through the offices of Walter Reuther, of the United Auto Workers Union, and his brother, Victor, who lived in Germany.

In the international trade union movement the CIA was equally active. In 1949 the British and American trade unions left the World Federation of Trade Unions, founded at the instigation of the Soviets in 1945, and established a new organization with CIA support, the International Confederation of Free Trade Unions. The agency received considerable help from American union leaders in the Congress of Industrial Organizations (CIO), who had had many bitter struggles with communist infiltration of their own unions in the United States.

A major clandestine operation was launched in order to ensure that officials with pro-Western sympathies secured key union positions. This was underpinned by detailed research and assessments of the trade union movement. Some of those involved in this operation were ex-communists, notably Jay Lovestone, who had been general secretary of the American Communist party in the 1920s. After the war he grew close to George Meany of the American Federation of Labor which formally merged with the Congress of Industrial Organizations to form the AFL-CIO in December 1955. Lovestone became director of international affairs of the AFL-CIO in which post he wielded considerable influence throughout the world trade union movement.

# THE BATTLE FOR PICASSO'S MIND

During the 1950s and 1960s the CIA gave support to a wide range of organizations, individuals, newspapers and periodicals throughout Europe in order to prevent any extension of communist influence. This was operated by the international organizations division of the DDP which was headed first by Tom Braden and then by Cord Meyer. Braden was particularly anxious to get the support of intellectuals:

> We had a vast project targeted on the intellectuals – 'the battle for Picasso's mind', if you will. The communists set up fronts which effectively enticed a great many – particularly the French – intellectuals to join. We tried to set up a counterfront.[4]

One of the most important anti-communist cultural organizations was the Congress for Cultural Freedom, and its magazines *Encounter* in Britain, *Die Monat* in West Germany, and *Preuves* in France. In one year, Braden recalled, the CIA's budget for the Congress was $800–900,000. The purpose of the Congress was to provide a gathering point for non-communist intellectuals in an organization which could also help them publish their work, and could hold conferences and seminars which would help influence journalists and critics in support. It was a high-class lobbying operation, in effect. It had the great advantage that many people readily agreed with its objectives and were willing to support it. Most of the people who worked for the Congress and its magazines, and who attended Congress functions and were published with Congress help, had no idea that they were in fact supported by the CIA. When this was revealed in 1967, at a time when the political atmosphere in the USA had changed radically, it led to the resignation of the Congress's director, and of Stephen Spender and Frank Kermode, two of *Encounter*'s three editors.

Radio Free Europe and Radio Liberty, which started in 1950 and 1951 respectively, also received massive financial support from the CIA. Although privately managed and owned, most of their annual $30–35 million budget came from the CIA. Braden and Meyer insisted on the journalistic independence of the two networks and resisted various attempts to use them for overt propaganda and disinformation campaigns.

The purpose of Radio Free Europe and Radio Liberty was to broadcast news and views from the west to the Soviet bloc in the various languages of the bloc.

They also broadcast talks by exiled writers and politicians. They were based in Germany, and on some occasions their broadcasts had considerable effect. In 1953, for example, RFE kept its listeners informed about the anti-communist demonstrations and riots which had broken out in Berlin and spread to the rest of East Germany. In 1956 RFE and Radio Liberty beamed the contents of Khrushchev's secret speech denouncing Stalin to Eastern Europe and the Soviet Union. RFE also accurately predicted the uprisings in Hungary and Poland which took place that year. Some of its broadcasts convinced freedom fighters in Hungary that US aid was coming, which it never did. After the uprising, many Hungarians blamed RFE for recklessly encouraging them.

Besides the trade unions and the intellectuals, Braden and Mayer devoted particular attention to the student movement. The International Union of Students had been founded in Prague in 1946 and was used by the Soviets in much the same way as the trade union movement was. The first Soviet vice-president of the IUS, Aleksandr Shelepin, later became head of the KGB. The IUS, Cord Meyer discovered, was:

> backed by virtually unlimited funds from the treasury of the Soviet Union. Owing a supranational allegiance to the Soviet Communist Party, disciplined young party activists throughout the world provided an interlocking directorate through which to influence the decisions of national student federations on matters ranging from policy positions to the selection of delegates, to the orchestration of propaganda campaigns.[5]

In 1947 the National Student Association was founded as a representative American student organization. The following year when the IUS refused to condemn the imposition of communist dictatorship in Czechoslovakia, the Association left the IUS and in 1950 established the International Student Conference with non-communist European student unions.

## GERMANY

Germany was at the heart of the Cold War in Europe. No one wanted a reunited Germany outside their control in the 1945–55 period.

From before the end of the war, the Western Allies quickly came to experience ruthless Soviet enslavements and expropriations, especially with factories and technical and industrial intelligence. Western technical experts made a thorough analysis of Germany's wartime scientific and industrial research, and made their findings freely available to the Russians who signally failed to reciprocate. The Soviet zone of Germany was closed to the West and the Soviet experts sent all their discoveries straight to Moscow without sharing them. Thousands of German scientists were sent to Russia, many of whom never returned. Exploiting the Potsdam agreement on German war reparations, the Russians dismantled all the main research centres in their zone and shipped them back to Russia.

The Russians already had the basis of an espionage service in West Germany. This was the Rote Kapelle (Red Orchestra), one of the most effective anti-Nazi networks during the war. Within days of the fall of Berlin, Lavrenti Beria, head of the NKVD, the Soviet secret police and forerunner of the KGB, established headquarters at Karlshorst in East Berlin. Soviet military intelligence, GRU, also opened an office in Berlin. Both services immediately began to penetrate and infiltrate the Western zones.

The partition of Germany gave them ample opportunity to recruit agents. Millions of Germans had served in Nazi organizations. The records of these organizations provided documents that could be used to blackmail people starting new lives. There were additional blackmail levers in the form of divided families and possessions. People with a mother or a father, say, in East Germany, could be persuaded to spy for the Soviets in return for better treatment for their parents. SS Obersturmführer Heinz Felfe, who became head of counterintelligence in the Gehlen organization, had a mother in Dresden in East Germany, his SS record was in Soviet hands, and he spied for the Russians. Berlin became known as 'kidnap town' in intelligence circles because of the frequency with which the Russians and the East German secret police kidnapped people and took them across the border into East Berlin. There were assassinations as well.

One kidnap victim was Otto John, head of the West German Federal Office for the Protection of the Constitution, the *Bundesamt für Verfassungsschutz* (BfV), who was taken to East Berlin in 1954. John had been a member of the 20 July 1944 plot against Hitler, and had strong anti-Nazi credentials. At the time it was believed that John had defected. John returned to West Germany four years later and was tried and found guilty of treason – a charge he always denied.

The CIA's Office of Special Operations developed a close relationship with the West German foreign intelligence service, the *Bundesnachrichtendienst* (BND), headed by Reinhard Gehlen, the former Wehrmacht protégé of the US Army, who was to remain in that post until 1968. The BND became something of a haven for ex-senior Wehrmacht officers, and for a number of ex-SS men – many of whom it later emerged were in fact Soviet spies. The CIA liaison officer who dealt with Gehlen, James Critchfield, had offices in the Gehlen headquarters at Pullach near Munich. Critchfield urged Gehlen to concentrate on espionage rather than on order-of-battle intelligence since Gehlen had contacts and agents in the east dating from the war. Gehlen, however, depended far more on signals intelligence and monitoring than on reports from agents in the field. He was bedevilled by bureaucratic intrigues involving Britain's SIS which supported BfV (indeed, some suspected that Otto John's 'defection' to the East was arranged by members of the Gehlen organization in order to discredit both John and the BfV). Horst Eitner, one of Gehlen's agents, was hired by SIS to obtain information about the Gehlen organization and its contacts in the East and was exposed as a Soviet spy in 1961.

Gehlen had several highly placed agents in East Germany. One, Hermann Kastner, was close to the East German leader, Walter Ulbricht, and subsequently became a member of the East German cabinet. Another, Walter Gramsch, was a member of the East German intelligence service. Yet another of Gehlen's agents managed to obtain the plans and test-flight records of Russia's first jet plane, the MiG-15.

Despite such successes, and despite the close working relationship which Gehlen's service had with CIA, the fact remained that for decades West Germany was one of the weakest links in NATO security.

In April 1961 the West German minister of the interior revealed to the Bundestag that there were approximately 16,000 known East German agents in West Germany. Between 1950 and 1960, 2186 agents had been caught and convicted of treason charges; a further 19,000 had confessed to espionage missions but were not prosecuted. In August 1968, six known East German agents fled back to the East after the defection to the West of the Czech general, Jan Sejna, who revealed several spy nets. The Soviets decided to secure a propaganda victory, and instead of pulling their agents out, left them in place. They calculated that the number of spies, and their positions in West Germany, would rock NATO and West German confidence. In October 1968, Rear Admiral Hermann Luedke was revealed as a Soviet agent. Within days he was dead: shot in the base of his spine with a soft-nosed bullet. He was almost certainly murdered. His was the first of thirteen deaths of West German officials, all dying in a two-week period, all revealed as Soviet spies. It was presumed in intelligence circles that they had all been murdered or driven to suicide by the Soviets in pursuit of their propaganda coup. In 1974, the Chancellor, Willy Brandt, resigned after the discovery that Gunther and Christel Guillaume were East German spies: Gunther, the son of a friend of Brandt's, was his political aide in the Chancellor's office.

In the 1970s, as the war generation retired, seduction became a major element in the Soviet spy game. In March 1979 six secretaries – all working for senior politicians and in government ministries – defected: they had been seduced and turned into spies by agents from the Soviet Union and East Germany. Every year a number of German women working in government, military establishments, and industry were compromised in this way. Germany was totally penetrated by both sides. It was a lesson in ambiguity that acted to mature the CIA.

By the early 1950s the situation in Germany could be described as one of stand-off and brinkmanship as the threat of war receded. This was vividly demonstrated in June 1953 when anti-communist demonstrations and riots erupted in East Berlin and then spread to the rest of East Germany. The CIA station immediately cabled Washington for permission to give arms to the demonstrators. John A. Bross, chief of the division dealing with Eastern and Central Europe, consulted his boss Frank Wisner, the Deputy Director of Plans. The Berlin station was told that while it should encourage expressions of sympathy and praise for the demonstrators and circulate offers of asylum in West Berlin, it was not to distribute weapons.

The Bross-Wisner telegram caused considerable dissatisfaction among some Washington officials who felt that the CIA should have seized the chance to make trouble for the Soviets and promote disorder in East Germany. Wisner and Bross believed that since the USA had no intention of going to war to protect the demonstrators, giving arms to them would only have led to useless bloodshed.

## ASSASSINS

Bloodshed was a feature of the early Cold War years in Germany. Agents on both sides were killed in Berlin, and CIA officers were often armed. The Soviets had developed assassination techniques and had trained killers since 1917. At Kuchino, just outside Moscow, two secret laboratories were devoted to developing poisons and murder weapons. Until the Cold War began, Soviet assassins were used principally against domestic opponents and defectors. In 1954 one of the assassins, Nikolai Khoklov, gave himself up to the CIA.

Khoklov had been sent to Frankfurt to kill Georgi Sergeevich Okolovich, a leader of the anti-communist Russian émigré group, NTS. But instead of completing his mission, he warned Okolovich that he was on a death list and showed him the death warrant issued by the central committee of the Communist party of the Soviet Union. Okolovich contacted the CIA, and the next day they took Khoklov into custody. Khoklov's two accomplices were arrested, and the assassination weapon – a miniature electric gun disguised as a packet of cigarettes that noiselessly fired soft-nosed bullets coated in potassium cyanide – was found. Khoklov and Okolovich gave a press conference revealing the whole story and showing the cigarette packet gun.

Three years later, a Soviet assassin managed to poison Khoklov in Frankfurt. He had cramps, then his skin turned blotchy and developed brown stripes. Blood started to seep through his skin, and doctors were baffled as to what was wrong. US army doctors treated Khoklov with constant blood transfusions, massive doses of cortisone and a number of experimental drugs. Gradually he began to recover: toxicologists discovered that he had been poisoned with radioactive thallium that destroyed white blood cells and body fluids.

Bogdan Stashinsky was another Soviet assassin. In 1957 in Munich he killed Lev Rebet, a Ukrainian exile leader. In 1959, again in Munich, he killed Stefan Bandera, another Ukrainian exile. In both cases he had used a specially developed gas gun that fired a glass ampoule filled with prussic acid that exploded in his victims' faces. Stashinsky was given the Order of the Red Banner in Moscow for his work. On 12 August 1961 – a day before the Berlin Wall went up – he defected to West Berlin, confessed to the murders, and was tried. Found guilty, he was sentenced to eight years in gaol as an accomplice to murder: the court held that the principal guilt lay with unnamed men in Moscow and the Soviet system who saw political murder as a state necessity.

The CIA, naturally, was influenced by such experiences and sought to develop an assassination – 'executive action', it was euphemistically termed – capability of its own. Some freelance agents were trained and toxins and weapons were developed in an attempt to match the Soviets. Assassination plots were hatched, and plans were actually made (almost certainly with presidential authority) against Patrice Lumumba in the Congo and Fidel Castro in Cuba. In 1975 Castro himself

*Overleaf* President Kennedy with Chancellor Konrad Adenauer and Mayor of West Berlin Willy Brandt by the Berlin Wall – symbol of a divided Germany and the East–West conflict – on 27 June 1963. Between August 1961, when the Wall went up, until its opening in December 1990, 191 people were killed and around 5000 were captured trying to escape from the East.

reckoned that there had been over thirty CIA-inspired attempts on his life. No CIA assassination, however, has ever been found out. This may be because they have been successfully disguised (a heart attack can be mistaken for a prussic acid death, as happened in the case of Stefan Bandera), or because none have succeeded. William Colby, who investigated such activities inside the agency in the 1970s, indicated that the executive action capacity had been there, but had been unsuccessful: there were no assassinations, he said, but 'it wasn't for want of trying'.

## TAPPING THE LINES

Vienna and Berlin were the paradigm Western Cold War cities whose extraordinary atmosphere of menace and intrigue inspired a generation of spies in films and novels, ranging from Graham Greene's Harry Lime in *The Third Man* to John le Carré's George Smiley. Like Berlin, Vienna was occupied by the four wartime allies – France, Britain, the United States and the Soviet Union – and was to remain so until 1955, when the Austrian State Treaty was signed making Austria a neutral state, leading to the end of the Allied occupation. This cheek-by-jowl proximity inspired some of the most daring and innovative operations of the Cold War in Europe.

The headquarters of the Soviet occupation forces in Austria was at the Imperial Hotel on the Ringstrasse, the main Viennese thoroughfare. To discover what went on in the Imperial Hotel became the prime object of the agency's Vienna station as well as SIS. The British had realized that since administrative centralization had been one of the chief characteristics of the old European empires, all major roads and telephone lines tended to converge on their capitals. Thus, in order to make a telephone call from one city in Austria to another, the chances were that the call would be routed through Vienna. By linking into the main telephone land lines near a private house in a Vienna suburb, the British found that they could tap into Soviet communications.

This operation, codenamed 'Silver', had been in progress since 1949, unknown to the CIA. It was only when Carl Nelson, an officer in the CIA's Office of Communications, started his own investigation into Vienna's underground cable routes that SIS disclosed 'Silver' to him.

Nelson's involvement with 'Silver' led to an important discovery which increased its value enormously. He found out that Sigtot, a cipher machine used by the CIA, gave off electronic echoes of the clear text as it was typed in to the encoder, at a distance of up to twenty miles down the line. Sigtot was quickly jettisoned by the agency. Nelson, however, discovered that Soviet communications had the same fault. The CIA kept this information to itself. When the British agreed to share 'Silver' with the agency, Nelson's discovery enabled the Office of Communications to break a whole range of Soviet codes and to gather a mass of vital information, the most important of which was that the Soviets did not intend to invade Tito's Yugoslavia, enabling the United States to show support for Tito knowing that its words would not be tested. After the outbreak of the Korean war in June 1950, this intelligence was particularly useful in determining American troop deployments in Europe and the Far East.

The success of 'Silver' led directly to a similar operation in Berlin – operation 'Gold' – the tapping of Soviet landlines from Karlshorst in East Berlin. This was done in collaboration with the British who had the original idea. SIS and the CIA drew up a plan for the construction of a tunnel to be drilled from the southern West Berlin suburb of Altglienecke, five hundred yards from the Soviet headquarters' landlines. The tunnel posed complex problems which tested the ingenuity of the Americans and the British to the limit.

The Soviets learned about the Berlin tunnel in its planning stage: one of the British team, George Blake, was a Soviet agent. But they knew nothing of Carl Nelson's echo-effect discovery because of the CIA's decision not to tell the British. The prime Soviet concern was the security of their codes and they believed them to be safe. So they took the view that it would be better to protect their spy than to stop the tunnel, and kept their knowledge to themselves. The tunnel was finished in February 1955. Three landlines were tapped, each one carrying one telegraph and four telephone lines, which could carry up to four communications each at a time. The volume of the material was staggering and at times threatened to swamp the operation. Up to 1200 hours of material a day was recorded, using 800 reels of tape. Airplane-loads of tapes were flown out of Berlin every week for examination in London and in Washington by fifty CIA officers fluent in Russian and German. The translators and analysts had to work two weeks on and one day off to keep up with the accumulating material.

The tunnel was discovered by the East Germans in April 1956. Heavy rain had seeped into the landlines, requiring maintenance work. When the East German telephone engineers dug up the cable to repair it they found the tap.

The CIA thought that when the tunnel was discovered, the Soviets would not dare reveal the fact that Western intelligence had been reading their high level communications circuits. In fact, the commandant of the Soviet garrison

A Soviet photograph of the interior of the Berlin tunnel in the Altglienecke section of Berlin. The tunnel was an Anglo-American espionage coup and engineering feat, tapping into the telephone lines from the Soviet headquarters at Karlshorst in East Berlin. It operated for eleven months until it was discovered in April 1956.

in East Berlin was absent at the time and his deputy invited the entire Berlin press corps to a tour of the tunnel and its facilities, pointing them out as examples of Western perfidy. The press reaction was not what he expected. The tunnel was hailed as a wonderful example of American ingenuity and, in the words of one Berlin editor, was 'the best publicity the US has had in Berlin for a long time'.[6] It took the agency another two and a half years to get through the backlog of tapes.

## BETRAYAL

Although the CIA had worked closely with their SIS colleagues in Vienna and Berlin, both operations had undercurrents of strain in their collaboration. The CIA was not sure that British intelligence was free of Soviet spies. This was just one of the ripple effects of the Burgess-Maclean-Philby scandal which had such momentous consequences for British-American intelligence relations.

In July 1947 Bill Harvey, a senior FBI officer who had been investigating Soviet spy rings within the US, joined the CIA's Office of Special Operations. With his experience in counterespionage and knowledge of FBI operations, Harvey was a very valuable recruit for the new agency and he spent two years building up a counterintelligence group, Staff C. In 1949, Harvey went over the Soviet codes which Donovan and the OSS had obtained from the Finns in November 1944. It was only then that a 1945 message sent by a Soviet agent in New York to Moscow was deciphered. It contained the complete text of a telegram from Churchill to Truman, sent from London via the British Embassy in Washington and containing various embassy reference numbers. It was very strong evidence that there had been a spy working at a senior level in the embassy. Who was he? And where was he now?

At the time these revelations were emerging, Kim Philby was British intelligence's liaison officer with the CIA. In 1938 and again in 1945 two Soviet defectors, Krivitsky and Volkov, had mentioned the presence of high-level moles in British intelligence, but Krivitsky died (probably murdered by Soviet agents) before he could give details, and Kim Philby alerted the Soviets to Volkov who kidnapped and murdered him. Bill Harvey, however, pursued the codebreaking leads and early in 1951 identified the British diplomat, Donald Maclean, as the Soviet spy in the British Embassy in 1945. By that time, Maclean was on the American desk in the Foreign Office in London.

In Washington, Philby learned of Bill Harvey's suspicions and evidence. He told another Soviet spy in the Foreign Office, Anthony Burgess, who was staying with him in Washington. Burgess, Maclean and Philby had all been at Cambridge together in the mid-1930s, and had become secret members of the Communist party there. Burgess returned to London and warned Maclean that arrest was imminent, and the two fled to Moscow in May 1951. Burgess' flight was not planned – it seems to have been a spontaneous decision – and it immediately cast suspicion on his friend, Philby. Bill Harvey categorically stated that Philby was a Soviet spy three weeks after Burgess and Maclean absconded.

The reaction of the CIA was immediate. Bedell Smith told Sir Stewart Menzies of SIS, 'Fire Philby or we break off the intelligence relationship.' Philby was recalled to London. He managed to bluff his way out of being arrested, but he had to leave the SIS. It was to be another twelve years before the scale of Philby's treachery was fully appreciated when he finally defected to Moscow.

There was considerable speculation then, and since, about the extent of the damage which Maclean and Philby wreaked on American intelligence. Maclean was aware of economic and political plans for post-war Europe: he knew the details of Anglo-American intelligence agreements with NATO; he knew about uranium requirements for atomic-energy schemes; he had access to several diplomatic codes. But nothing caused the agency greater anguish than Maclean's knowledge of Anglo-American policy at a sensitive stage in the Korean war. It was suspected that Maclean had told the Chinese, through their Russian contacts, that the United Nations had decided that they would not retaliate against China if Chinese troops entered the Korean war. Maclean was in a position to know that in October 1950, Truman had ordered General Douglas MacArthur, commander of UN forces in Korea, not to attack Chinese territory without prior authority from Washington.

Maclean was bad enough but what was the extent of Philby's betrayal? It could be argued that Maclean's base of operations concerned diplomacy, a more 'open' area of national strategy where a secret did not remain a secret for very long because a country's intentions soon became clear. Philby's milieu, on the other hand, consisted of unofficial, high-level contacts with the FBI and the CIA, briefings with the most powerful people in Washington. It was an informal, fluid world and as a result it proved extremely difficult to gauge the extent of the damage Philby did. Where Philby was known to have caused harm was in Anglo-American intelligence operations in Albania, the Baltic states, and the Ukraine. In Albania, an attempt was made to overthrow the communist regime of Enver Hoxha. Albanian exiles were trained and then dropped on the Albanian coast to move inland and organize resistance. Every single one was captured and most were killed: the operation had been betrayed from within by Philby. In the Baltic and the Ukraine, military and material support for nationalist movements and agents was sent in. In both cases most of those involved in the operations were also captured and executed. William Sloane Coffin, a CIA officer responsible in the early 1950s for training émigrés to parachute into the Soviet Union as agents, recalled that not one of the operations in which he had been involved had been successful.

In the aftermath of the Maclean-Burgess-Philby treachery, there were scores of such painful post-mortems. Worst of all were the depths of bitterness and distrust which had such a corrosive effect on the Anglo-American intelligence relationship. For many in the CIA who had been in the wartime OSS, and who respected the British, the scale of Philby's treason in particular was devastating. He had been considered a friend by many of them, and had been trusted with the most sensitive information. How had he disguised his true allegiance for so long? How could he have betrayed friends and allies in such a cold-blooded fashion? There was a lurking belief that the old boy network of the British establishment had protected their own. Ten years later Philby's successor as British intelligence liaison in Washington, Maurice Oldfield, was still finding resounding echoes of the scandal. Within two weeks of his arrival in Washington he was shown a memorandum by the Joint Chiefs of Staff which claimed that the British had done little or nothing to prevent a repetition of those events and that Burgess and Maclean 'were apparently protected by others in high places, some allegedly still in key positions'.[7]

Ray Cline, who was one of the CIA's estimates liaison officers in London from October 1951 to November 1953 – the period in the immediate aftermath of the scandal – noted realistically:

There was no other major service in the world with which to collaborate. The Germans were penetrated more badly. The Israelis had a limited service of high quality. If we were to have any serious collaboration, we had to have it with the British. We had early on split the world with the Brits on code-breaking and monitoring ... We had a lot of benefits from the operation and I would argue it was well worth taking the risks we took ... The people who criticized only had one major argument in their favour: the unique case of the Cambridge cell ... It could happen in America too: feelings of utopianism, alienation, depression in the 1930s. It was an historical accident ... We had [Alger] Hiss – not as bad as the Philby case, but there ... I don't think our system worked any better except for the one damning thing of the Cambridge spies.[8]

Cline's assessment proved accurate: American intelligence was not immune to treason. At the very time of the Burgess-Maclean defection, the FBI had tracked down a traitor in the Armed Forces Security Agency who sold the Russians the information that the CIA possessed their 1944 code book. In 1960 two homosexual cryptologists employed by the National Security Agency defected to Moscow, having joined the Communist party two years before, a fact of which the NSA was unaware.

Nevertheless, to many in the American military and intelligence establishment, the Cambridge spies were a potent symbol of British political and moral decline, of a country living beyond its means and cracking apart. The Profumo scandal of 1963 (when the Secretary for War was found to have had an affair with a party girl who also had a relationship with a Soviet military attaché in London) and the Jellicoe-Lambton scandal ten years later (when two government ministers were found to have had relationships with prostitutes, opening them to potential blackmail) did nothing to lessen that belief. The imperial lion had become motheaten and was in retreat on all fronts.

# 5
# COUPS
## *1953–1959*

*A*s 1953 opened there was a new President, a new Secretary of State, and a new Director of the CIA. The working relationship between the three was to be extraordinarily close and effective. The shrewd, cautious Eisenhower, with his glittering war record, was the first Republican President since Herbert Hoover. He took a traditional Republican line on domestic issues, but on foreign policy he differed noticeably from the Congressional Republicans. Many of them still nourished a strong distrust of Britain, and their isolationism, as so often in the past, took the form of a desire to act alone in the Far East and to ignore Europe. Eisenhower, with his wartime and NATO experience, knew that Europe could not be ignored. He also thought that the popular cries about rolling back communism should remain just hot air. Refusing to enter into an all-out arms race with the Soviets, he preferred to concentrate on deterrence, placing particular emphasis on élite high-tech forces such as Strategic Air Command.

As his Secretary of State, Eisenhower appointed John Foster Dulles; as his Director of Central Intelligence he appointed Foster's brother Allen. The Dulles brothers came from a family with a long and distinguished background in diplomacy and the law. Their maternal grandfather, John Foster, had been Secretary of State under Benjamin Harrison. Their uncle, Robert Lansing, had been Woodrow Wilson's Secretary of State. John Foster Dulles had been a member of the US team at the Versailles peace conference where he was a chief negotiator on war reparations. His New York law firm, Sullivan & Cromwell (where Allen also worked), was deeply involved in arranging American loans to Europe and he kept in close contact with European politics during the interwar period. Eisenhower and Dulles thus had impeccable foreign policy credentials and they taught something new to the Republicans: that an activist, liberal foreign policy could go hand in hand with conservatism at home.[1]

Next to his outwardly conservative and sombre brother, Allen Dulles had a more adventurous and romantic aspect. He graduated from Princeton in 1914, and then taught English for a year in India, developing a dislike of the British empire in the process. In 1916 he entered the State Department and was posted to Vienna. The following year he was sent to Berne. He liked to tell the story of his time in Switzerland when a Mr Lenin sent a message saying that he would like to meet him urgently. Dulles had an engagement to play tennis with friends, and so ignored the message. Only later did he realize that the exiled Lenin would probably have told him that he was returning to Russia. Who knows, Dulles later mused, if the course of history would have been different if he had met Lenin.

In 1919 he joined his brother as a member of the US delegation to the Paris peace conference. Then he served in Berlin and Constantinople, before returning to Washington as head of the State Department's Near East division. In 1926 he left the foreign service and joined Sullivan & Cromwell. He kept a connection with the State Department, however, and served as legal adviser to the US delegations at the League of Nations' Geneva conferences of 1927 and 1932. In 1942 William Donovan recruited him for the OSS, and from October 1942 until November 1945 he was head of clandestine operations in Europe, and of the OSS mission in Germany. In April 1945 he negotiated the surrender of German forces in northern Italy.

He was the American closest to being a professional intelligence officer. He was friendly, warm and outgoing in personality and under his directorship the agency had a high profile which he relished. He gave an interview to *Time* which put him on the cover, and he insisted that DDI officers should have the opportunity to publish. Good lawyers know that you gain by disclosing as much as possible: Dulles was a DCI unimpressed by the cult of secrecy. He was also responsible for the construction of the new CIA headquarters at Langley in Virginia, a building which was even signposted on the George Washington Parkway.

Allen Dulles also had a well-earned reputation for being loyal to subordinates: he had protected CIA officers against McCarthy's witch hunt, and he was insistent that the agency's academic analysts should be able to publish their work in declassified form so that they could gain the respect of their peers. If they were not able to do this, he argued, the CIA would not be able to attract and retain high-quality staff. One of his greatest contributions to the agency was the high morale he created.

The role of the Director of Central Intelligence was established during the Eisenhower presidency. He was the President's man in the intelligence community, and unquestionably the President's foremost adviser on intelligence matters. As head of the CIA, he was also in charge of the most active and apparently effective arm of US foreign policy. The range of the agency's activities – collection, analysis, espionage and operations – challenged the power and authority of State and Defense. This was much less of a problem for Allen Dulles as long as his brother was Secretary of State, but it was to bedevil his successors. If a DCI ever came into serious conflict with a Secretary of State or the Secretary of Defense, he knew he could not win without the President's support. The secretaries had the power, the budget and the pull in Congress. As R. Jack Smith, CIA Deputy Director of Intelligence, put it succinctly, 'Congressmen are naturally interested all the time for things in their local constituencies which the military can grant, for favours which State can grant. So if it comes to that kind of contest, the director can never win.'[2]

Eisenhower always gave Allen Dulles his full support, and rejected pleas from the military and some Congressmen to dismiss him: they were worried by CIA operations. 'I'm not going to be able to change Allen,' Eisenhower admitted. 'I have two alternatives, either to get rid of him and appoint someone who will assert more authority or keep him with his limitations. I'd rather have Allen as my chief intelligence officer with his limitations than anyone else I know.'[3]

Eisenhower's support explains why Dulles was not much bothered about territorial rivalries. He preferred to work alone, depending on his close personal contacts within the governing élite. His brother, after all, was Secretary of State and he had Eisenhower's complete confidence. A simple telephone call or meeting at home could sort out problems. For example, Tom Braden was having trouble with the French desk at the State Department. He went to see his chief to complain: 'I said, "Allen, French in the State Department doesn't want to do this," and Allen said "What?!" then picked up the phone: "Foster, one of your people seems to be a little less than cooperative." That's power.'[4]

With this kind of support Dulles was able to concentrate on covert operations – the part of his job which he enjoyed most and which attracted most praise from Eisenhower and from Foster. After his experiences in World War I and World War II, clandestine activities in all their forms were meat and drink to Dulles. Espionage was part of the very fabric of his life and under Eisenhower's presidency he was given the opportunity to exploit it to the full.

Because of Dulles' personal preference for the cloak-and-dagger side of intelligence, Frank Wisner had easy and frequent access to him. Wisner and Dulles had known each other in the OSS and there was nothing better both men enjoyed than concocting various plans and schemes together.

The élite in the DDP were often swashbucklers and buccaneers, with the connivance of Allen Dulles drawing up projects without consulting other sections of the agency. This caused friction. Richard Bissell, who succeeded Wisner as DDP in 1958, recalled:

> After I became DDP I began to see Allen's managerial practices from a slightly different standpoint. He would quite often call someone who was two or three echelons down from me. He would call them about a cable that had come in, and he would sometimes tell them how to answer it. I finally blew up at Allen ... [his] instant reaction on the phone was quite violent. He said 'I'm going to speak to anybody I want to in this agency about anything I want to speak to them about... If your people haven't been telling you about their conversations with me, that's because you're not enforcing the rules!' He was right. I came to live with it, and I realized it was part of his way, and it was a perfectly good way to run the place.[5]

## COVERT OPERATIONS

When the CIA was set up in 1947 it was not expected that it would be responsible for covert actions. That situation changed within a year and the agency entered the operational field. The OPC and OSO, which in 1952 were merged under the Directorate of Plans, were soon engaged in covert action in Europe. Because covert action came about as an immediate response to an emergency, little thought was given at the time to its potential hazards. In January 1949, the NSC directive which set up OPC stated that its operations must be: 'so planned and conducted that any US government responsibility for them is not evident to unauthorized persons and that if uncovered the US government can plausibly disclaim any responsibility for them'.[6]

The message was clear: don't get caught, but if you do make sure you don't cause any trouble for Washington. It was a remarkably naïve and simpleminded message. What would happen when agents were captured and forced to make public confessions? Later, after the shooting-down of the U-2 spy plane and the failure of the Bay of Pigs, the true meaning of this message would be learned publicly and painfully. In 1949, however, as the Cold War escalated, no one had time to study the possible implications.

As covert operations increased, so did the coordination problems between the agency, the White House, the State and Defense departments and the NSC. In 1955 the NSC issued two directives on control procedures for covert activities. A group of designated representatives was set up, consisting of the nominees of the President and the Secretaries of State and Defense, to review and approve projects. This group survived into the 1970s. The chairman of the Joint Chiefs of Staff attended, as did others on an ad hoc basis depending on projects and policies. The National Security Adviser, McGeorge Bundy under Kennedy, Walt Rostow under Johnson and Henry Kissinger under Nixon, attended all meetings and represented the White House.

## THE PHILIPPINES

The agency's definition of covert operations was 'any clandestine operation or activity designed to influence foreign governments, organizations, persons or events in support of United States foreign policy'. They had been in progress for two years in Cold War Europe when the outbreak of the Korean war provided the impetus for a huge increase in paramilitary and covert activities. Even before the North Korean attack in June 1950 the agency had established a base in Taiwan, under the guise of a company called Western Enterprises Inc., to train Nationalist Chinese guerrillas for raids on the communist mainland. In 1952, two CIA agents were captured in China where they were trying to organize anti-communist guerrilla groups.

The Chinese operation was one of several undertaken in the Far East to keep out the communists. Lieutenant Colonel Edward Lansdale arrived in Manila in 1950 as head of an OPC team, under cover of being an adviser to the Philippine army. In fact his task was to develop an effective counter to the communist Hukbalahap ('Huk') rebellion which had begun in 1948. The Hukbalahaps, meaning 'anti-Japanese army', was a World War II group that had resisted Japanese occupation. It was reformed in 1948 to become one of several communist insurgencies which had broken out in the Far East after the war, notably in Malaya where the British were waging a hard-fought campaign against the communists there.

Like the Malayans, the Huks had started in 1942 as a 'peoples' army' to fight the Japanese but had refused to surrender their arms to the Philippine government when the war ended. By 1950 they controlled most of central Luzon and even part of Manila.

Lansdale drew up a sophisticated programme of military, political and psychological measures to counter the Huks. These focused on Ramón Magsaysay as the national figure most able to present an alternative to both the communists and the politicians who had collaborated with the Japanese during World War II. As the agency had done in Italy in 1948, Lansdale gave Magsaysay help in the form of election funds, propaganda leaflets, posters and broadcasts. In August Magsaysay was appointed Secretary of National Defense and, working closely with Lansdale, launched an effective military and psychological campaign against the Huks. CIA analysts concluded that the Huks would only give up fighting if they were given a worthwhile alternative. The Huks were offered the choice of constant warfare or economic stability with resettlement and land ownership. The son of a poor blacksmith, Magsaysay appreciated the attractiveness of this plan: if a farmer owns his own piece of property, he will resist anyone who tries to take it away from him.[7] He and Lansdale established the Economic Development Corps through which Huks who surrendered were given a piece of land, tools, seeds and a cash loan to be repaid over a five-year term.

In the Philippines, support for the resettlement scheme was non-existent outside the Department of National Defense, but as the 1953 presidential elections approached, Lansdale embarked on a more active military campaign against the Huks who still resisted resettlement, and thus gave Magsaysay additional electoral appeal. The technique of working through second and third parties was developed by Lansdale in the Philippines into a high art of counterinsurgency, and it became a hallmark of CIA methodology, notably in Laos and Vietnam. Philippine army units were even disguised as Huks, attacking villages, so as to generate more support for the government. To back up Magsaysay's candidacy, two organizations were formed with CIA backing, the National Movement for Free Elections and the Magsaysay for President movement.

Magsaysay easily won the election in September 1953, a victory hailed by the *New York Times* as making the Philippines 'the showcase of democracy in Asia' and by Eisenhower who declared, 'This is the way we like to see an election being carried out.' His victory coincided with the ceasefire in the Korean war.

The work and the approach to counterguerrilla warfare of Lansdale and his team represented an important and distinguishing element of the CIA: it was a *liberal* American institution, seeking to establish liberal democratic principles in its operations.

In the Philippines, with Magsaysay, the agency had succeeded in checking the communist insurgency and placing an able, non-communist leader in power. But what would it do when there were already radically nationalist governments in power, as in Iran and Guatemala?

## IRAN

In many ways Iran was to be a nemesis for the agency, but when it first intervened in Iranian affairs, in the early 1950s, confidence and a fierce rivalry with the British characterized American involvement, rather than foreboding. In 1951 the Nationalist Party led by Muhammad Mussadegh came to power and soon sidelined the young Shah, Muhammad Reza Pahlevi, who had ruled under British auspices since 1941. For decades, the British had extensive interests in Iran, first, attempting to prevent Russian expansion into the Gulf and the Indian Ocean, and secondly, the protection of oil supplies which were managed by the Anglo-Iranian Oil Company. The company had been founded in 1901 by an Englishman who was given a sixty-year monopoly. In 1914 the British government purchased a substantial share in the company which had a contract to supply the Royal Navy. The Shah was given production royalties by the company and these were increased in 1933 when its monopoly was extended for a further sixty years.

Early in 1951, Mussadegh expropriated the company and when compensation was not forthcoming, the British began to apply pressure which effectively amounted to a blockade of Iranian oil supplies. Mussadegh refused to bow to British pressure although the effects on the Iranian economy were devastating. The British were anxious to secure American support to regain their oil monopoly and played up Mussadegh's nationalistic attempt to assert Iranian authority as pro-Soviet. But they soon realized that British and American interests did not coincide.

Shortly after Mussadegh's expropriation of Anglo-Iranian Oil, John Foster Dulles visited the Middle East and concluded that Soviet influence was gaining in the area. He was not particularly impressed with British policies in the Gulf and believed that there might be more to gain from the American point of view by convincing the Arabs that the USA was not on the side of the old imperial powers, Britain and France. Naturally, this would also be an opportunity to extend American commercial interests into valuable new markets.

Initially, the US government took no action against Mussadegh, but in 1953, after reports of a Soviet-Iranian loan and alliance, Eisenhower and Dulles agreed

Muhammad Mussadegh, Prime Minister of Iran (1951–3), was popular with Iranians and unpopular with Britain and the United States. He nationalized the Anglo-Iranian Oil Company and seemed friendly towards the USSR. He was toppled in a coup organized by the CIA and the British Secret Intelligence Service.

to cooperate with the British in a clandestine operation to remove Mussadegh from power. This was the immediate aim. Their long-term motives were somewhat different. The British wanted to regain their oil concession whereas the United States was more worried about the Soviet threat.

In the CIA, responsibility for what became known as Operation Ajax was given to Kermit Roosevelt, grandson of Theodore Roosevelt, and an OSS veteran with extensive experience in covert operations. Roosevelt was charming, resourceful, understated, possessing great energy and a phenomenal range of contacts. He applied his skills to strengthening internal Iranian opposition to Mussadegh.

The plan which Roosevelt drew up in consultation with Dulles and the British envisaged a *coup d'état* based on assessments by the CIA and British intelligence that there were powerful sections of popular opinion and the army which favoured the overthrow of Mussadegh. The American ambassador in Tehran, Loy Henderson, was unhappy with the plan but saw no other alternative. He told Roosevelt: 'I don't like this kind of business at all . . . But we are confronted by a desperate, a dangerous situation and a madman who would ally himself with the Russians. We have no choice but to proceed with this undertaking.'[8]

Within two months Mussadegh was overthrown and the coup proved that the predictions of popular and army support were correct. To replace Mussadegh, Roosevelt chose General Fazlollah Zahedi, a person deeply unwelcome to the British since Zahedi had been arrested by them in 1941 as a Nazi sympathizer and interned in Palestine for the rest of the war. Zahedi, like Mussadegh, had been reaching for any balance to British interests in Iran: in 1941, Nazism was to hand; in 1951, communism. When the news was broken to Sir Patrick Dean, a senior foreign office official who was in Washington for Operation Ajax, there was an uncomfortable silence. But Dean realized that the British had no choice. By seeking American help to overthrow Mussadegh, it was axiomatic that American interests would come first. Zahedi became Prime Minister in 1953 and a new nationalized company was established, the National Iranian Oil Company, in which the British – who had previously enjoyed a monopoly – held an equal stake of 40 per cent with US oil companies.

Operation Ajax was a major triumph for the agency. The financial cost was less than $200,000, although the budget had been four times that, and at most eight agency personnel were involved. Eisenhower and John Foster Dulles were ecstatic. Roosevelt, however, was less happy. When he briefed the President and Secretary of State about the operation on his return to Washington, he was disturbed by their reaction and by the conclusions which they drew from the success of Ajax:

> Foster Dulles had been so pleased and mesmerized by the success I'd had in Iran that he just figured I could solve any problem anywhere in the world ... I could see Foster Dulles sitting there licking his chops. I said, if you don't want something that the people and the army want, don't give it to clandestine operations, give it to the marines. And Foster Dulles sat there, just obviously not accepting that at all.[9]

Roosevelt's warning should have been inscribed in stone at the White House. Unfortunately, the long-term effects of Operation Ajax meant that the agency became a victim of its own success: the politicians were falling in love with covert operations. Victor Marchetti, who worked in the office of the DCI for four years before leaving in 1969, charted the development:

> Once I got upstairs and started working for Helms, I found out how the agency really works. I found that one boasted of intelligence but what rings the cash registers is clandestine operations, and within clandestine operations it isn't spying: it's covert action – overthrowing governments; manipulating governments; doing this, that, and the other, including assassinations. And in order to achieve these goals, anything goes. I could see how it worked. I was dealing with Congress and the White House.[10]

## GUATEMALA

In 1950, George Kennan addressed the second regional conference of US chiefs of mission which was being held in Rio de Janeiro. The subject of his address was Latin America and its importance to the United States.

Kennan had great prestige. He was recognized as the person who had accurately foretold the coming of the Cold War, and was credited with developing the US policy of 'containment' to deal with the expansionism of the Soviet Union. American policy, he declared to the diplomats, had three aims: to protect the vital supplies of raw materials which Latin American countries exported to the USA; to prevent the 'military exploitation of Latin America by the enemy'; and to avert 'the psychological mobilization of Latin America against us'. Latin America, Kennan argued, would be the last area of support left to the US if

Europe turned anti-American. As a result, Kennan said, American policy toward Latin America had to put US security interests first:

> The final answer might be an unpleasant one, but ... we should not hesitate before police repression by the local government. This is not shameful, since the communists are essentially traitors ... It is better to have a strong regime in power than a liberal government if it is indulgent and relaxed and penetrated by communists.[11]

These were fateful and prophetic words.

US business interests had a large economic stake in Latin America and by the end of the 1950s US-Latin American trade accounted for a third of the imports and a quarter of the exports of the United States. Of the foreign capital invested in Latin America, 80 per cent was from the USA. The trade had been advantageous to Latin Americans during the war when the USA paid high prices for raw materials, but after 1945 the volume fell. However, there was a post-war assumption that primary products would to a large extent govern terms of trade, and Kennan was reflecting this view.

Guatemala was a microcosm of these problems. Its economy was dominated by the American-owned United Fruit Company and when, in 1952, the Guatemalan government threatened United Fruit's interests, the US government was all too willing to see an ideological aspect in the 'persecution' of US business interests. United Fruit's record in Guatemala made it unsurprising that it should be threatened: if reform of land and working conditions were to be achieved, either United Fruit had to agree or it had to go. Shortly after his return to Washington from Iran, Kermit Roosevelt was asked to take charge of another covert operation: the overthrow of Jacobo Arbenz's government in Guatemala. Roosevelt refused and left the CIA, believing the love affair with coups was misplaced. But the scheme had the enthusiastic support of Foster Dulles who pressed ahead.

Arbenz came to power in March 1951, after an election in which he had won 65 per cent of the votes cast. He was determined to continue the social and economic reforms initiated by his predecessor, and in this he had the support of the Communist party and the working people's organizations. But he also incurred the hostility of the conservative opposition within Guatemala which regarded him as a crypto-communist. A plan to overthrow Arbenz, with the backing of Nicaragua's Anastasio Somoza, had been prepared during the last months of Truman's presidency but had been jettisoned after strong objections from Dean Acheson and his Undersecretary, David Bruce. The Eisenhower administration did not object.

In 1952 Arbenz expropriated United Fruit's holdings and, when he refused to offer compensation and to agree to arbitration at the International Court at The Hague, the company began to put pressure on the US government to act. United Fruit had powerful friends in Washington. Foster Dulles had been United Fruit's legal counsel; Allen Dulles was a shareholder; Robert Cutler, head of the National Security Council staff, had been a director; Thomas Corcoran was a paid consultant of the company while simultaneously working for the CIA, and Spruille Braden, Assistant Secretary of State for Latin American affairs, later joined United Fruit as a director.[12]

When Roosevelt declined to take charge of the Guatemalan plan, Wisner appointed his deputy, Tracy Barnes, to head Operation Success, as it now became known. For the first six months of 1954 the agency spent an estimated $20 million preparing for the coup. It set up a guerrilla army, a secret air force and secret radio stations. It also selected the man who would replace Arbenz – Colonel Carlos Castillo Armas. On 18 June, Armas attacked Guatemala City. Initially things did not go well for Armas and the CIA. The Guatemalan army pushed him back and there was no popular uprising to support him. It was then that crucial air support was given to Armas by the CIA, and this led to the overthrow of Arbenz within days.

This second CIA triumph, following so soon after Iran, was not greeted with universal enthusiasm. The State Department had bitterly opposed Success, claiming that such US intervention would have serious repercussions throughout the rest of Latin America. The British also took a jaundiced view. There was also CIA resentment at a request made by the station chief in London to the British Secret Intelligence Service that Britain should waive the rights of free passage for their ships in areas near the Guatemalan coast in order to allow US vessels to search any incoming vessels. The British Foreign Secretary, Anthony Eden, later said that, 'it was a proud right which the British had never before given up even in wartime and the Americans never even said thank you. Or gave us quid pro quo later, when we asked for one.'[13]

But Eisenhower, who had taken a keen interest in the progress of Operation Success, was delighted with the result, yet another example of CIA ingenuity. 'Thanks, Allen, and thanks to all of you', he told Allen Dulles when Dulles and other senior agency officials gave him a personal briefing at the White House, 'You've averted a Soviet beachhead in our hemisphere.'[14]

An effigy of Jacobo Arbenz, President of Guatemala (1950–4), surrounded by members of the 'Liberation Army' that deposed him with CIA help. Arbenz, the country's second democratically elected leader (he won 65 per cent of the votes cast), had confiscated the American-owned United Fruit Company's holdings, refusing to pay compensation. This prompted the CIA-backed coup effort led by Colonel Carlos Castillo Armas.

But had they? Evidence of Soviet involvement was tenuous to say the least, as even Foster Dulles admitted. Mussadegh's dealings with the Russians were not disputed, but Arbenz had simply been trying to reform his country and had not sought foreign help for this. The *coup d'état* which removed him from power was a warning to Latin America (and the Soviets) that US interests would receive US protection, but it was also a challenge to the national self-esteem of each Latin American country.

By the end of 1954 thirteen of the twenty countries of Latin America were military dictatorships. Regimes which delivered raw materials for American industry as well as support for US policies at the United Nations, benefited in turn from US aid. The CIA was the channel of support, training police forces, temporarily assigning advisers, exchanging information and intelligence.

Guatemala was to be a mirror image of Chile twenty years later when President Nixon ordered the CIA to topple Allende's government there, but by then the political atmosphere in Central and Latin America had changed dramatically, as the CIA appreciated.

# 6
# CASTRO

' I don't run for the office of the presidency to tell you what you want to hear. I run for the office of president because in a dangerous time we need to be told what we must do if we are going to maintain our freedom.' This was a theme of many of Kennedy's speeches during the 1960 presidential campaign. 'When Jack laid it out like that,' remembered William Manchester, an old friend of the future President, 'you felt challenged. We were perhaps the last liberal patriots to stride down the campaign trail. This was our country, and it was on the wrong track, and we were going to set it right.'[1]

The Kennedy family was reared in a competitive ethos. Their father, Joe, Roosevelt's ambassador to Britain in 1937–40, was tough, ambitious and dictatorial. He had made several dubious fortunes, one from bootlegging during Prohibition, which he was determined to use to advance his sons' political careers.

The Kennedys were Irish, Catholic and south Boston in origin and although Jack had been to Choate and Harvard, in the 1940s when Jack and Bobby started out on the political train, the Catholic-Irish label was still a stigma in many parts of the USA and was used against Jack during the 1960 campaign. The determination to prove the doubters wrong, the drive to win, the belief in muscular laissez faire – all these factors ensured that the Kennedy White House would be action-oriented.

There was not much difference in substance between Kennedy and Eisenhower in foreign policy, but Kennedy thought that his predecessor had been too cautious. Kennedy was a young and vigorous Cold War warrior, willing to rethink traditional arguments and positions in the struggle against communism. He was fascinated by the opportunities which American power and influence offered him, a fascination all the more potent because of his lack of experience. Rejecting his father's isolationism, he was very much a product of the post-war era, a period in which New Deal principles of mobilization were put into action in foreign policy. He was influenced by the ideals of Woodrow Wilson and Franklin Roosevelt but he was determined to make his own mark.

The excitement generated by a new activist President found ready echoes in the CIA. Dulles quickly realized the kind of impression the agency would have to make on a White House concerned with energy and management. He and his Director of Plans, Richard Bissell, moved rapidly to demonstrate their power and skill to key Kennedy officials. They invited a dozen White House aides close to the President to dinner with ten top CIA men. As one of the Kennedy aides present recalled:

> After most had relaxed with several cocktails, the inside stories of past secret exploits were recounted: it was heady wine. Bissell was asked to introduce himself and talk about his work. 'I'm your man-eating shark', he said. CIA man Robert Amory thought that Bissell had set just the right note… Before long, McGeorge Bundy reported to Amory that the President had said, 'By gosh, I don't care what it is but if I need some material fast or an idea fast, CIA is the place to go. The State Department takes four or five days to answer a simple yes or no.'[2]

It was indeed heady wine, all the more heady because the Kennedy brothers were in love with all the mystery and excitement of clandestine operations. Not for nothing were Ian Fleming's James Bond thrillers among the President's favourite books.

## BAY OF PIGS

One of the first items on Kennedy's foreign policy agenda was the newly established regime of Fidel Castro in Cuba. Castro's predecessor, the dictator Fulgencio Batista, had been supported by the US government, although Batista ignored advice to reform his government and its pervasive corruption. In January 1959, not entirely to American surprise, Batista was overthrown by Fidel Castro who had been waging a long guerrilla campaign against Batista's regime.

At first Castro was something of an unknown quantity. A CIA man, Jerome Droller, met him in 1959 but did not think he was pro-communist, a view shared by others in the agency. However, over the next year Castro turned increasingly left and American anxiety mounted. He confiscated $1 billion worth of US property and when no compensation was offered the USA retaliated with a ban on imports of Cuban sugar. More ominous were Castro's moves towards the Soviets. In 1960, he met Khrushchev for the first time at the United Nations and made a four-and-a-half-hour speech accusing the Americans of economic aggression. He agreed to exchange Cuban sugar for Soviet arms, while Khrushchev declared that if the USA took any hostile action against Cuba he would 'support Cuba with rocket fire'. Castro also began sending out guerrilla invasion teams to the Dominican Republic, Panama, Haiti and Nicaragua.

In January 1961, just before John Fitzgerald Kennedy's inauguration, Castro ordered the US Embassy staff in Havana to be cut from eighty-seven to eleven. In one of his last acts in office, Eisenhower ordered diplomatic relations with Cuba to be severed.

Plans to oust Castro had been in preparation for a full year before Eisenhower left the White House and were in place by the time Kennedy took office. They reflected the same tangled, lurid, and occasionally comic developments which were to dog the agency's long involvement with Cuba. The CIA had prepared a plan for Castro's 'elimination' as early as December 1959, and in January 1961 Kennedy directed that the agency should start 'covert contingency planning to accomplish the fall of the Castro government'. In March Colonel J. C. King, chief of the CIA's western hemisphere division in the Directorate of Plans, had organized a task force and had made it clear that assassination was being considered. In July, the CIA station in Havana was given authorization to assassinate Castro's brother, Raul, but the authorization was withdrawn within hours of being granted. Such stop-go, last-minute orders were to be a marked feature of the whole anti-Castro operation.

Soon after the cancellation of the assassination plan, an even more sinister and murky thread was woven into the anti-Castro plot which was to have far-reaching repercussions – the Mafia connection. In September 1960 Robert Maheu, a former FBI officer turned private investigator and occasional CIA go-between, approached three prominent underworld figures, John Rosselli, Santos Trafficante and Sam Giancana, offering them $150,000 to kill Castro.

The Mafia connection bristled with danger. There were the deeply unsavoury backgrounds of the trio, but what was worse was that one of Jack Kennedy's many mistresses, Judith Campbell, was also Giancana's mistress. Giancana was not slow to sniff the blackmail potential of that relationship, particularly since the new President's brother Robert, appointed Attorney General, was determined to crack down on organized crime and had targeted Giancana. The Mafia connection was soon discovered by J. Edgar Hoover who told Richard Bissell

September 1960: Fidel Castro and Nikita Khrushchev meet for the first time at the United Nations in New York. Castro had just nationalized all US companies in Cuba. From this time, planning in the CIA for the overthrow of Castro began in earnest.

on 18 October 1961 that Giancana and his friends were being indiscreet about their Castro assassination plans. Although several attempts were made to kill Castro over the next few months by means of poison pills, none of them succeeded because the Cubans involved got cold feet.

Assassination was one track but from March 1960 onwards plans were also being prepared for a major covert operation. Bissell's Directorate of Plans was in charge. He described the outline succinctly:

> What was approved was a plan to take about twenty-five Cuban refugees, young and well-motivated, and train them in sabotage and communications techniques – train them to be guerrillas – then to insert them into Cuba. In the first class there were twenty-five, and in subsequent classes there might have been thirty to forty-five, not more than that. The design was a classic World War II underground activity. Our operation was to train eventually up to seventy-five or more individuals who would first of all have communications techniques and equipment, and second, have some skill in sabotage. Their primary function was to enter the country, join guerrilla groups or resistance groups already there, and put them in direct communications with an external headquarters, partly to exercise command control and partly to enable them to receive logistic supplies by boat and aircraft.[3]

But was a 'classic World War II underground activity' really suitable for Cuba in 1961? Kermit Roosevelt's warning in 1953 that covert actions must be finely geared towards particular conditions in the country concerned appeared to have been forgotten. Colonel King and others in the western hemisphere division had failed to take into account the importance of social reform in Central and Latin America and the role it had played in Castro's coming to power. This myopia also existed in the White House. Arthur Schlesinger, Jr, one of Kennedy's advisers, recalled that a Cold War atmosphere pervaded White House discussions about Latin America, with the result that the communist threat to Latin America was seen in the same terms as the Nazi menace in the 1930s. Latin America was regarded with such contempt that it was viewed as an obvious target for any totalitarian bully. There was little understanding in Washington that Latin American resistance to US power and influence meant that Latin Americans would 'talk' communism, because communism was the great rival to the United States. The Soviets did understand this, and helped: they did not export Marxism, they exported organization.

There were others in the agency who recognized that Castro was something new in Latin American politics and that he would not be dislodged as easily as Arbenz. In any operation against Castro, it was clear that there was no chance of any uprising against him, first because he had by now firmly consolidated his power and second because he was genuinely popular.

It was this and other reasons which made several officials in the DDP increasingly doubtful of the efficacy of a major operation against Castro. Their doubts were realized when some of the first trainees were infiltrated into Cuba at the end of 1960. Many of them were picked up and most of the air drops also ended up with Castro's forces.

After Kennedy came to power, plans to undermine Castro changed dramatically and became focused on an overt military operation. It was devised by Tracy Barnes, Bissell's special deputy who had been in charge of the Guatemalan coup, and by a marine colonel, Jack Hawkins, who was temporarily assigned to the CIA at Allen Dulles' request to give military advice. They did not make a good team. Their plans were logistically weak, and took it for granted that the United States would intervene directly if necessary.

The new plan provoked even more criticism within the agency. Richard Helms, Bissell's chief of operations, thought it had got out of hand and complained that Bissell had made sure that other senior agency officials, notably Robert Amory of intelligence and Sherman Kent of estimates, were kept away from it. Helms was also concerned at the lack of security which had reached farcical levels of incompetence. A CIA courier had lost a briefcase full of top secret papers including a list of agents and contacts in Cuba. On another occasion a secretary, whose brother was in the FBI, was staying in a hotel room next to that of the CIA linkman with the Cuban exiles in Miami. When she overheard the CIA man discussing the operation she made notes which she passed on to her brother. They eventually found their way to Hoover's desk. The FBI director promptly passed them on to the agency, no doubt with considerable satisfaction. It was hardly surprising that Helms told friends to have nothing to do with the operation. Relations between him and Bissell disintegrated, which did nothing for the overall coherence of the anti-Castro plan. At this point Allen Dulles should have intervened: he was DCI and had ultimate responsibility for its activities.

But where was Dulles? At crucial stages while the plan was evolving the fact remains that he was simply not around. It was not that he was against the operation: on the contrary, Dulles believed that the plan would both establish the CIA's reputation with the new President and get rid of Castro. But Dulles should have seen to it that Amory and Kent were involved in the planning. His successor as DCI, John McCone, was certainly of this opinion and made sure that in future their involvement in operations planning became an established part of CIA methodology.

Faced with these inter-office intrigues, Bissell and Barnes pressed ahead with their plans for the operation. The principal points were clear: there would be a landing to establish a beachhead with a defendable perimeter; the landing force would have its own air protection; once the beachhead was secure the Cuban government-in-exile, consisting of anti-Batista, anti-Castro democrats waiting in Florida, would return and be recognized by the USA; once this government had established itself, its army, with some overt American support, would advance on Havana and take over the country. Bissell told Kennedy and his National Security Adviser, McGeorge Bundy, that the exiles had a 'good fighting chance, and no more'. This was a point of considerable controversy after the failure of the operation, when critics accused the agency of misleading the White House about the possibility of an extensive anti-Castro uprising. But this prospect, although discussed in the agency, had never been seriously entertained by either Bissell or Dulles.

In retrospect Dulles placed most of the blame for the subsequent failure on vacillation by the White House where Kennedy's lack of military experience and his growing sensitivity to the political hazards of the operation had increasingly serious consequences. More likely, Kennedy simply would not accept that a full US military operation would be necessary to achieve victory; the Bay of Pigs planners, in contrast, probably assumed that Kennedy would send in the marines if necessary. Kennedy refused to be led by the nose, and the result was disaster.

It had been Kennedy's decision to go for a military rather than a traditional covert operation, but he was anxious that it should not be seen to have American backing. Given the scale of a military operation, however, this was virtually impossible. What kind of cover stories could explain away the B-26 bombers which were providing air support? An American connection would be obvious to everyone.

Kennedy's solution to this was to reduce the role of air support. As the time drew near for the start of the operation in mid-April 1961, major changes like this were introduced almost casually. David Atlee Phillips, who had been closely involved in the anti-Arbenz coup, arrived at the War Room one day at the beginning of April and found that the landing place for the Cuban-exile task force had been changed from the coastal town of Trinidad to the Bay of Pigs, a hundred miles along the Cuban coast, because Kennedy thought there would be fewer people there and thus that the landing could be more secret. He was also astounded to hear that the first ships to land would be carrying tanks. 'Tanks!' Phillips exclaimed when he was told. 'We're going to mount a secret operation in the Caribbean with tanks?'[4]

As the countdown to the operation on 17 April 1961 proceeded, there was more and more conflicting pressure. Senator William Fulbright and Arthur Schlesinger, Jr, advised against the operation as did Adlai Stevenson, US Ambassador at the UN, and Chester Bowles, Under Secretary of State. Dulles and Bissell argued that any further delay would be fatal, and that the operation either had to start or be cancelled. The Cuban exiles in the task force, 'La Brigada', pressed for the operation to go ahead from their bases in Guatemala where they had been trained.

The operation was based on two key objectives: the destruction of Castro's air force, which had been concentrated at one base, and US air support for the invading task force. The first air strike was due to take place on 15 April, but in order to prepare the cover story that the United States was not involved in the invasion, Kennedy made a speech on 12 April stating that the USA had no intention of intervening militarily in Cuba. The following day he ordered that the air strike must appear as if it had originated in Cuba with defecting pilots. This was done, but when two B-26 bombers arrived at Key West in Florida, having supposedly attacked their own air fields in Cuba, one reporter noticed that the machine guns had tape on them: they had never been fired. The Cuban Ambassador at the United Nations made a furious denunciation of the attack, claiming that it was an American plot. Adlai Stevenson, unaware that the invasion was proceeding, poured scorn on the Cuban allegations.

At midday on 16 April, the last moment at which the operation could be cancelled, Kennedy gave the final go-ahead but with the critical proviso that there were to be no air strikes after the first one. Why did the President do this? Various sources have ascribed the decision to bitter opposition from Stevenson, who found out that the invasion was imminent but was unable to have it cancelled, and from Secretary of State Dean Rusk who warned that air strikes would have a bad effect in the rest of Latin America.

For everyone in the agency the cancellation of air support dealt a body blow to the success of the invasion. Richard Helms said that once the air cover was removed: 'they denuded [the operation]. Whether it would have worked according to the original plan I have no idea. But one thing is for sure: it had no chance of working the way it was finally whittled down.'[5]

Bissell was even more forthright about the vacillation in the White House. He succeeded in convincing Kennedy to allow some more air strikes, but these were then either cancelled or much reduced in the number of planes that flew:

> So from an expectation of some forty sorties, we were down to eight or nine actually accomplished. I cannot avoid the impression that if we'd had anything like the forty sorties, we really would have knocked out Castro's air. We would have been effective by a factor of four. I think that did have a definite bearing on the outcome.[6]

Even Castro agreed. Some years later when asked by a reporter why the Americans failed, he replied, 'they had no air support'.

Bissell, aware that the prospects of success were receding with the air strike restrictions, did his best to persuade people not to quit, arguing that the operation was too far advanced to be abandoned: '[We never] seriously contemplated calling the whole thing off. This is probably where we made the big mistake. But one becomes emotionally and psychologically committed, and things have a momentum of their own.'[7]

When 'La Brigada' landed on Monday 17 April at Zapata on the Bay of Pigs, Castro's air force, unopposed, sank two brigade transports, one of which was carrying most of the task force's ammunition. On Tuesday morning, after urgent requests, Kennedy approved an air strike but low clouds protected the targets. Three B-26s were shot down and others were damaged. On Tuesday night when the President was hosting a black-tie dinner for Congressmen, Bissell asked to see him and pleaded with him for two hours to send more air support. But once again, faced with opposition from Dean Rusk and other civilian advisers, Kennedy compromised: US Navy planes could protect Brigade B-26s but they could not fire at Cuban planes or ground targets.

Besides the problems with air support, the Brigade also experienced major difficulties with the terrain. They fought for three grim days before surrendering to Castro's army. One hundred and fourteen were killed and many others wounded, of whom thirty-six died later in Cuban camps. Some of those captured were to spend over twenty years in Cuban jails.

The decision to withhold air support was part of a much wider miscalculation which Bissell, Dulles and others acknowledged. This was the extraordinarily naïve assumption that, as Bissell said, 'If an operation couldn't be tied in a court of law to the US government, it would be disclaimable, and that was important.'[8] For his part, though Dulles (and others in the CIA) had doubts about the deniability of the operation from the American point of view, Bissell had believed that once it was underway the President would do what was necessary to help it succeed.

Bissell and Dulles were held responsible for the fiasco. Dulles resigned as DCI in November 1961. Bissell also submitted his resignation. President Kennedy said to Bissell, 'In a parliamentary government I would resign. In this government the President can't and doesn't and so you and Allen must go.'

## POST MORTEM

In the immediate aftermath of the Bay of Pigs, Kennedy displayed the same vacillation as he had while it was in progress, alternately blaming himself and the agency, threatening to redefine its mandate, reduce its budget, restrict the Directorate of Plans and transfer paramilitary operations to the Department of Defense. In the event he did none of these things, but no one in the agency was under the illusion that the debacle at the Bay of Pigs was anything other than a watershed for the CIA. There was a pessimistic belief that the agency's luck had simply run out at last, and if it hadn't been the Bay of Pigs it would have been something else. They had grown too cocksure, too certain of success under Truman and Eisenhower. Now the day of reckoning had come. Kermit Roosevelt's warning about covert operations rang in many CIA ears.

Kennedy wanted his brother Robert to run the CIA after Dulles, but Bobby refused, arguing that it was a bad idea to appoint him to a non-political post. John McCone, a Republican who had been an assistant to James Forrestal in 1947, became the new DCI. McCone was a devout Catholic and an equally devout cold warrior. Nevertheless, the President made sure that his brother, as Attorney General, played a key role in supervising the whole intelligence community, and Bobby Kennedy became the effective head of covert operations.

Bobby Kennedy was the driving force in toughening up the agency and making it more effective. Despite the Bay of Pigs, the brothers both realized that alone of the government agencies, the CIA had been willing to act and to do what the President wanted. They saw the Bay of Pigs as a failure of management, not of policy.

The agency never recovered from the light that was cast upon it in the wake of the Bay of Pigs. It had thought of itself as a secret service in the British tradition: it found it was not.

## CUBAN MISSILE CRISIS

The most serious implications of the Bay of Pigs were felt immediately in US-Soviet relations, as Kennedy and his advisers had feared. The Soviets saw the new President as weak and indecisive because of his failure to force the Bay of Pigs operation through to success, and quickly moved to take advantage of this.

On 22 April 1961, just three days after the surrender of the Cuban task force, Kennedy met Eisenhower to ask his advice about the Soviet reaction. Eisenhower advised him to keep his position strong at the conference table and to 'let the enemy see that our country was not afraid. We believe in what is right and attempt to insist upon it.'[9]

Khrushchev and Kennedy met for the first time in Vienna in June 1961, two months after the Bay of Pigs. It was a bruising encounter which left Kennedy in no doubt as to Khrushchev's contempt for him and his government. Nursing his wounds, he told the distinguished columnist James Reston somewhat ruefully:

> I think he did it because of the Bay of Pigs. I think he thought that anyone who was so young and inexperienced as to get into that mess could be taken, and anyone who got into it, and didn't see it through had no guts. So he just beat the hell out of me. So I've got a terrible problem. If he thinks I'm inexperienced and have no guts, until we remove those ideas we won't get anywhere with him. So we have to act . . . Now we have a problem to make our power credible, and Vietnam looks like the credible place.[10]

Khrushchev's belligerent boasting and truculence increased the tension dramatically. He told every Western visitor to Moscow that Russian missiles were ready to force the Allies out of West Berlin. There were incidents in Berlin which led to fears that the situation would explode. In August 1961 the Berlin Wall was constructed.

Soviet arms build-up had commenced in Cuba in 1960 with considerable shipments of conventional weapons for the Cuban army, along with Soviet technicians and training personnel. It was in August 1962 that a U-2 spyplane on a reconnaissance flight over the island took photographs of a surface-to-air

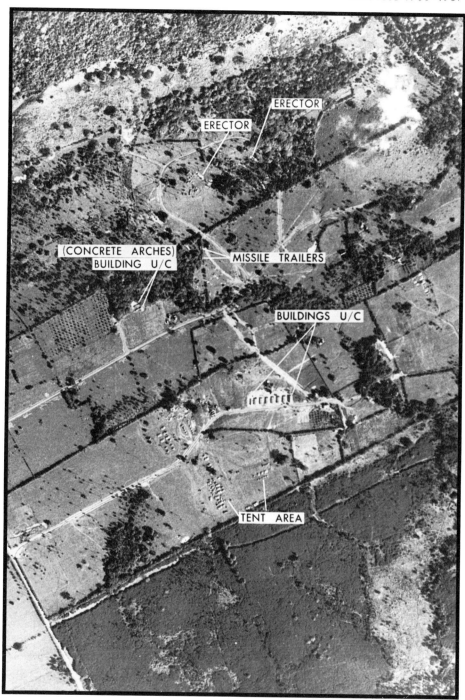

October 1962: Cuban missile crisis. U-2 photograph of a Soviet medium-range missile base under construction in Cuba. This and similar photographs were made public by President Kennedy. They revealed the quality of the information that the U-2, flying up to thirteen miles high, could bring back.

An official US Navy photograph of fuselage crates on the Soviet freighter *Kasimov*, sailing back from Cuba after the missile crisis. The crates were opened by the Soviet crew to prove that they were withdrawing weapons systems from Cuba.

missile site under construction. On 14 October another U-2 flight brought back evidence of a ballistic missile site under construction at San Cristobal. This immediately set the alarm bells ringing at the CIA and the White House was alerted that a major crisis was at hand.

The agency's handling of the crisis helped it to win back all the reputation it had lost the previous year. The new DCI, McCone, had already warned the President in September that in his opinion the Soviets were not just installing anti-aircraft missiles. He pointed out that anti-aircraft missiles were defensive, and that therefore they were there to defend something more sinister. When this was confirmed, McCone's stock at the White House soared.

On 22 October Kennedy gave a dramatic televised address to the nation, revealing the findings of the U-2 reconnaissance flights and demanding the removal of the missiles. In the meantime, he announced, there would be a naval blockade of Cuba to ensure that no further weapons were brought in. One hundred and eighty US warships circled the island. Khrushchev replied on 26 October offering to remove the missiles in return for a pledge not to invade Cuba. The next day there was another message, this time demanding the dismantling of

US missile sites in Turkey. The President, prompted by his brother Robert, decided to answer the first reply and ignore the second, although Kennedy later removed the sites in Turkey. Sixteen Soviet ships, some with crated missiles on their decks, turned round in mid-Atlantic and headed for home.

## OPERATION MONGOOSE

The humiliation of the Bay of Pigs, and the narrow escape of the missile crisis, helped to revive the idea of Castro's assassination. Richard Helms, giving evidence to Congress fourteen years later, recalled that in October and November 1961 the CIA was instructed to draw up plans to get rid of Castro. These plans would obviously have to be covert because 'nobody had any stomach anymore for any invasions or any military fiascos of that kind'. The atmosphere, Helms remembered, 'was pretty intense ... Nutty schemes were born of the pressure ... No doubt about it, it was white heat.'[11]

The driving force behind plans for the assassination, and for the disruption of the Cuban economy, Operation Mongoose, was Robert Kennedy, who had announced in January 1962 that it was a 'top priority ... all else is secondary'.[12]

The Mongoose team, led by Bill Harvey, came up with no less than thirty-three different plans to deal with Castro which became increasingly desperate and bizarre as failure followed upon failure. Plans included an exploding seashell which would be placed on the sea floor near the place where Castro was known to swim; impregnating Castro's wet suit with poison coating; dusting Castro's shoes with thallium salts in the expectation that this would cause his beard to fall out and so destroy his charisma. A mistress of Castro agreed to give him two poison capsules and hid them in her jar of cold cream. They melted. Another more creative plan involved an attempt to convince Cuba's large Roman Catholic population that the Second Coming was imminent but only if they got rid of Castro first. A US submarine was to surface off Havana and shoot star shells into the night sky, heralding the return of the Lord. The theology was even more dubious than the plan itself. It was sheer *opera buffa*.

Other attempts were more serious. In the autumn of 1963, a major in the Cuban army close to Castro, Rolando Cubela, who had been working for the CIA since 1961, was given encouragement to launch a coup and attempt the assassination of Castro and other Cuban leaders. On 22 November 1963 he was given a poison pen device, which he rejected in favour of something more sophisticated, but he was also told that he would be given rifles with telescopic sights. That day Kennedy was assassinated in Daly Plaza, Dallas.

Castro was with a French journalist when he heard the news of Kennedy's murder. '*Es una mala noticia*' ['It's bad news'], he kept repeating, saying that while he held Kennedy responsible for everything, nevertheless Kennedy had come 'to understand many things over the past few months'.[13] Kennedy's death was unpleasantly close to the murky story of the attempts to kill Castro. It led to all kinds of horrifying speculations. Was it a Mafia job? Was it retaliation by Castro? For a time Lyndon Johnson thought this was the case. What about the contacts between Lee Harvey Oswald, the assassin, and the anti-Castro Cubans, contacts which were never revealed to the commission investigating the murder? Could it have been a CIA-inspired murder, with the agency seeking revenge for the Bay of Pigs? Bobby Kennedy took this thought so seriously that he asked John McCone to convince him it was not so.

After Kennedy's death there were no further direct CIA attempts to kill Castro. But the Cuban connection provided the agency with a number of freelance agents who were to be involved in operations worldwide.

## CHE

Cuban exile pilots, trained for the Bay of Pigs and for Mongoose missions into Cuba, later flew in Africa and the Far East on CIA missions. Others became important operatives in the Spanish-speaking world, notably in Latin America.

Felix Rodriguez was such an operative. His family had prospered under Batista – his uncle had been the Minister of Public Works – and settled in Mexico when Castro took over. Aged seventeen in 1959, Felix joined the Cuban exile anti-Castro movement. He trained as a guerrilla in the Dominican Republic. Six weeks before the Bay of Pigs in 1961, he was one of thirty-five 'Grey Team' exiles in seven five-man groups infiltrated into Cuba. After the failure of the invasion, he successfully escaped from the island to become a CIA freelance agent. In 1967 he was an adviser to the Bolivian Army chasing Che Guevara.

Che had been the second figure in the Cuban revolution that brought Castro to power in 1959. In 1965 he left Cuba, going to Latin America to stir up revolutions. In 1967 he was reported to be in Bolivia, and on 9 October that year was captured by a unit of the Bolivian Army to which Felix Rodriguez was attached. Che could have been a formidable enemy indeed, if he had not lost all tactical judgement and tried to campaign on the *alti plano*, the open country of Bolivia. Helicopters and airplanes could – and did – shadow him: it was not like

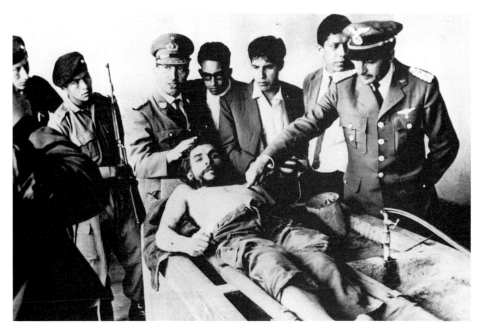

The body of Che Guevara in the morgue at the Valle Grande Hospital in Bolivia. Guevara had been captured by a Bolivian Army unit, but the Bolivian high command ordered that he be killed immediately, without trial. At the time the Army claimed that Guevara had been shot in an armed clash.

fighting in a jungle. To cap it all, he was asthmatic, and going up to that height was not good for him.

The Bolivian high command ordered Che to be shot the same day that he was captured: they were fearful that if he lived he might successfully foment revolution at a later date. Rodriguez carried the death order to Che:

> '*Comandante*,' I said, 'I have done everything in my power, but orders have come from the Supreme Bolivian Command . . .'
>
> His face turned as white as writing paper. 'It is better like this, Felix. I should never have been captured alive.'
>
> When I asked him if he had any message for his family, he said, 'Tell Fidel that he will soon see a triumphant revolution in America.' He said it in a way that, to me, seemed to mock the Cuban dictator for abandoning him in the Bolivian jungle. Then Che added, 'And tell my wife to get remarried and try to be happy.'
>
> Then we embraced, and it was a tremendously emotional moment for me. I no longer hated him. . . . He was facing his death with courage and grace.[14]

# 7

# DOMINOES

## *1950–1964*

T he end of World War II led to the break-up of the centuries-old British, French and Dutch empires in the Far East. The British, economically devastated by the war, left India in 1947 and, by the mid-1950s, after successfully defeating a long communist insurgency, had laid the groundwork for the independence of Malaysia. In 1949 Indonesia gained independence from the Dutch. France with its protectorates in Vietnam and Laos took longer to adjust to the end of empire.

Both Presidents Roosevelt and Truman were openly contemptuous and distrustful of European imperialism. Even before the end of the war the United States had established contact with many of the new nationalist movements in the colonies of the Far East. In 1942, the OSS decided to extend its activities into as many Japanese-occupied areas as possible, and forged operational alliances with nationalists and communists fighting the Japanese. In 1943, the OSS considered working with Ho Chi Minh, the Vietnamese communist leader, who had successfully appealed to Vietnamese nationalism and organized a guerrilla army that was fighting the Japanese. As the war progressed, contact with Ho was made.

Once the colonial peoples rejected European overlords, the historian Hugh Brogan observed, 'they could make it agonizingly expensive, in lives, credit and treasure, for any power which tried to keep them in subjection'.[1] The British, after their experience of guerrilla warfare in Ireland in 1916–21, and Gandhi's passive resistance national movement in India in the 1930s and 1940s, absorbed this truth and retired from the business of empire with some dignity. So did the Dutch. The French took a different path. After 1945, instead of handing over power to the people in their colonies, they sought to re-establish their pre-war supremacy. In Vietnam, the principal French colony in the Far East, this enabled Ho Chi Minh to present himself as the national leader who had fought the

Japanese and was now fighting against French rule and for Vietnam's independence.

The contact with the OSS played an important part in Ho's tactics. By early 1945 the OSS 'Deer Team' and Ho's forces were secretly working together rescuing Allied pilots who had been shot down, and sabotaging Japanese supplies and communications. The French were very suspicious of this collaboration, warning and complaining about it to the US government. In 1945, the French attempted to reassert their authority in Vietnam through the puppet regime of the ex-Emperor Bao Dai in Saigon. In 1946, Ho announced the creation of the Democratic Republic of North Vietnam with Hanoi as his capital, and he began a guerrilla war with his Vietminh forces to unify the country under him. Ho had tried to obtain American recognition of North Vietnam, and had strong support in many quarters in Washington, not least among OSS men who had worked with him and others who felt that the United States should not support the old empires, but instead should support national movements and independent states. What swung American support away from Ho was the fact that he was a communist – indeed, he was a Moscow-trained revolutionary agitator who had worked in France and China as an agent – and in 1946 the civil war in China was reaching its climax with the prospect of a communist takeover there. In 1948, the Truman administration gave military support to the French in Vietnam as part of the US effort to contain communist expansion.

For some of the OSS men who had fought alongside Ho during the war, the failure to build upon the good relations then developed with the Vietminh was disastrous. Archimedes Patti, the leader of the OSS-Indochina mission to Ho in 1945, believed that if President Truman had backed Ho instead of the French, Ho would not have turned to Mao Tse-tung and Moscow for support.[2] Though a communist, Ho might easily have become an 'Asian Tito' and a *de facto* ally of the West. The course of Vietnamese foreign policy after 1975, when the communist government of unified Vietnam began to seek economic and political agreements with the West rather than the Soviet Union, and fought a border war with Red China, lends support to Patti's view.

US support for the French, Mao Tse-tung's victory in China in 1949, and the worldwide Cold War ended any prospect of a change in American policy in favour of Ho. The prime objective of American policy during the Truman administration became the prevention of any further communist expansion anywhere in the world. In February 1950 the US National Security Council stated that if Vietnam, Cambodia and Laos fell to the communists, then Thailand,

Burma and Malaysia might follow. The theory was that if one 'domino' fell, it would have a knock-on effect.

There was a general assumption after China fell to Mao Tse-tung in 1949 that there was an inevitability to peasant communism in the Third World. South Korea was defended because it was a defensible place. So, too, was Japan. But the crash of decolonization suddenly put the whole of South East Asia into the melting pot at the same time. After China, it looked as if Indonesia might go, then Malaya and the other countries of Indochina. And then quite possibly India. The Dutch, French, and especially the British were very strong in their urging the USA to finance their operations in Indochina.

Behind the domino theory was the conviction that Moscow was the centre of a worldwide controlling network of every communist movement. Mao Tse-tung in China was seen as a puppet of Stalin, and Stalin was seen as being hellbent on world domination. This view was challenged by the China desk of the State Department which pointed to serious differences between Soviet and Chinese communism. But after 1949 and Mao's victory, this desk was a particular target for the McCarthy witch hunts and led to the departure from the State Department of most of the senior China hands. With them went any serious doubts within the US policy-making establishment about Mao being Stalin's puppet. Not until a decade later was the view that Mao was a Soviet stooge challenged in Washington – this time by the analysts in the CIA. The departure of the State Department's China hands prevented the vital internal debate so necessary for developing and fine-tuning policies in government, and had the effect of locking US policy in the Far East into a hard Cold War stance throughout the 1950s.

Eisenhower continued Truman's support of the French in Vietnam which, by 1954, amounted to $1 billion a year: over three-quarters of the entire French military budget there. But it made little difference to the outcome of their war with the Vietminh. In May 1954 the French suffered a major defeat at Dien Bien Phu in North Vietnam. In Geneva, the two sides made peace. Vietnam was provisionally divided in two at the 17th parallel. North Vietnam was Ho's; South Vietnam remained under Bao Dai who appointed Ngo Dinh Diem as prime minister. General elections were scheduled to take place in both parts of the country in July 1956.

Eisenhower's Secretary of State, John Foster Dulles, was deeply dissatisfied with the Geneva Accords, condemning them as a French capitulation. He knew that Ho was the only Vietnamese leader who had fought the Japanese and the French, and thus was seen by his countrymen as a national leader. Time was needed to build up a non-communist counterweight to Ho, another leader who could attract national support. So Dulles encouraged Diem in Saigon to take every step to delay the general elections: within a month of the Accords being signed, the CIA had predicted that Ho would probably win.

## EISENHOWER AND VIETNAM

The fear of constant communist expansion was at the heart of Eisenhower's Vietnam policy, but he was cautious about US military engagement on the Asian mainland, especially after Korea. As a soldier he understood the nature of the guerrilla war that France had unsuccessfully fought in Vietnam. As President he recognized the danger of spurring tens of millions of Red Chinese troops into action in Indochina. His caution was backed up by the CIA analysts who warned that the danger of Chinese involvement in support of Ho was real. An additional factor in Eisenhower's decision to support South Vietnam was that Ho's regime in the North was by no means popular with the North Vietnamese. Millions of people fled the North for the South after 1954. Eisenhower's overall policy gained broad support in Congress and in US policy-making circles because the fact was that Moscow and Peking were supporting all manner of communist and nationalist movements around the world. What was not appreciated at the time was that Moscow and Peking were becoming rivals. Moscow supported Ho in Vietnam, for example, in large part because it did not want to see Peking grow more powerful.

Eisenhower ruled out direct US military involvement in favour of con-

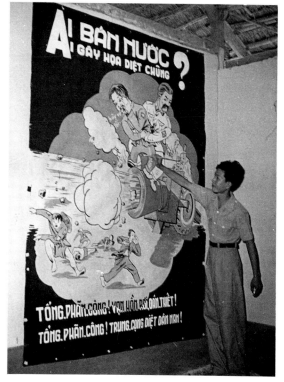

Cao Dai was a political and religious movement which developed in Indo-China in the 1920s. A mixture of Roman Catholicism and Eastern beliefs, it was strongly anti-Communist and so was supported and encouraged by the CIA. Here a Cao Dai artist in South Vietnam finishes a poster depicting Stalin and Ho Chi Minh as blowing death and destruction on their people.

tinuing Truman's policy of supporting the Saigon government with money and supplies. He also agreed to send special advisers to help direct Saigon's efforts to withstand Ho, who was continuing his guerrilla war in the South. Colonel Edward Lansdale was sent to Vietnam in June 1954 as head of the Saigon Military Mission, working in association with the CIA, straight from his success against the Huks in the Philippines. Lansdale quickly decided that Diem was the strongest South Vietnamese leader, and he backed him fully. A year later, Bao Dai was deposed and Diem became President of the new Republic of South Vietnam.

The CIA agreed with Lansdale that Diem was the best anti-communist bet, the only figure on the South Vietnamese political scene behind whom genuine nationalist support could be mobilized. The CIA reported that Diem was 'confronted with the usual problems of inefficiency, disunity, and corruption in Vietnamese politics', but that he had the character and ability to overcome these obstacles. Eisenhower and Dulles became convinced that this was so. But all along the dilemma in US policy showed: it grated with America's image of itself that it should have been on the side of the old empires against a national independence movement. Ho being a communist was a key element in Truman's decision to support the French. And the fact that South Vietnam was not democratic, and that American policy was to delay democratic elections, also grated. Diem was offered US aid on the following terms:

> The Government of the United States expects that this aid will be met by performance on the part of the Government of Vietnam in undertaking needed reforms [so that it will be] so responsive to the nationalist aspirations of its people, so enlightened in purpose and effective in performance that it will be respected both at home and abroad and discourage any who might wish to impose a foreign ideology on your free people.[3]

Diem accepted Eisenhower's terms, and the United States, in 1955, effectively replaced France as the protecting power in the South. With US support, Diem refused to hold the 1956 elections.

Over the next five years the CIA became involved in a number of operations designed to strengthen Diem's rule in South Vietnam. The agency set up a $25 million scheme with Michigan State University to train rural administrators, the national police and the civil guard. Drawing from his experience in the Philippines, Lansdale organized the first effort to undermine Vietminh support amongst the people of South Vietnam through 'pacification': establishing strategic hamlets

or 'agrovilles' in the countryside, protected by South Vietnamese forces, coun-
tering communist infiltration by guaranteeing security and the rule of law to
villagers.

Diem, however, was not Magsaysay. His police and civil guard paid far more
attention to the arrest and torture of anyone who opposed his regime than to
the pursuit of 'needed reforms' and the 'aspirations' of the South Vietnamese
people. The agroville system, which Diem promised to be the herald of land
ownership reform, frequently aroused the discontent of the peasantry because,
instead of securing peasant ownership of land, it was used to sustain the estates
of the wealthy, old pro-French landlords.

Diem was an astute politician, and he calculated that with US support he did
not have to introduce extensive domestic reform. Instead, he thought, he could
gain the support of the wealthy sections of South Vietnam and defuse discontent
by appealing to rural conservatism and anti-communist national feeling. During
the Eisenhower presidency, with its fear of communist expansion, Diem's calculation worked. South Vietnam rapidly improved economically, and Diem
proved to be an effective administrator. For a time, these factors compensated
for the lack of democracy in the eyes of Washington, and US attention on
Vietnam diminished. This was to be the fatal weakness. By 1960 Diem had
concentrated enormous power in the hands of himself, his brother, Ngo Dinh
Nhu, and his brother's wife. US support for his regime had become automatic,
but even the wealthy sections of South Vietnamese society were becoming
increasingly resentful of Diem's dictatorship and his family's power, while in the
countryside communist promises of land reform were becoming more and more
seductive. Ho Chi Minh saw his chance and formed the National Liberation
Front, or Vietcong, to launch a full-scale guerrilla war against the South. By
1961 the CIA estimated that the Vietcong in the South numbered 10,000 and were
receiving arms and supplies from China. But two other Far Eastern countries –
Indonesia and Laos – caused more concern in Washington than Vietnam did.

## INDONESIA

Vietnam was not the first 'domino' at risk in the eyes of Washington. In the mid-
1950s, President Sukarno in Indonesia attracted the attention of the Eisenhower
administration because of his attempts to court the Soviet Union and to involve
communists in his government.

Under the Dutch, and continuing with independence in 1949, Indonesia was

Achmed Sukarno, President of Indonesia (1949–67). His grandiose military spending and triumphalist building bankrupted the country. He came to depend more and more on the support of the Indonesian Communist party. In 1965 he lost power in a military coup that also involved the slaughter of about 500,000 communists.

run for the benefit of its most populous component: Java. In Sumatra and Borneo there was considerable resentment with Java, and in Borneo especially there was also Christian discontent with Javanese Muslim supremacy.

In the elections of 1955, Indonesian communists won about one-quarter of the votes, and Sukarno argued that therefore one-quarter of the Cabinet should be communist too. Sukarno was not a communist, but he saw the Indonesian Communist party as a way of counterbalancing his generals. He was also attracted to the communists because he wanted organization in a disorganized society. And he was moving away from democracy towards a personal dictatorship, what he called 'guided democracy'. This was enough to convince Eisenhower that Indonesia, the most populous country outside China in the Far East, would at the least become a Soviet communist ally if Sukarno remained in power. In November 1957, the CIA was ordered to aid rebel Indonesian colonels on the island of Sumatra, and to prepare a Guatemala-style coup to overthrow Sukarno.

The CIA gave the rebel colonels arms and organized B-26 bombers flown by contract pilots. A pornographic film was made by the CIA with a Sukarno look-alike in order to discredit him with his supporters. In February 1958, while Sukarno was on a visit to Japan, the colonels launched their attack. Sukarno, however, enjoyed strong support in Java, and his army remained loyal to him. CIA assessments of his resourcefulness and determination were shown to be way off the mark. After five months the rebellion collapsed.

In victory, Sukarno played his hand skilfully. Although the USA had denied any involvement with the rebels, the CIA's support for them was public know-ledge: a B-26 on a rebel bombing mission crashed, and the American contract pilot was captured. Instead of making propaganda from this, however, Sukarno pretended that the USA had not been involved, calculating – correctly – that there was more benefit to be had from Eisenhower's gratitude than from his continued hostility.

In the years that followed, US economic aid to the Far East substantially increased, with the majority of it going to Burma, South Vietnam, and Indonesia. In 1965, the Indonesian army suppressed a Chinese communist-backed coup attempt, slaughtering tens of thousands of Chinese and communists. In 1967,

*Overleaf* In the early 1960s Laos, not South Vietnam, was seen in Washington as the country in Indochina most likely to fall to communist insurgency. Here, President Kennedy briefs the White House press corps about US military and diplomatic moves being planned to help the Laotian government.

when the Indonesian military asserted their power, and took over the government, US influence was applied to ensure that Sukarno was not assassinated.

Indonesia was the first major exercise of agency power in East Asia. It had trained raiding parties in Taiwan before, and had supply and training camps in Thailand for anti-communist groups from the countries of Indochina, but such activities were small compared to the direct coup attempt against Sukarno. The CIA effort in Indonesia provides a dismal record of failure. The big question was: would the agency learn from its mistakes and develop a finesse for operating in different countries and cultures? Or would it remain a coup-making machine designed to satisfy presidents and policymakers in Washington?

## LAOS

When Eisenhower left office in January 1961, of all the 'dominoes' in the Far East, Vietnam's neighbour Laos was causing the greatest concern. The talk of war in 1960–1 was of world war over Laos, and Eisenhower warned Kennedy that Laos was the major crisis point in South East Asia. It looked as if it would fall before South Vietnam did.

The 1954 Geneva Accords had applied to Laos as well as Vietnam: it was agreed that the country should have a neutral coalition government that would side with neither the North Vietnamese-supported communist Pathet Lao, nor the old pro-French ruling élite. However, as in Vietnam, the USA found that its support was necessary against the guerrilla activities of the Pathet Lao in order to buy time for non-communist Lao politicians and political groupings to gain strength. Between 1954 and 1961 the USA spent over $300 million trying to keep the Pathet Lao at bay, most of which went to General Phoumi Nosavan, in all but name the dictator of Laos. As with Vietnam, US policy was to support the strongest anti-communist leader to be found.

Phoumi Nosavan came into power with the support of the CIA. In 1958 the Pathet Lao won a majority of the seats in the Laotian Parliament and joined a coalition government headed by Prime Minister Souvanna Phouma. This sounded alarm bells in Washington and, as in Indonesia, the CIA was again ordered to intervene to prevent communist participation in government. Henry Heckscher, the CIA station chief in Vientiane, the Laotian capital, instigated the resignation of Souvanna Phouma and a reconstituted government under Phoumi Nosavan that excluded the Pathet Lao. Pathet Lao forces, which had been

Pathet Lao militia at the wreck of a burning US plane shot down by rifles in the Plain of Jars-Xieng Khoand area of central Laos. The CIA managed to keep the struggle in Laos at stalemate.

integrated in the national army following the Geneva Accords, rebelled and civil war ensued.

The role of the CIA in Laos reflected the secret reality of the agency's position in Washington. The State Department had formal responsibility for US relations with Vientiane, but it was effectively excluded from policy in Laos. CIA station chiefs were often regarded as being more important than ambassadors, and this was the case with Henry Heckscher. The US Ambassador to Laos, who had favoured adherence to the Geneva Accords and the coalition government of Souvanna Phouma, complained about Heckscher's actions: the Ambassador was transferred.

From 1958 the USA secretly supported Phoumi Nosavan through the CIA while the Pathet Lao and neutralists received aid from Moscow. A temporary ceasefire was arranged between the Pathet Lao and Vientiane forces in 1961, but it proved impossible for all sides to agree on a coalition government. In May 1962 the Pathet Lao launched a major anti-government offensive, and rapidly controlled most of the country. Laos, in effect, became a province of North Vietnam, and the Vietcong used large parts of the country for supply routes to South Vietnam. The CIA was given the green light to organize and run a secret war, and it did so to considerable effect. Anti-communist government troops were trained and supplied, as were hill tribesmen. The calculation was that fighting in Laos would force the Vietcong to divert resources from their efforts in South Vietnam. By 1966, CIA officers controlled an army of 30,000 Laotian tribesmen that successfully harried Pathet Lao and Vietcong forces.

The agency's involvement in Laos was a stark contrast to its involvement in Vietnam. It began with one remit – to prevent the country falling to the Pathet Lao – and found it had to develop another in order to perform. In consequence, the agency took on an imperial role. It became the single most powerful player in the country, acting with the full support of the President, the Joint Chiefs of Staff, and to a lesser degree the State Department.

There were, as a result, two agencies at work in South East Asia: an imperial agency in Laos and a bureaucratic agency in Vietnam. There was nothing proconsular about the agency in Saigon. In Laos, it was dominating and on the ground: it was war for a country, and the agency had armies and an air force, camps and airbases. In Vietnam, the agency was fitting into a mess.

## DRAWING THE LINE

The first US soldiers – Major Dale Buis and Sergeant Chester Ovnand – were killed in Vietnam on 8 July 1959, but war in Vietnam did not become a painful issue until Kennedy started drawing the line there. From the perspective of the early 1960s, it looked as if South East Asia would fall apart like wet paper unless the USA did something. Thailand was particularly weak: corrupt and unstable. Malaysia was having severe racial problems: Singapore, a Chinese émigré city, was thrown out in 1965 to become a sovereign city state. It looked as if there was going to be a communist takeover in Indonesia and Laos, and a communist occupation of South Vietnam. There was a considerable case for stalling events by fighting in Vietnam.

But what did it mean, 'Communism is growing!'? Had communist expansion been decided in Moscow or Peking? Policy-makers in Washington had no real sense of whether they were dealing with a centrally controlled world communist insurgency, or if they were dealing with genuinely nationalist movements that had taken on communism as a way of attracting Soviet–Chinese support. It was a problem that bedevilled the whole story of US involvement: the only people the USA could find to support against communist insurgency were either dictators or faction leaders who could not command national support, or both.

# 8
# WAR

## *1960–1966*

Vietnam was of secondary importance for the USA until about 1960. In 1959, intercepted signals made it clear that the North Vietnamese Politburo had determined to go for broke and colonize the South.

When Eisenhower briefed Kennedy in December 1960 and again in January 1961, he was very anxious that the incoming President would give way to pressure for more direct US involvement in Indochina. The whole of Eisenhower's style was to prepare for as many options as possible, but only as a last resort to commit the United States to direct intervention anywhere. He far preferred to provide US support in the form of money, food, weapons, CIA officers and military advisers so that native governments and people could themselves fight.

It is not clear whether Kennedy actively wanted a more direct US role in conflict zones around the world, or if he considered that there was no alternative to direct US involvement if anti-communist regimes were to survive. In 1962, still smarting from the failure of the Bay of Pigs and the Vienna summit, he determined to draw a firm line with the Soviets. His was an arrogance, born of ignorance of what the world was really like, assuming that American energy and power, applied with conviction, could change the world. At the moment when the United States could have maintained an arm's length Vietnam policy without political embarrassment, here was a President who decided to test his political virility.

In May 1961, four months after being sworn in as President of the United States, Kennedy sent Vice-President Lyndon Johnson on a fact-finding mission to Saigon. Johnson, whose whole adult life had been spent in US domestic politics, was bowled over by Diem, calling him the 'Winston Churchill of Asia', and recommending increased support for his regime. In October 1961, another fact-finding mission arrived in Saigon led by General Maxwell Taylor, chairman of the Joint Chiefs of Staff, and Walt Rostow, a member of the National Security

Council staff. Diem's reputation as a tyrannical ruler was considered to be a serious obstacle to US support for his regime. He arrested tens of thousands of political opponents; he established military courts to try them and, said the official newspaper, 'All must suffer execution'; he forced 300,000 Chinese either to become Vietnamese citizens or to cease doing business. The Taylor-Rostow report seconded Johnson's view that Diem be given full support to withstand the Vietcong, including an increase in the number of US military advisers. It simultaneously recommended that US pressure should be applied to force Diem to introduce democratic reforms. The double helix of US policy – supporting democracy and anti-communists – was to ride roughshod over political realities in South Vietnam, taking no account of Vietnamese history and culture (neither of which featured democratic impulses), and ultimately forcing even greater instability upon South Vietnam at the very time when strong government was needed for the war with the Vietcong to be successful.

The Taylor-Rostow report provoked considerable argument. Should the USA continue to support Diem or some other South Vietnamese leader? Should US support remain advisory, or should it become direct and military? US allies in the Far East took the view that the weakness of Diem's regime was largely Diem's fault: if he had introduced land reform and been less dictatorial, they thought, then his government would be more popular. At the State Department, George Ball, the Under Secretary, was an outspoken opponent of direct US involvement, arguing that the essential point was the attitude of the South Vietnamese toward their government and that in this respect Diem was clearly an obstacle to a democratic settlement that would have popular support.

Kennedy's solution was a compromise with the Taylor-Rostow report's recommendations. While agreeing that Diem should be pushed to more reform, Kennedy established the Military Assistance Command, Vietnam (MACV), in February 1962, under General Paul Harkins. The Pentagon was now directly involved. 'It is fashionable in some quarters,' said a future chairman of the Joint Chiefs, Earle G. Wheeler, in November 1962, 'to say that the problems of South East Asia are primarily political and economic rather than military. I do not agree. The essence of the problem is military.' By December 1962 there were 11,000 regular US troops in South Vietnam.

The CIA was simultaneously given a more active role in training counter-insurgency forces, both military and police, and in producing an anti-guerrilla strategy. Here, its developing experience in Laos began to prove valuable. In April 1962 strategic hamlets were established in the Mekong delta, with help from US Special Forces and the Agency for International Development, to combat the Vietcong technique of murdering doctors, nurses, teachers, effective administrators and anti-communist village headmen.

By June 1963, 67 per cent of South Vietnam's rural population was concentrated in such hamlets. But since the people in the countryside found themselves inside these hamlets, not outside them where their land and farms and livelihood were, the operation had a contrary effect, as US analysts noted:

> Despite its relative sophistication, the strategic hamlet program, like its predecessors, drove a wedge not between the insurgents and the farmers but between the farmers and the GVN [Government of Vietnam], and eventuated in less rather than more security in the countryside.'[1]

The first twenty-one months of direct, but limited, US involvement thus witnessed a deterioration in Saigon's authority. Between the establishment of MACV and the overthrow and murder of Diem and his brother, Nhu, by an army coup in November 1963, support in the South for the Vietcong was generally conceded as having substantially increased. The South Vietnamese generals who plotted Diem's removal promised the USA that they would introduce democratic reforms: they had seen US policy as meaning that they would benefit from even more US military support and involvement if they got rid of Diem. Lou Conein, a CIA officer in Saigon, acted as go-between for the plotters and the US Embassy where the Ambassador, Henry Cabot Lodge, mindful of the experience of other US ambassadors with the CIA, had successfully insisted that Conein report to him about the plot, and not to the station chief. Lodge and senior members of the Kennedy administration gave clear indications to the plotters that Diem's removal – but not his death – would be welcome in Washington.

Diem was a Roman Catholic in an overwhelmingly non-Christian society. He was a narrow-minded mandarin, thoroughly crooked, arrogant, foolish. He smoked a lot of opium and had virtually no personal qualities except extreme courage. And while it was not possible to build an ordered system of grass-roots resistance to the North on that, Diem did have nationalist credentials that denied the USA the responsibility for being the full protector and organizer of Vietnam.

*Overleaf* The civil war in Vietnam, into which the United States injected itself, was ruthless and unrelenting. Torture and harsh treatment were routine for the Vietcong, North and South Vietnamese. Here, at An Ninh in 1965, a South Vietnamese kicks a captured Vietcong.

After Diem's murder, it was never possible to put someone in charge in Saigon who could obviously operate independently of US goodwill. The last ten years of US involvement in Vietnam stemmed from the liquidation of Diem.

The agency maintained a distance from the death of Diem and his brother, and it would be quite wrong to say that it assassinated them. But it was an open secret in South East Asia in the months before their deaths that the agency was making Kennedy's displeasure with Diem widely known, and was talking to coup plotters. Subsequently, however, their contacts with the plotters, and the role of Conein, sustained the suspicion that Kennedy and the CIA were behind the murders.

Kennedy seems to have felt that all he had to do was snap his fingers and some new Vietnamese official would appear as leader, and no one would see that the USA had done anything but throw its weight behind one faction or another. Instead, thereafter, the USA was perpetually shoring up the tottering wall of South Vietnam. To warn of this likelihood should have been the function first and foremost of the Embassy, and secondly of the CIA.

None of the various generals who succeeded Diem enjoyed wide popular support, with the result that South Vietnamese leaders became both more dependent on the United States, and more obstinate in resisting peace proposals that threatened their positions. South Vietnamese government authority declined, reforms were forgotten, and there were eleven changes in Saigon leadership between November 1963 and the summer of 1965.

As the Kennedy and subsequent Johnson administrations became more and more involved in Vietnam the discrepancy between policy and intelligence became increasingly acute. It was a perennial problem for the CIA: it did the intelligence work, analysed it, and watched helplessly as the preconceptions of policymakers set aside its conclusions. Eisenhower avoided such differences. He looked to the CIA for National Intelligence Estimates on key issues, and through him the CIA's analysts had a clear effect on policy. The importance that Eisenhower attached to accurate intelligence enabled the CIA to take an independent stand against the military, and policymakers in the State Department and elsewhere because it enjoyed the backing of the President.

Kennedy never read an estimate, and after the Bay of Pigs he resolved to manage everything from the Oval Office, bypassing the National Security Council (which never met during his presidency) and its committees where so much of the Eisenhower administration took place. He did not give the CIA his full backing, but he respected its analysts, and at the time of his death in November

1963 was wondering to friends if US involvement in Vietnam should not, in fact, be broken off. Under Johnson, the CIA's pessimistic analysis of the Vietnam war, increasingly at odds with policy, became more and more difficult for the President to accept.

## SHOOT THE MESSENGER

John McCone was the first DCI to feel Johnson's pressure for the CIA's analysis to conform to his policy. Johnson was a highly intelligent man who had clear ideas about where he was going and what he was doing. His 'Great Society' reforms of domestic, political and economic conditions came from his deep belief that the United States was the land of equal opportunity. He was completely at ease with domestic politics, but not with foreign policy. After Kennedy's assassination, Johnson was content to follow the policy already laid down in Vietnam, believing that the best brains in the US foreign policy establishment had worked everything out. He kept many of Kennedy's aides and Cabinet officers in place, including Secretary of State Dean Rusk, Secretary of Defense Robert McNamara, head of the National Security Council staff McGeorge Bundy, and Bundy's deputy (and later his replacement), Walt Rostow.

While Kennedy was prepared to listen to bad news, Johnson was not. He was angry with the CIA for its pessimism about the war – and, as it turned out, its accuracy. In June 1964, in response to his request for an assessment of whether the other countries of South East Asia would fall to the communists if Vietnam and Laos did, the agency estimated that 'with the possible exception of Cambodia, it is likely that no nation in the area would quickly succumb to communism as a result'.[2] The Vietcong, it said, further enraging the President who wanted consensus within his administration on the war, drew their strength not – as the US military thought – from North Vietnam, but from nationalist sentiment and from popular pressure for land reform in the countryside in the South. In November 1964 the agency disagreed with Walt Rostow, McNamara, McGeorge Bundy and other Johnson advisers, who felt that North Vietnam was vulnerable to air raids because it would not be prepared to see its industry ruined, and instead said that it 'did not concede very strong chances for breaking the will of Hanoi' with bombing campaigns. North Vietnam was fundamentally agricultural; losing its industry would hurt, but would not be fatal.[3] Johnson became increasingly angry about press leaks and criticism of the war, withdrawing into a tight circle of trusted advisers in 'Tuesday lunch' sessions when policy would be worked out and decisions made.

As the war and protests about it became more intense, the 'Tuesday lunches' became more frequent and occurred on different days and different times. It was a haphazard method of administration, and it caused great difficulties for the military, the State Department, and the CIA. Ray Cline, CIA Deputy Director for Intelligence, watched this process with concern:

> As the Vietnam war became more worrisome, Johnson retreated more and more from orderly reviewing of evidence and systematic consultation. Kennedy had converted Eisenhower's methodical NSC process to a fast-break, executive task-force process, which worked well if the President really focused on the problem. Lyndon Johnson further narrowed the circle of participants in the NSC to the principals, whom he began to meet at a weekly luncheon – Dean Rusk, McNamara, and Bundy, who was replaced later by Walt Rostow. There were other groups: but this was the critical policy forum, and intelligence did not have a place at the table.[4]

It was ironic that it was this group of men, who prided themselves on being practical and placed their faith in management-as-a-science and in technocracy, and insisted in quantifying everything, who intensified the gap between policy and intelligence. It was a classic example of not seeing the woods for the trees, vividly recalled by Peer de Silva, CIA station chief in Saigon in 1964–5. Early in 1964 McNamara attended a MACV briefing in Saigon at which de Silva was present:

> The briefing concluded, McNamara dropped his pencil, pushed his chair back from the table, and began to bombard at large the MACV senior staff... How many more strategic hamlets have been constructed since I was last here? How many more yards of barbed wire for these new hamlets have been issued since my last visit? What are the latest POL [petrol, oil and lubrication] requirements for ARVN [Army of the Republic of Vietnam]? Tire requirements? I sat there amazed, and thought to myself, what in the world is this man thinking about? This is not a problem of logistics and, in any event, there are plenty of people here at MACV fully competent to handle the material side of the war. This is a war that needs discussion of strategic purpose and of strategy itself. What is he talking about?...

The man simply had no comprehension of the nature of the conflict in Vietnam, let alone any idea of how it should be handled. As time wore on, he demonstrated that he believed only in the application of military force. A rational man himself, he tended to view the world as being populated by rational people: surely once the Vietcong perceived the fact that an overwhelming military force could not be stopped, McNamara logically believed, then they would, as rational men, cease their violence. How wrong he was.[5]

The agency's consistent pessimism about the war (it never said the war was unwinnable: it said that it would be a long, hard slog to win and that it was not being won) constantly endangered its standing in the Johnson White House. By the beginning of 1965 John McCone decided he had had enough: he felt that the President was no longer listening to him and therefore it would be better for everyone to have a DCI who did have the President's ear. So he resigned. On 11 April 1965, Johnson appointed Vice Admiral William Raborn as McCone's successor, with Richard Helms, who had been in the OSS and in the CIA since its start, rising to become Deputy Director of Plans.

Johnson hoped that Raborn would make the agency less pessimistic about Vietnam, but this did not happen. Raborn had a reputation as an efficient manager – he had overseen the Navy's Polaris submarine development – and was a simple, patriotic officer. The complexities of foreign policy and strategic hamlets were beyond him. Stories of his gaffes and ignorance soon became a Washington talking point. 'Who's this fellow Oligarchy anyway?' he once asked. On another occasion he thought 'Kuwait' was an agency codename. 'What do you do?' said one CIA man in frustration. 'You gasp.' Such was Raborn's ineptitude that whenever he was asked to attend a NSC meeting, he was also asked by the White House to bring Helms with him, a situation which brought equal embarrassment to both men.

Raborn also failed to make a good impression in Congress, and this was a serious blow to Johnson who counted on the DCI being able to convince Congress of the viability of the war. After barely a year at the agency, Johnson replaced Raborn with Richard Helms, the first professional CIA officer to hold the post. Johnson told Helms that he had only ever intended Raborn as a temporary appointment until Helms became known to Congress and could take over as DCI.

Nevertheless, Raborn's period at Langley, though short, was important.

During 1965 Johnson involved the CIA more and more in the operational side of the Vietnam war. This in turn required more and more agency officers to sustain the involvement, and it became the common wisdom inside the CIA that the fast track to career advancement was to serve in Vietnam.

## HEARTS AND MINDS

'Pacification' became the watchword of the attempt to stimulate South Vietnamese opposition to the Vietcong in the countryside. Ever since Lansdale and his team set up the first strategic hamlets in the mid-1950s, the CIA always placed emphasis on generating and supporting native resistance to the communists.

In the mid-1960s, the hamlets were followed by People's Action Teams – local militias, in effect – that were village-based, wore no uniforms, and lived where they fought. The PATs were well-trained and had considerable success in dealing with local grievances and withstanding Vietcong attacks and propaganda. The CIA established a PAT training base on the Vung Tau peninsula, and by early 1966 had trained 16,000 Vietnamese villagers in 59-man teams. The success of the PAT teams attracted the attention of MACV which, to the anger of the CIA, took them over in November 1966.

William Colby, known in the agency as the 'Godfather of Vietnam', because of his long involvement with the war there, was responsible for several of the agency's most effective counter-guerrilla policies. He was station chief in Saigon, 1959–62; chief of the Far East Division of the DDP, 1962–7, and on leave from the CIA from 1968 to 1971 as South Vietnam director of Civil Operations and Rural Development Support (CORDS) for the Agency for International Development.

A substantial amount of the CIA's budget was going into South East Asia by 1964. Its operation in Vietnam was very large, very different from any other: it was not typical of the agency. In Bill Colby, the CIA had an atypical officer, a man of great subtlety of operation, in charge for most of the 1960s. He had fantastic drive, and this was needed to compensate for the agency's weak language capability (not many CIA officers spoke Vietnamese). And Colby was willing to risk failure. His energy and bravery were heavily involved. He was one of the very few people prepared really to have a go.

In agency terms, Colby did well. In Vietnam in the 1960s, the agency consistently appeared to be the organization getting the best return on its investment, both in terms of damage done to the enemy, and in terms of relative incon-

William Colby, known in the CIA as the 'Godfather of Vietnam' because of his long involvement with the country, went on leave from the agency in 1968 for three years to become head of counter-guerrilla operations with the rank of ambassador. Here he examines a shotgun of a self-defence group in northern Thua Thien province in June 1969.

spicuousness. Proportionate to effort – enemy killed and captured; US casualties minimized; resources employed; and, not least, minimization of publicity and therefore of unpopularity both at home and abroad – the CIA got top marks. So did Colby. He became DCI five years after leaving Vietnam.

As chief of the Far East Division, in 1965 Colby set up the Counter Terror (CT) units, later called the Provincial Reconnaissance Units (PRUs), which concentrated on conflict in the countryside. The CT units were funded and masterminded by the CIA, but commanded by the South Vietnamese security forces. CT interrogation blocks were built throughout the country, and soon had a frightening reputation. According to a former State Department officer, Wayne Cooper, who spent eighteen months as an adviser to the South Vietnamese security police, the CT units were:

a unilateral American program, never recognized by the South Vietnamese government. CIA representatives recruited, organized, supplied, and directly paid CT teams, whose function was to use Vietcong techniques of terror – assassination, abuses, kidnappings and intimidation – against the Vietcong leadership.[6]

A major problem for Americans involved in fighting the Vietnam war was the great cultural differences between them and the Vietnamese. Murder, corruption, blood feuds, torture, terror, and a generally lower valuation of human life were more commonplace in Vietnam than in the United States. This meant, in turn, that Americans working with Vietnamese during the war had to be prepared for involvement – if only by association – with morally repugnant actions close up: a fact which had a direct effect on the contemptuous attitude of GIs towards their allies, and which undoubtedly affected the soldiers involved in the My Lai atrocity of 16 March 1968 when at least 450 unarmed South Vietnamese civilians – men, women, and children – were massacred by US troops.

However, the CIA was not full of soldiers who could go into the jungles and shoot: that was not the agency's business. The CIA employed about 18,000 people in total worldwide during the period of the Vietnam war, including the agency's own security staff, personnel staff, secretaries, communication staff – amounting to several thousand – and the analytical side based at Langley, and which composed the majority of the agency's employees. Thus at any one time the agency had at most about 700 of its own staff in Vietnam.

By the end of 1966, it was recognized that the strategic hamlets by themselves were not working. McNamara told President Johnson in October 1966 that: 'Success in pacification depends on the interrelated functions of providing physical security, destroying the VC apparatus, motivating the people to cooperate and establishing responsive local government.'

To achieve this, civilian and military operations were integrated into CORDS under Robert Komer, with Bill Colby as his deputy. Komer had been an analyst in the CIA in the 1950s, but had left to join the National Security Council staff in the Kennedy White House. In March 1966, Johnson appointed Komer as his special representative in Vietnam. Komer called himself 'The high panjandrum of pacification'; in Saigon he was called 'Blowtorch' because of the energy he applied in his job.

# *9*
# FIGHTING
## *1967–1975*

*I*n July 1967, Robert Komer set up the Intelligence Coordination and
Exploitation (ICEX) operation, aimed at correlating intelligence information from all sources to identify and then root out the Vietcong infrastructure (VCI) – the Vietcong leadership in the South; chain of command;
agents; informers. Komer and Colby tried to impress on the Saigon government
and MACV the importance of identifying the VCI, but made little impact.
Because of this, they developed the Phoenix plan out of ICEX as a way of
getting on with the job themselves, utilizing CIA information to the full, with
the help of cooperative South Vietnamese commanders in the field. Bowing to
the inevitable, the South Vietnamese government formally endorsed Phoenix in
December 1967.

### PHOENIX

Phoenix was set in motion at the end of 1967 with the aim of carrying the war
to the VCI. US intelligence – from MACV and the CIA – was to be pooled
with South Vietnamese intelligence. South Vietnamese security forces were then
to go into action to identify members of the Vietcong chain of command, arrest
and interrogate them, and if possible turn them into informers. Bill Colby
described the aims of Phoenix as:

> To re-establish local territorial security in a gradually expanding number
> of hamlets and villages. As this expansion occurred, increasing attention
> could be placed on the re-establishment of local government through village
> and hamlet elections and the reconstruction of roads, schools, etc. This
> was followed by the initiation of local economic development and the
> reinforcement of community defense.[1]

Phoenix, however, was never at the forefront of the war and always had to fight for resources and support. Komer returned to Washington in November 1968, leaving Bill Colby in charge.

As CORDS chief, Colby was responsible for a huge bureaucracy which between 1968 and 1970 cost $4 billion, of which Phoenix was a substantial part. Six hundred and thirty-seven US military personnel worked with South Vietnamese units in Phoenix operations throughout South Vietnam. About 100 CIA officers were also involved.

After the war was over, the Vietcong said that Phoenix had been the most effective operation against them. But it had probably impaired less than 10 per cent of their effort.

The drive to quantify everything in the war, to produce statistics of Vietcong 'neutralization', resulted in corrupt reporting procedures by Vietnamese forces who invented body counts in order to fulfil quotas (and thus get paid). Phoenix often acted as a cover for personal vendettas. It soon acquired a reputation for murder and terror, second only to that of the Vietcong, and became a focus of anti-war protests in the United States. Once arrested, prisoners were routinely tortured and killed, and no action was taken against those responsible. Of the 81,740 individuals captured in Phoenix operations by August 1972, 23,369 were killed. After 1972, with US commitment to the war fast disappearing, Phoenix collapsed.

Phoenix showed the agency that nothing but very heavy killing would resolve the guerrilla war: 23,000 plus dead had not worked; 300–400,000 would probably need to be killed in order to win. But it produced tactical intelligence, and demonstrated the agency's commitment to the war to the satisfaction of Washington. The operation conformed to Washington expectations of the CIA, buying the agency the right to question the conduct of the war. It won the agency credibility when it came to advice and estimates.

However, the generals in Vietnam made perfectly sure that the agency was not going to be allowed to become big enough to win the war. In bureaucratic terms it was 'their' war, and defeat at the agency's hands would have been a devastating blow to their standing. Thus keeping Phoenix weak suited their bureaucratic objectives. For Phoenix to have been decisive it would have to have been multiplied about twenty times. Since it was not allowed to pay off, it is remembered as a murder plan.

## HIGH WIRE

In February 1965, President Johnson approved the 'Rolling Thunder' bombing campaign against North Vietnam, and in July major reinforcements for MACV began to arrive. The agency, walking a high wire, discreetly cautioned against greater direct US involvement in the war, but under Raborn its views were not presented strongly either to Congress or the White House.

When Richard Helms was sworn in as DCI on 30 June 1966, Johnson had already made the critical decision to wage all-out war in Vietnam. Helms' job, as far as Johnson was concerned, was to sustain the war effort in Vietnam and in Congress. Johnson, with the most agonized reluctance, having determined to go into Vietnam, did not want his intimate counsel darkened by 'yets', 'buts', 'ifs', and 'if you don't minds'. Helms knew that in being pessimistic about the Vietnam war the agency was going up against LBJ arm-in-arm with his Secretary of Defense, Robert McNamara, and the Joint Chiefs. And, at that moment in 1966, no one could be certain whether Bobby Kennedy – who was expected to run for the presidency – would oppose the war.

At the top level in US policymaking circles, support for the war was almost complete. Johnson's policymakers disagreed on the matter later – although before the vast majority of the country did – when the war became a political issue. They came from a cadre of people who were very conscious of their own children, and pressure from their children (especially in the case of McNamara and Cyrus Vance), and young people generally, had a direct effect: they thought that by pursuing the war they were alienating the future.

It was constructive of Helms to choose the agency's ground within the tent where it argued for complexity, subtlety, for the degree to which Vietnam was not an ordinary war – or at least unlike any war the United States had had occasion to fight so far – rather than to argue directly against the war. The agency would have engaged in hara-kiri if it had gone up against the LBJ-McNamara-Joint Chiefs combination in 1965–7. Not until McNamara's nerve started cracking in the spring/summer of 1967, as he realized that his quantitative approach to the war was not succeeding, could the agency really speak out to any degree. By that time, too, the war had become the major political issue in the United States.

The high-wire act of the agency, under Helms, caused worry amongst middle levels of agency staff, who were concerned that their intelligence analysis of the war seemingly had no effect on policy. Ray Cline experienced this when he was asked by McNamara and McGeorge Bundy to conduct a study of the 'Rolling Thunder' bombings. Cline's report was pessimistic and argued that the bombing would not change North Vietnamese policy and, 'if anything, the strikes to date have hardened their attitude'. Cline also warned of the effect that the bombings might have on US public opinion, particularly if direct US military escalation proved ineffective in apparently winning the war. On all counts, he said, the USA should avoid becoming 'mired down in combat in the jungle in a military effort that we cannot win, and from which we will have extreme difficulty in extracting ourselves'.

McNamara and Bundy received Cline's report, and said nothing. But McNamara continued to ask the agency for its assessments: he knew that whether or not he liked the conclusions, he needed good intelligence analysis. R. Jack Smith, who wrote many of the reports and estimates in this period, noted with resignation that although McNamara expressed his confidence in agency conclusions, that confidence tended to evaporate whenever he went to Vietnam and experienced 'that treatment that the military boys put on so well'. The war, and the constant increase in direct US involvement, continued. Richard Helms, knowing that his agency's caution about the war was the backdrop to everything he said, concentrated on gaining LBJ's confidence and using his position to seek the best practical alternatives for the United States in making the war winnable in some way – perhaps a patient, longer way – or in securing an acceptable end to it.

In order to deal with the concern within the agency over Vietnam, Sherman Kent and his successor as head of the Board of National Estimates, Abbot Smith, assembled analysts from different sections of the CIA to report on matters of controversy and to hear different arguments. A major controversy concerned the estimates of the numbers of Vietcong and North Vietnamese involved in the war.

## NUMBERS

Sam Adams, an analyst in the CIA on the staff of George Carver, Helms' special assistant for Vietnam, specialized in estimating the numbers. MACV estimated the total enemy troops and other categories as coming to about 270,000. Captured documents and intelligence reports led Sam Adams to a different total. Adams thought that a more accurate number for the other categories was 330,000, and he also reckoned that regular troop numbers were higher than MACV's estimate.

His total was about 600,000, more than double MACV's.

As it happened, in 1967 MACV was also revising its estimates, and when Carver and Adams had an order of battle conference with the military in Saigon, they were able to compromise on a new total of 500,000. The importance of agreeing on the numbers was that they then provided a common basis for analysis and discussion of the war within the US government. If different totals were used by the Pentagon and the CIA, then the President and his advisers would always have to make their own assessment. Thus, agreement on the numbers also suited the bureaucratic interests of the military and the CIA because it meant that their 'control' of the basic facts would not be questioned.

The problem with the new agreement on the total number of Vietcong and North Vietnamese personnel engaged in the war was that doubling the figure had major political consequences in the USA. Simply put – and politicians tend to put things simply – it meant that the war was twice as difficult to win. Johnson was banking on a military breakthrough in Vietnam to help his campaign for the presidency in 1968, and everyone was reluctant to break the news of the new figure to him. The implication of the new total also sank in at the Pentagon, and MACV began to back track on it. In May 1967 the Board of National Estimates was due to present the National Estimate on Vietnam, and Helms knew that he could be faced with a bruising battle over the numbers. R. Jack Smith put his finger on the emotional quality of the numbers debate:

> Never before had a civilian intelligence organization challenged an army in the field about its orders of battle. There is one principle which military men hold dearest to their hearts, and it is the security-of-forces principle. Any time you presume to tell them their forces are or are not in danger to the extent they say they are, they get outraged. Their job is to keep their forces secure. But here were a bunch of civilians telling not only the Pentagon but also the forces in the field that the number they were facing was higher. That created a very difficult position: it was their war. They were the ones getting killed. There was a lot of emotion involved in that.[2]

Helms delayed the presentation of the Estimate, and in September sent Carver, Adams and another analyst to Saigon to try to reach another agreement with MACV on the figures. The result was the 'Saigon agreement' which accepted a common figure for the enemy regular and Vietcong forces, but did not add service troops and political cadres to the total. A range of 299,000–334,000 was accepted as the new total, with everyone free to differ over the forces in the other two categories. In itself, this agreement was symptomatic of the increasing differences within the United States over the war. MACV was killing thousands of North Vietnamese soldiers and Vietcong, but as many seemed to sprout out of the ground. Vietcong morale remained high. This made the decisions about the war facing Johnson in 1967 far more political than military. The debate over numbers served simply to reinforce the obvious difficulty of winning the war.

On the basis of the Saigon compromise, Helms signed the Vietnam Estimate on 13 November 1967. Adams was bitter: he failed to appreciate that Helms was trying to wean Johnson away from the view that the war was quickly winnable and that a bureaucratic battle about the numbers would simply undermine Helms' standing in the White House. It was also the case, as an internal agency inquiry showed, that it was not easy to quantify enemy strength since so much of it consisted of undeclared supporters and guerrillas.

Nine days after Helms signed the Estimate, however, General William Westmoreland, the MACV commander, said in a press conference that enemy strength 'had declined from 285,000 down to 248,000'. He failed to mention that he was talking about only part of the enemy strength. This spurred Adams to further research. He was becoming increasingly distraught at the way in which his work was not having effect, and became convinced that Helms was holding it back. Within two months Adams had collected further evidence to back up his original assessment that there were probably as many as 600,000 enemy of one sort or another. His findings were independently supported by another analyst, Joe Hovey, working in Saigon and using communications intelligence. Hovey also concluded that a major North Vietnamese and Vietcong offensive was imminent.

He was right. In January 1968 North Vietnam and the Vietcong launched the Tet offensive. In ten weeks, Tet was over, with the North Vietnamese and Vietcong suffering heavy losses. Indeed, military analysts subsequently determined that Tet was a massive miscalculation by North Vietnam, and that after its failure the communists lost any hope of a military victory. Politically, however, Tet was a success for the communists, convincing US public opinion that the USA should get out of Vietnam. The sight on television of the US Embassy in Saigon under siege, and the fact that Vietcong guerrillas attacked in provinces and cities that had been thought to be entirely communist-free throughout South Vietnam, broke faith in MACV's estimates and assertions. Just six weeks before

The Vietcong and North Vietnamese Army launched a massive attack on South Vietnam during the Tet – Vietnamese New Year – celebration in February 1968. Vietcong guerrillas successfully infiltrated the US Embassy and other strongpoints in Saigon. The attack was a military failure but a propaganda success. Here captured Vietcong and their weapons are put on display.

the offensive, Bob Komer was quoted in *Newsweek* as saying that 'our information is that they can't put more than a company-sized unit into the field anywhere in South Vietnam'.

The scale of the Tet attacks was such a shock that it forced MACV and the CIA to reconsider assessments of the strength of the Vietcong. Sam Adams pressed for an inquiry into why his analysis had not been acted upon, eventually leaving the CIA convinced that there had been a cover-up between the agency and MACV to hide their combined inefficiency in not following up his work. Inquiries, however, found that Adams' work, while good, had not been conclusive, and that Adams had become somewhat fanatical about his case.

Helms understood that there would have to be a public reckoning after Tet. Johnson painfully accepted that the war could not be quickly won. MACV read the results differently, and pressed for a further 206,000 US troops to be sent to Vietnam in addition to the 543,000 already there. From a military perspective, after Tet the Vietcong were significantly weakened and therefore it was the time to push even harder.

Within days of Tet ending, Johnson asked his new Secretary of Defense, Clark Clifford, who replaced McNamara on 1 March 1968, to make a recommendation on MACV's request. Clifford's staff spent three days going over the CIA's studies, and concluded that even if the extra troops were sent, the war would still be stalemated in 1969. Clifford recommended to the President that MACV's request be denied, and that instead plans should be made for a withdrawal from the war. At the end of March 1968, Clifford's view was supported by the 'Wise Men', a group of senior statesmen assembled by Johnson to advise him. Previously the 'Wise Men' had supported the war; now they turned against it. Three days after their conclusions were presented, Johnson went on television and announced that he would not be running for the presidency and would devote the rest of his term to trying to end the war.

By pulverizing the country with bombing and artillery and mining and defoliation, the infrastructure of Vietnam was grossly eroded, and understandably the locals wanted to end the war on virtually any terms. The Sam Adams affair revealed this. Adams also argued that if the pacification programmes, including Phoenix, were properly developed, they could win the war. His complaint was that his evidence was suppressed, and so the best opportunity of winning the war was lost.

Helms' problem was that he could not present a plan for victory ten years or so in the future. His – and the agency's – whole position depended upon his being a bridge between two time frames. The people who wanted a quick victory were already angry enough at the agency for qualifying their vision so markedly, while the people who argued for a long-term approach to victory lacked any mass constituency and did not appreciate the difficulty of presenting their case to an élite looking for immediate results. Helms was on the receiving end from both sides.

## FINAL ACT

The war did not end for another seven years, but from 1968 it was clear that the United States had lost the will to fight and then it was only a matter of time before it withdrew. Even after 1973, when the vast bulk of US presence in Vietnam was gone, it was by no means certain that North Vietnam and the Vietcong would win. It was only after Congress voted to stop US financial and military aid to South Vietnam that the Saigon government collapsed.

In that collapse, many South Vietnamese who had worked for the CIA suffered. Frank Snepp, a CIA officer in Saigon at the time of the South's fall, contended in his book, *Decent Interval*, that many agents were betrayed through inefficiency when CIA files were abandoned in the evacuation. Tom Polgar, the CIA chief of station in Saigon at the time of the fall, vigorously contests Snepp's claims.

A very tough decision was involved in the Saigon evacuation. If people had been evacuated early while there was still a US military presence to manage it, it would have signalled that America was determined to end the war at any cost and its leverage at the table would have been attenuated. If the USA had started to evacuate its people months or even weeks earlier, it would have been saying that South Vietnam was doomed, and doomed almost at once – something not even North Vietnam believed. Hanoi seems to have been genuinely surprised at how fast South Vietnam came apart in 1975.

If North Vietnam was determined on a unified Vietnam under Hanoi's control, and the United States was determined against union, talk about a peaceful, prosperous South Vietnam went out the window until the resolution of war. The USA was then caught between the odious Diem regime that was dismantling half of what was worthwhile in Vietnam, and the communists. In the war, the agency was fundamentally engaged in buying time and expanding the imagination of policymakers, which under the circumstances was all that it could do.

On 29 and 30 April 1975, about 8000 Americans and South Vietnamese were flown from rooftops in the final US evacuation from Saigon. This was the house of the CIA deputy chief of station. Vietnamese agents and intelligence officers are seen queuing to be flown from here to waiting US ships and safety.

## FINAL SUM

In Vietnam, the generals were saying 'Can do, can do' and asking for 'More, more, more'. Their trouble was that they were never given (and never asked for) an adequate definition of their mission. They pursued an entirely conventional military policy when a much more complex doctrine was called for.

McNamara saw the Vietnam war as a bargaining affair: he detested the killing and the cost, and he sought to use numbers of men, weapons, bombings etc., in a contest in which the North Vietnamese and their allies were expected to respond in kind at first, but ultimately with withdrawals and moves towards making peace. He – and most others – believed that a certain level of pain would bring the North to the table. But the Viets were an incredibly determined, hard, tough people.

Below the level of the President, the agency was outspoken in its pessimistic view of the war: at the assistant secretary and journalistic level, agency people let their views be known. Also, Vietnam was neither McCone's nor Raborn's type of operation, and the agency had to wait until they went, before it acquired a proper bureaucratic voice. McCone was a very fine administrative DCI, but he consciously avoided questions of high policy. Raborn had other things on his mind, in particular his forlorn attempt to keep Johnson and Congress happy, and in any event, naval – not land or air or police or intelligence – operations were his forte.

Under Helms, the agency came into its own. His handling of Vietnam intelligence and operations was possible because the agency was very good. He likes to tell the story of when in 1967 Arthur Goldberg (and others) were pressing Johnson to supply Israel with more of everything, the President asked Helms for an estimate of Israeli capability. The analysts said that Israel would win a war against any combination of Arab states in two weeks. Johnson asked, 'Are you sure?' Helms came back: 'We've revised our estimate. Israel would win in a week.' This provided Johnson with the ammunition he needed to withstand the Israeli lobby on the Hill and in private. In the event it took Israel six days. Helms had a proper confidence in the quality of the agency.

Most institutions become less energetic and less capable of innovation within ten or fifteen years. The agency that had been formed in the direct emergency of 1947–9 was going to be worn out by 1970 at the latest in the normal course of events. But Vietnam, in a very real sense, rejuvenated the CIA.

Today, Vietnam is slowly being forgotten. Hollywood has been exorcizing the ghosts for a decade. Phoenix, which aroused very strong emotions even a few years ago, does not do so any longer. The agency has not been in the proconsular business since the early 1970s. Founded as a response to surprise attack, and energized by the Soviet threat, the agency had intervened around the world on the assumption – mistaken or not – that benefits would flow to the Soviets from its inaction. Vietnam changed all that.

# 10
# SPIES

Within the Directorate of Plans was the counterintelligence division (CI), an hermetic, secretive fiefdom which for over thirty years was headed by one of the most controversial personalities in the history of the CIA, James Jesus Angleton. Angleton was a legend within the agency. He was a skilled fly-fisherman, orchid grower, and leather tooler. He would give fishing flies and leather cigarette boxes that he made himself as presents to friends. His nicknames testified to his reputation. 'Virginia Slim' after the cigarettes he chain-smoked; 'Skinny Jim', a man who looks 'like his ectoplasm has run out', said a colleague; the 'Delphic Oracle', and 'The Ghost'. Officers could work for years at Langley without ever setting eyes on him.

Counterintelligence is a very specialized and sophisticated activity. It has an in-built institutional paranoia which sooner or later overwhelms every counterintelligence officer and Angleton himself was not immune. As head of the counterintelligence staff, Angleton's task was to police the CIA, to frustrate attempts to penetrate the agency and confuse it with disinformation. Because of connections he made with Israelis in the 1940s in Italy, he was personally given responsibility for liaison with the Israeli intelligence services.

Angleton came from Idaho and was half-Mexican through his mother, a fact about which he was extremely sensitive and which he tried to hide in a WASP upbringing. He was educated in England and then went to Yale. In 1938, when travelling in Europe, he met Ezra Pound who later visited Yale and contributed to the literary magazine Angleton edited, *Furioso*. During the war, his cosmopolitan background led him to the OSS where he was involved in liaison with the British in London during the war. He also became friendly with Allen Dulles. They were both fascinated by counterintelligence, for which Angleton had a real flair. When Angleton became head of counterintelligence in 1954, largely thanks to Allen Dulles who was by then DCI, he reported directly to Dulles to whom he

James Jesus Angleton, head of CIA counterintelligence for twenty years, became convinced that the KGB had successfully penetrated the agency. His 'mole hunts' found no moles. In 1974 William Colby, then DCI, decided that Angleton had become counterproductive and sacked him.

had complete access.

Throughout the 1950s Angleton formed very close contacts not only with the main Western European intelligence services but also with the Turkish, South African, Yugoslav, Taiwanese, Thai and, especially, the Israeli organizations.

Angleton's job, part policeman, part spycatcher, required him to be intensely suspicious of his closest colleagues and had a very isolating effect. Friendship was a luxury. But during his wartime stint in London he did make friends with Kim Philby of SIS. When Philby arrived in Washington after the war as SIS liaison with US intelligence, Angleton showed him around and smoothed his way with introductions and contacts in the Washington bureaucracy. They

Harold Philby, Stalin's spy at the heart of British and US intelligence, responsible for the deaths of hundreds of British and American agents. He was nicknamed 'Kim' after Rudyard Kipling's boy spy hero of the same name. In 1951 evidence accumulated that he was a Soviet spy, and he was forced to resign from the British service. He fled to Moscow twelve years later.

lunched together frequently and dined at each other's houses. When Philby fell under suspicion in 1951, after Burgess and Maclean absconded, Angleton vehemently defended his friend to the DCI, Bedell Smith, claiming that Philby had been duped by Burgess. When confirmation of Philby's treachery finally came in 1963, Angleton was devastated. He became even more withdrawn and isolated as a result. If Philby could betray on such a scale, he concluded, then nobody could be trusted. From that point he conducted an increasingly obsessive mole hunt in the CIA.

At its start, the agency experienced Soviet spies, although only one (and that for China, not the Soviet Union) was ever found to have really penetrated it. James Speyer Kronthal was probably the first. He had served with Allen Dulles in the OSS in Switzerland during World War II. When the CIA was created, Kronthal became the agency's first station chief in Switzerland. There he was blackmailed into becoming a Soviet spy: he was homosexual. In 1953 he committed suicide, apparently hopelessly torn between a real loyalty to the United States and his treachery.

John Arthur Paisley joined the CIA in 1953. He had been a sailor, specializing in signalling. In the agency, he worked in the DDI's electronic branch, becoming expert in Soviet communications. In 1974 he retired from the agency. Four years later he disappeared sailing off the Maryland coast just as investigations had begun to try to determine whether or not he had spied for the Soviets.

Karl and Hana Koecher were a Czechoslovak couple who came to the United States in 1965 claiming to be political refugees. In 1973, for four years, Karl was hired as a translator by the agency. In 1984 he was arrested for spying for Czechoslovakia, with his wife acting as his go-between. It was thought by some of the CIA and FBI investigators that the Koechers had worked with Paisley.

David H. Barnett joined the agency in 1958. He resigned twelve years later. Then, in 1976, he became a Soviet agent, selling Moscow his knowledge of the agency and actively seeking to join the staff of the Senate intelligence committee in order to obtain more information for his paymasters. He was arrested in 1980. He confessed and was sentenced to ten years in gaol for espionage.

In 1985, Larry Wu-tai Chin, a naturalized US citizen, was arrested for spying for Red China. He was an early CIA analyst, reaching senior position in the China section of the DDI. Before committing suicide weeks after his arrest, he admitted that he had been an agent for Peking for the whole of his career.

Over a thirty-year period until the mid-1970s when Angleton left the agency, tens of thousands of individuals had passed through the CIA. The handful of identified penetration agents was a testimony to something – the efficiency or inefficiency of the CI staff; the effectiveness of the agency's screening procedures; the inefficiency or efficiency of Red Chinese and Soviet bloc intelligence services. Angleton fundamentally regarded it as evidence of the cleverness of the other side, and was convinced that there was at least one high-level, long-term Soviet spy in the CIA who had not yet been caught. Suspicion, after all, was his job.

## EARLY AGENTS

The CI staff was not responsible for handling agents or defectors: that was the job of the Soviet bloc division of the DDP. The problems arose when counterintelligence came to assess the value of agent and defector information and the possibility that they might be disinformation agents.

Allen Dulles made the recruitment of penetration agents a prime objective of the CIA. The best ones, he considered after his wartime experience with Kolbe and Gisevius in Switzerland, were what he usually termed 'walk-ins', people who out of the blue offered their services. However, it was not until 1952 that the first Soviet official was recruited: Major Vladimir Popov of the GRU, Soviet military intelligence.

William Hood, Popov's case officer in the CIA, summed up Popov's contribution until he was finally arrested in 1958:

> For six years he trundled bales of top-secret information out of the top-secret centres of Soviet power. In the process he shattered the Soviet military intelligence service, caused the transfer of the KGB chief (a four-star general and one of the most powerful men in the USSR), and saved the United States half a billion dollars in military research.[1]

A year after Popov was recruited, an officer serving under him in the GRU, Major Peter Deriabin, asked for asylum at American military headquarters in Vienna and gave his debriefers a wealth of information about the KGB and about the Kremlin intrigues which followed Stalin's death in March 1953.

In 1954 Soviet defectors to the West included the KGB chief in Australia; a KGB officer stationed in Tokyo; Nikolai Kholkov, a member of the KGB's assassination section, SMERSH, who defected in West Germany; and a senior officer from the Polish intelligence service.

Over the years scores of defectors from the Soviet Union and Eastern Europe contributed to the agency's knowledge of Soviet activities and plans, enabling vital cross-checking to take place. Emigrants to the West also helped with information and with such mundane items as clothes and documents that could be used to disguise agents being sent behind the iron curtain.

## PENKOVSKY

One of the most important Soviet agents recruited by Western intelligence was Colonel Oleg Penkovsky of GRU who approached the British in 1961. When the CIA was informed, Bissell was initially wary. 'How do we know this guy is on the level?' he asked Jack Maury, head of the Soviet division. Angleton thought he was a double agent but Maurice Oldfield, SIS liaison in Washington, persuaded the Americans of his authenticity. He was, Oldfield said:

> the answer to a prayer. What he provided seemed like a miracle too. That is why for so long he was mistrusted on both sides of the Atlantic. It seemed incredible that he could take such risks – not merely photographing top

The 44-year-old Colonel Oleg Penkovsky photographed in 1963 as he was sentenced to death for
espionage by a military court in Moscow. Penkovsky was a Russian patriot who believed that
the Soviet system was destroying his country, and he volunteered his services to the British and
Americans. He supplied valuable intelligence during the October 1962 Cuban missile crisis.

secret documents, but actually giving us the original documents in some instances.[2]

Penkovsky soon proved his worth to the agency during the Cuban missile crisis where his information was invaluable in complementing and verifying the intelligence obtained from the U-2. He said that Soviet missile technology in 1962 could not yet attack the USA with intercontinental nuclear missiles. This confirmed the technical intelligence on the subject.

Penkovsky corroborated the technical intelligence finding that Soviet missiles were vulnerable to US anti-missile systems. It was information that helped to convince Kennedy that Khruschev would back down over Cuba. Penkovsky also confirmed that the chief of Soviet missile forces and 300 officers had been killed when a missile had exploded at a test site.

Penkovsky and his British contact, Greville Wynne, were arrested in Moscow in 1963 and found guilty of espionage. Penkovsky was immediately executed. In 1964 Wynne was exchanged for the Soviet spy, Gordon Lonsdale, who had been unmasked in London in 1960.

A controversy surrounds the handling of Penkovsky. Several of those involved, particularly in the CIA, subsequently stated that he should have been asked to do much less: the quantity of information that he passed to SIS and the CIA involved frequent and difficult meetings in Moscow. In London when he was with a visiting Soviet delegation, he spent most of the night with his debriefers. It all heightened the chances that he would be observed and caught. During the Cuban missile crisis he worked overtime, and did excite suspicion leading to his arrest.

How to handle Penkovsky was recognized as a problem at the time. He was a frenetic spy: having made the decision to betray his country's secrets, he did so all the time. He saw himself as a patriot and the Soviet government and system as the real betrayer of Russia. The British took the view that he was unstoppable, and that any attempt to rein him in would be counterproductive. They thought he would be caught, sooner rather than later, but that for his sake he should be fully used until then. This was the view that prevailed.

The handling of agents and defectors requires special personal skills: firmness, sympathy, understanding. Because of the fear of sudden disclosure, agents in place live under considerable strain which often manifests itself in odd ways: self importance, a foolhardy recklessness which almost invites exposure, and occasional eccentricity. Penkovsky was a classic example. He made endless requests to meet the British Queen and the President of the United States. He kept incriminating photographs of himself in British and American uniforms in a secret drawer in his Moscow flat.

As head of counterintelligence, it was Angleton's job to play devil's advocate in assessing the worth of information about the CIA produced by agents and defectors. Were they the real thing or not? The problem was that Angleton himself was poorly equipped for such a sensitive job. He did not speak Russian; he had never been to the Soviet Union; he had never run an agent.

## MONSTER PLOT

Anatoly Golytsin defected to the CIA in December 1961 from Finland, where he had been working as a major in the KGB's first chief directorate (responsible for foreign operations) concentrating on NATO targets. He had been planning to defect for some time and had collected all the information he could on Soviet agents and operations. Golytsin produced a vast amount of information which helped to provide leads to over 100 Soviet spies and sources within the NATO alliance.

Information from Michael Goleniewski, a Polish intelligence officer who defected in 1960 giving the agency the names of several hundred Soviet bloc agents in the West, tied into Golytsin's, corroborating many specifics. It was the time of the Berlin Wall, the Cuban missile crisis, growing involvement in Vietnam. In that atmosphere, coupled with Goleniewski's and Golytsin's revelations of the extent of Soviet spying, it was not surprising that paranoia about the agency being penetrated should loom so large.

The main thrust of Golytsin's evidence was that there was a huge Soviet disinformation campaign operating in the West and he predicted that the KGB would do their best to discredit him. Within a few months, three Soviet disinformation agents had appeared to cast doubt on Golytsin, thus seeming to provide convincing proof that his allegations were genuine. This gained Golytsin access to the top levels of the agency before he was fully debriefed.

Golytsin called his conspiracy theory 'the master plot' but critics soon dubbed it 'the monster plot'. A CIA psychiatrist conducted a routine examination of Golytsin and concluded that besides exhibiting signs of a 'severe paranoid disorder', Golytsin was also a megalomaniac.

Angleton was sympathetic to Golytsin's claims, but when Golytsin started to rubbish every other defector who followed him, some experienced agency people began to wonder whether he himself might not be an *agent provocateur*. According to one CIA officer who dealt with him:

> Golytsin is a very suspicious, very withdrawn, very difficult man ... after a while he came to realize that he didn't have to tell the truth in order to get attention. His later information, from the fall of 1962, lacked an element of veracity. It was about that time that Angleton took over, and apologized to him for the behaviour of people who had tried to get him to straighten up a little bit, and Golytsin at that point realized he had a nice situation he could control, and he has travelled with it ever since.[3]

It was this combination of fact and fiction which made Golytsin's evidence so problematical and created so much havoc in Western intelligence services.

In England he helped to unmask three Soviet agents and warned that there had been another two agents besides Burgess, Maclean and Philby. In 1964 Anthony Blunt, and in 1967 John Cairncross confessed to being the 'fourth' and 'fifth' men. Blunt had been in British intelligence during World War II, and had remained on the fringes after 1945. He had helped Maclean and Burgess flee to Moscow in 1951. Subsequently he had become Master of the Queen's pictures, for which he was knighted in 1956.

Cairncross was an economist who, by his own admission, spied for the Soviet Union from the mid-1930s until 1952. He had worked in the top secret 'Ultra' intelligence unit breaking German codes during the war, and had regularly passed decrypts to the Soviets. After the war he served in SIS and gave Moscow British-US plans for the future of Yugoslavia. Later he worked in the Foreign Office and the Treasury.

Golytsin and Angleton, and some like-minded individuals in British intelligence, were convinced that Sir Roger Hollis, head of MI5 (British counterintelligence), was a Soviet agent. There was no proof that Hollis was ever a Soviet agent (and every other Soviet defector in a position to know has said that he was not). However, the determination of his critics led to two separate investigations of him. He was cleared on both occasions. But the investigations created turmoil in the British security services and many of those involved believed that Golytsin could not have done more damage by way of disruption and casting suspicions than if he had been a Soviet agent.

There was a similar story in France. Golytsin revealed that there was a network, codenamed Sapphire, of Soviet spies in the French government. A senior French official at NATO was indeed revealed to be a Soviet spy, and this gave weight to Golytsin's claim that there was an even more senior spy still at large. Kennedy took the extraordinary step of writing a personal letter to de Gaulle, warning him of the spy. As in Britain, there was an inconclusive mole hunt. Jacques Foccart, who was on de Gaulle's personal staff and was an adviser on intelligence matters, was accused of being the 'French Philby' as a result. He sued the newspaper which published the charge and won damages.

To general consternation, Golytsin's allegations also extended to the CIA itself. He claimed that not only did the KGB have a source, codenamed 'Sasha', who had penetrated the agency's German operations, but also that there was a high-level Soviet mole in Langley. None of these supposed moles was ever found but Angleton hunted for them relentlessly. On the basis of unsubstantiated information from Golytsin, Angleton told the astonished head of French intelligence that the CIA station chief in Paris, David Murphy, was a Soviet agent. Some officers found their careers blighted and promotion denied: others resigned in frustration. Some were fired because they could not prove their innocence. Richard Helms took the hard but correct view that if an officer was suspect, it was safer for all concerned for him to leave the agency. FBI officers reckoned that in the mid-1960s they were carrying out surveillance on more CIA officers in the USA than on KGB agents.

There was also considerable disquiet within the agency over the handling of some Soviet defectors as a result of Golytsin's allegations. One was Nikolai Fedorovich Artamonov, who took the cover name Nick Shadrin, a Soviet Navy commander who defected in 1961, impressing the CIA and the US Navy with his knowledge. In 1965 Golytsin denounced him as a plant. In 1975, Artamonov disappeared in Vienna, being used by the CIA as a double agent. Another accused by Golytsin was Yuri Nosenko who defected from the KGB in 1964. Golytsin said he was a disinformation agent, and since Nosenko's information was that the KGB was not involved in the Kennedy assassination, there was intense pressure to establish his bona fides. If he was a disinformation agent, then his story suggested that the KGB *was* involved in the assassination, and this would be a most serious matter that could affect world peace. Angleton termed such conundrums the 'wilderness of mirrors'.

Golytsin's allegations impressed CIA officers other than Angleton. For nearly three and a half years Nosenko was kept isolated under close arrest by the Soviet bloc division of the DDP, with the approval of the DCI, and was interrogated at length, sometimes with hallucinogenic drugs, as if he were a KGB agent.

Angleton had no direct involvement in the treatment of Nosenko and, according to Raymond G. Rocca, Angleton's deputy, thought it was a mistake:

> I was, in fact, present when Jim Angleton learned from Dave Murphy [then head of the Soviet bloc division] that the director of CIA, on the recommendation of Mr Murphy and his staff, had authorized that course of action forthwith ... Jim Angleton's reaction: 'It was a mistake'. I remember those words because I agreed with them.[4]

Opinion in the agency was divided as to whether Nosenko was genuine or not and two enquiries conducted by the agency were similarly inconclusive. Subsequently, however, the consensus was that Nosenko was genuine and his information accurate. He was given money, employment, US citizenship, and an apology from the CIA.

More disturbing than Nosenko was the case of Yuri Loginov, a KGB man who had been recruited by the CIA. Golytsin denounced him as a disinformation agent, and he was subsequently handed over to the Soviets in Germany. In 1979 a top-secret agency investigation concluded that Loginov was genuine.

To the horror of his colleagues, Angleton gave Golytsin access to privileged operational files in the hope that he could point to moles within the agency. By the late 1960s Golytsin's value was diminishing. He had denounced the Sino-Soviet split as a sham and in 1968 he assured agency experts that the Prague Spring was part of a Soviet plot to bring anti-communists into the open, and that Dubcek was party to the deception. The common wisdom in the agency was that Golytsin had started with solid information, but gradually had come to pursue the logic of his master plot theory to the point where he was making allegations from speculation. Angleton's support of Golytsin helped to protect him, but by the time William Colby became DCI in 1973, patience was running out. The Soviet division was paralysed and Colby felt that too many people had been hurt by Golytsin's suspicions and Angleton's mole hunts. In 1974 Colby telephoned Angleton and said simply, 'It's time to leave. It's over.'

Angleton's job was about suspicion. Many people felt that there had to be somebody like Angleton in the agency, someone who distrusted everyone and everything and was willing to push anyone out of the way in his search for penetration agents. Colby felt differently: that in Angleton the institutional paranoia had overreached itself, to the detriment of the agency's efficiency on the clandestine side. It was time for ghosts to be exorcized.

# 11
# TARGET
## *1946–1976*

T he Soviet Union in all respects was the principal intelligence target of the CIA. Even after its domestic upheavals, as the world's other major nuclear power, the Soviet Union remains a principal intelligence target. The agency seeks to monitor the Soviet economy, as well as Soviet armed forces, weapon systems, order of battle, geography, politics, leaders, population, space effort, health – everything. Langley is probably the foremost repository of accurate information on the Soviet Union in the world. Its analytical side, in which the Soviet Union is the largest single component, accounts for the majority of CIA staff.

For over forty years the agency has kept close watch on the Soviet Union and has informed and advised presidents and policymakers, but its message, as in Vietnam, has not been received with enthusiasm. Intelligence services are popularly believed to be hyper-suspicious of the other side, always finding new schemes and plots. The agency distinguished itself in being persistently sceptical about the Soviet Union's military and economic abilities. In a period of major US alarm after the launch of the first Soviet sputnik, the agency remained calm. In 1960, it published a landmark report on the Soviet economy, the message of which was: 'Relax, they're not ten feet tall!' But this was a view that was unpopular in US military circles, and in Kennedy's White House. It antagonized the military which had an institutional bias towards bigger budgets and it also antagonized some politicians who took hard Cold War positions. These were to be consistent factors in the agency's management of its analysis of the Soviet Union.

## THE ATOM THREAT

In September 1946, Clark Clifford, special counsel to President Truman, wrote a report for the President on the rapidly escalating Soviet threat in which he stressed the importance of full and accurate intelligence:

> Suspicious misunderstanding of the Soviet Union must be replaced by an accurate knowledge of the motives and methods of the Soviet government. Only through knowledge will we be able to appraise and forecast the military and political moves of the Kremlin: without that knowledge we shall be at the mercy of rumours and half-truths.[1]

Soviet communist ambitions were seen as the single greatest threat to US national security. But for most of the 1940s and early 1950s, the scale and nature of that threat were frustratingly difficult to measure. It was virtually impossible to obtain good information about the USSR and its Central and Eastern European regimes. Defectors and communications intelligence such as Operations Gold and Silver were the principal sources, and they were inadequate, as Richard Helms, who had long experience on the clandestine side of the house, admitted:

> For some years we used the same methods, learned from the British in World War II, that had been tried and proven. But the Soviet bloc in peacetime, particularly the Russians themselves – suspicious, disciplined, possessed of a formidable security police – proved a tough nut to crack.[2]

By the time the agency was founded the USA had already been subjected to intensive Soviet spying which was particularly targeted at the atomic project, and the burning question of when the Soviets would acquire their own bomb had exercised the CIA from its earliest days.

In December 1947, Hillenkoetter told Truman that although the full impact of the Soviet atom spy ring was not yet known, the Soviets were probably still some years away from acquiring their own bomb. In July 1948, the CIA estimated that the earliest possible date for this was mid-1950 but that a more probable date was mid-1953. The Air Force disagreed with the CIA's estimate and said that in their opinion the USSR was 'on the brink of success in the development of their bomb'. This was one of the first in a series of major disagreements between the agency and the Air Force over the next three decades.

Truman and his advisers knew that sooner or later the Russians would develop their own bomb, but it happened in August 1949, as predicted by the Air Force. Seven months later the CIA Office of Reports and Estimates presented a grim analysis of the implications of the Soviet bomb for the USA. It believed that the Soviets would not use the bomb to achieve a communist-dominated world, but it would continue to use all methods short of war to achieve this objective. The big difference was that if war was a result it could now involve the devastation of the USA.[3]

Because the Air Force was the first line of US security against attack, and the first line in any US attack, it was by far the most hawkish of all the services. Before the intercontinental missile age, it was particularly concerned with the bombers which the Soviets would need to drop their atom bombs. At the 1948 May Day parade in Moscow the fly-past of a new Russian bomber took place, the TU-4, which looked remarkably like the American B-29. The Air Force reasoned that if the Soviets had built a long-range bomber, then their atomic and bomber capabilities were probably more advanced than had been thought. This led to an argument with the CIA over the 'bomber gap', the forerunner of the 'missile gap' debates of the 1960s and 1970s.

In the agency's opinion, the Air Force's anxieties were not based on any hard evidence about the TU-4's real strategic capability, only on observation and defector information. Indeed, the agency thought that the Soviet bomber was much less advanced than it seemed. Six years later, at the 1954 May Day parade, a US Air Force attaché observed a new, much larger bomber, the Bison, and this convinced the Air Force that the Soviets were far more advanced than the CIA had estimated. The Air Force calculated that by 1959 the Soviet Union would have a strike force of over one thousand bombers. The Air Force Chief of Staff, General Curtis Le May, used this figure to press for an even bigger B-52 strike force, claiming that there was a bomber gap developing.

The agency's analysts, working from specialist technical and economic literature, argued that the Soviet Union's industrial base was not capable of building over one thousand Bison bombers since there were not enough tool production lines or aluminium forges to do the job. The argument was finally closed in 1956 when the CIA's U-2 spy plane demonstrated conclusively that the Soviets did not have a bomber fleet. There had been no 'bomber gap' at all. The Air Force attaché had witnessed a deception by the Russians: they had simply flown the same planes in different formations, giving the impression that there was a squadron of Bisons when in fact there were only eight.

## U-2

Richard Helms described the U-2 and its successors as 'the intelligence explosion of the century ... which turned analytical work on these so-called denied areas from famine to feast. Our best Russian agents ... suddenly seemed pale and inadequate.'[4]

The U-2 was the brainchild of Clarence 'Kelly' Johnson, Lockheed's brilliant aerospace engineer and president, but the idea for using it came from a committee chaired by Edwin H. Land of the Polaroid Corporation on methods of accurately monitoring Soviet military capabilities and dispositions. Land's committee re-commended that a new airplane be developed which could fly higher than Soviet anti-aircraft missiles, along a north-south path across the Soviet Union without refuelling. Kelly Johnson's design was to hand. The plane would carry a newly developed camera capable of high definition photography at an altitude of thirteen miles. It became known as the U-2 and was one of the most highly classified secrets in the agency, which had overall control of the project. Even the 'U' term was designed to disguise its real function: 'U' for utility.

Responsibility for the U-2 was given to Richard Bissell, special assistant to Allen Dulles, who had joined the agency only a few months earlier. Bissell's talent and abilities were formidable. An economist by training, he had studied at the London School of Economics, under Harold Laski, and returned to the USA to teach Keynesian economics at Yale – the first person in the United States to do so. He organized Allied shipping during the war and afterwards was closely involved in the implementation of the Marshall Plan. Bissell was also well connected, being acquainted with senior agency men like Dulles and Frank Wisner, and up-and-coming young politicians like John F. Kennedy.

Bissell was the pioneer technocrat who guided the CIA into the new age of intelligence. He was one of the first to realize that accurate factual information, rather than simply accurate political intelligence, was essential to counter the Soviet threat in a nuclear age. He turned this recognition into a bureaucratic programme and in the process brought about an intellectual and management revolution in intelligence.

Within nine months of the U-2 project being approved, Bissell supervised the first flight of the new plane in August 1955. The first operational flight took place nine months later in May 1956, seventeen months from the very start. It was a remarkable achievement.

In all, a fleet of twenty-two airplanes was eventually built and stationed at US

Air Force bases in Britain, Germany, Norway, Turkey, Taiwan, Japan, and Pakistan. The first operational flights over the Middle East and the Mediterranean took place in May and June and recorded for the US government the preparations being made by the British, the French and the Israelis for their invasion of the Suez Canal zone in October that year. In June Eisenhower gave permission for the first flights over Soviet territory. Within weeks the U-2 had detailed photographs of the Soviet Aviation Day fly past over Moscow.

The first U-2s had a range of 2200 miles which was increased to 3000 miles within three years. It could fly over 13 miles high and the normal operational altitude was over 70,000 feet. Each flight had specified targets, with the aim of avoiding repetition of areas photographed from flight to flight. Pilots were allowed to deviate from their flight course but not from their altitude. When one particular pilot decided to deviate because he saw something beyond the edge of his camera range, the results were spectacular, as Bissell recalled:

> He was flying over Turkestan, and off in the distance he saw something that looked quite interesting and that turned out to be the Tyuratam launch site – and unlike almost every other target we went after, not even the existence of that had been suspected ... He came back with the most beautiful photographs of this place, and within about five days the photo-interpreters had built a cardboard model of the whole Tyuratam site – roads, railway sidings, feeder roads, everything.[5]

Lawrence Houston, the CIA's general counsel, believed that sooner or later the Russians would have the capability of shooting down the planes and wanted to be sure that the flights were worth the risk. When he consulted the Air Force, the reply was unequivocal, he recalled: 'They said the U-2 information had forced them to completely retarget the USSR.'[6] U-2 photographs revealed new towns and cities, as well as military sites, that had been previously unknown to the United States. A result was the complete remapping of the USSR.

Eisenhower was also alert to the political and military repercussions of the project and carefully restricted the number of flights. Bissell managed to circumvent these restrictions by getting the British and the Germans to undertake U-2 missions of their own with planes supplied by the CIA.

Most of the flights were conducted during a two-year period between 1956 and 1958, by which time the bulk of military information had been assembled. In 1959 only a few flights took place and when Francis Gary Powers' U-2 was brought down on 1 May 1960, it was only the third flight that year. The risks to the U-2 had increased enormously by 1960. Powers' flight had been prompted by US anxiety over the speed in Soviet advances in missile technology and was to recheck some of the sites. Four hours into the flight, Powers came down in Soviet territory.

The flight had been scheduled for 1 May, because a summit conference was due to take place in Paris in mid-May between the Americans, British, French and Russian leaders, and Eisenhower did not want any flights while the summit was on. In the event, when the U-2 was shot down, Khrushchev cancelled the summit. Powers was captured, tried, and gaoled. In 1962 he was exchanged for Rudolf Abel, a KGB colonel who for nine years ran a network of Soviet agents in the USA until his arrest by the FBI in 1957.

The Powers incident marked the end of U-2 flights over Russia, but not elsewhere. Its utility was graphically demonstrated during the Cuban missile crisis. The plane continued to operate right into the 1980s with flights over China, the Far East and the Middle East.

In its very short history of deployment against the Soviet target, the U-2 had dramatically revised downwards the estimated numbers of Soviet long-range bombers; discovered the existence and method of deployment of Soviet medium and long-range bombers; revealed Soviet methods for storing nuclear weapons at air bases; provided evidence of Soviet ICBM deployment; provided information on Soviet intermediate and long-range missiles; revised downwards estimates of the numbers of Soviet ICBMs; provided information on the Soviet nuclear programme in general, and located uranium mining, processing and storage sites.

## MISSILE GAP

The launch of the first Soviet sputnik on 4 October 1957 provoked a wave of public alarm in the USA. The Soviets were seen to have overtaken American technology with their SS-6 intercontinental rocket, and sputnik was recognized as having a bombing capability. This gave credence to the political campaign launched by the Democrats during the presidential election the year before that played upon Air Force estimates that there was an enormous 'missile gap' in which the USA lagged seriously behind Soviet guided-missile development and production.

Given the Cold War atmosphere of the time, the missile gap controversy made

Francis Gary Powers, the U-2 pilot shot down over the Soviet Union on 1 May 1960, photographed during his trial for espionage in Moscow. In 1962 he was exchanged for the Soviet spy, Rudolph Abel, who had been arrested in New York in 1960.

a considerable impact and was a major issue in the 1958 midterm and 1960 presidential elections. In fact, as Eisenhower and the CIA were well aware, the Soviet missile threat was far less dangerous than the Democrats claimed. The U-2 had already disproved the existence of a 'bomber gap', and now U-2 photographs provided evidence that there was no great Soviet intercontinental missile force and that the few SS-6s constructed by the Soviets were being used for their space effort. Eisenhower was also aware of the technological superiority of the American space effort which, although some years away from being operational, was far more sophisticated than its Soviet equivalent.

With this knowledge behind him, after the launch of sputnik Eisenhower assured Congress and the American public that the USA would stay ahead in the missile race. However, his assurances seemed to smack of complacency. It was not until a Soviet moon capsule crashed into the moon in 1966 that the inadequacy of the Soviet system was clearly demonstrated, leaving the United States firmly ahead in the technological race.

In 1958 and 1960, the problem for both Eisenhower and the agency was that they could not reveal the U-2 information. This left the field open to critics of the administration and to the Air Force which consistently leaked estimates of a huge Soviet missile force. For frustrated agency analysts it was a phoney campaign of the 'bomber gap' type. In the 1960 estimate on Soviet capabilities and intentions, the CIA concluded that evidence from all sources indicated that the Soviets were far less advanced in missile technology and deployment than the Air Force believed and, indeed, the agency's own previous estimates had stated. By 1963, drawing on vastly improved technical intelligence, the agency calculated that the Soviets might have only about 200 intercontinental ballistic missiles.

Such information had little effect on the 1960 presidential election. Although Kennedy had received pre-election briefings from the agency on the missile gap, he continued to make extensive use of Air Force leaks to support his 'missile gap' allegations during the campaign. This was to have unforeseen and far-reaching consequences because Kennedy's opponent, Vice President Richard Nixon, believed bitterly that the agency had failed to convince Kennedy that the missile gap was a myth, thereby contributing to his losing the election. Nixon, ever alert to slights and conspiracies, did not forget.

## TECHNICAL INTELLIGENCE

The extraordinary shift from famine to feast that the U-2 and its camera made possible led to serious conflicts within the agency about the merits of technical intelligence versus human intelligence. The two protagonists were Helms and Bissell, the former believing that 'gadgets cannot divine man's intentions', and the latter convinced that gadgets were, in the main, preferable to agents. It was a dilemma which has remained persistent.

Bissell gathered around him a staff who, in those early experimental years of technical intelligence gathering, were aware of its limitations while never doubt-ing its ultimate potential. But later, the very ease and security with which information was acquired by technical means led to less speculative assessments, saying only what was certain. And what was certain was usually voluminous and often photographic, tending to make a great and immediate impression on the users of intelligence.

In 1958 Bissell succeeded Frank Wisner as Deputy Director of Plans, to the disappointment of others in the agency, particularly Wisner's number two, the Chief of Operations in the DDP, Richard Helms. Helms started out as a journalist, but had been in US intelligence since he joined the OSS in 1942, working almost continuously on the clandestine side in the DDP. He was

Richard M. Bissell, Jr, receiving the National Security Medal from President Kennedy in April 1962. As CIA Deputy Director of Plans, Bissell oversaw the development of the U-2, the first US satellites, and the SR-71 spy plane. He was responsible for the Bay of Pigs operation.

dedicated to the institution of the agency, seeking to further its role in informing decision-making, nurturing its relationships with the White House, Congress (where he was highly regarded), and other government departments. In Helms' view:

> Intelligence always has a policy effect, no matter what you say to a policy-maker ... You can't divorce intelligence from policy. The only thing you can do is what I did, which was to try not to get into the actual policy-making process by trying to influence it one way or another.[7]

Helms had long experience in handling agent networks and case officers. It was an arcane and often impenetrable world which, in the opinion of his senior colleagues, Helms knew better than anyone else except Allen Dulles.

Bissell had a more utilitarian approach: if U-2s and spy satellites were more efficient in providing accurate intelligence about the Soviet Union, then there was no need to risk agents' lives. Helms felt Bissell had scant regard for his work and this made his position as Bissell's deputy increasingly difficult.

The conflict between technical and human intelligence was personified by Bissell and Helms. Bissell later acknowledged that he was somewhat to blame for the tense relationship, saying in particular that he wished he had consulted Helms more on the Bay of Pigs operation:

> There was a large element of philosophic difference and the trouble was that the philosophic difference did not get brought out.... If I had been more effective and had tried to draw him in more, he could have given wise counsel. I sure as hell needed it. I don't think at the time I knew it.[8]

## DIRECTORATE OF SCIENCE AND TECHNOLOGY

After the Bay of Pigs and the departure of Allen Dulles and Richard Bissell from the agency, John McCone determined that Bissell's achievement in developing technical intelligence was such that a new Directorate of Science and Technology was required. A Directorate of Research was established in 1962. McCone asked Bissell to stay on as its head, but Bissell refused, preferring to leave the CIA altogether rather than accept a post that would be seen as lower than DDP, the unofficial No. 3 position in the agency. As first head of the Directorate, McCone appointed Herbert Scoville who left after a year. He then appointed Albert 'Bud' Wheelon, a young CIA officer and aeronautical engineer, who proved to be a brilliant manager and bureaucratic player, as head of a new Directorate of Science and Technology.

Wheelon inherited two key projects from Bissell: the SR-71 and Corona, both of which he ushered to success. In 1956, two years after the start of the U-2 project, the CIA's development project staff began research on a supersonic spy plane, the SR-71.

At the same time as the SR-71 project began, the Air Force started work on a programme code-named WS-117L: America's first spy satellite. In 1958, after his success with the U-2, Eisenhower gave Bissell effective control of the project, developing a reconnaissance satellite called Corona which would send back to earth a recoverable photographic capsule. The first Corona satellite was launched in February 1959. Despite the initial success of the satellite, subsequent launches were disastrous failures, and it took two years for Bissell to iron out the problems.

Once the programme was underway, the results were spectacular and galvanized the agency's analytical work in the same way the U-2 had until Powers'

The TR-1, the ultimate development of the Lockheed U-2 high-altitude photo- and multisensor-reconnaissance aircraft, began production for the USAF in 1980. It could fly above 70,000 feet at a speed of 430 mph, carrying nearly two tons of sensors in its fuselage and wing pods.

The Lockheed SR-71 'Blackbird' prototype first flew in 1962. It holds the world speed (2193 mph) and height (85,069 feet) records, and could cruise at about 2000 mph at 79,000 feet for 2900 miles without being refuelled. It could carry a one megaton bomb, but was used exclusively for reconnaissance purposes. The USAF SR-71 Wing was decommissioned in 1990.

flight. There was a huge need for photo-interpreters and eventually over 1200 agency employees were involved in photo-interpretation. In 1961, the CIA combined with the military to create the National Photographic Interpretation Center under the control of the DDI, thus establishing close working ties with the other departmental intelligence services.

Wheelon left the agency in 1967, having started a major development of satellite intelligence collection systems. His successor, Carl Duckett, DDS & T from 1967 to 1976, another effective manager, pursued this development, with the result that by the early 1970s the United States was receiving extraordinarily detailed photographic, telemetry, and communications intelligence, and the DDS & T was firmly established at the hub of the intelligence system, outshining the analysts of the DDI.

During Duckett's time, several of the most effective technical intelligence systems became operational. The *Samos* (launched under Bissell and operational into the early 1970s), *Keyhole – KH-8*, and the two 'Big Birds' *KH-9* (launched first in January 1971) that used a telephoto lens camera, and the *KH-11* (launched first in December 1976) that used a television camera giving high-resolution, directly transmitted visual intelligence and also monitored communications and other satellite systems developed with the National Reconnaissance Office (a joint CIA-military organization responsible for SR-71 and satellite intelligence), enabled US analysts to listen to conversations and telephone calls to and from the Kremlin. The *KH-8* could photograph objects of about six inches in length from 70 miles; the *KH-9* could resolve detail of under twelve inches from over 100 miles; the *KH-11* used digital imaging cameras to enhance its pictures to the point where they could detect missiles inside silos.

Other technical intelligence collection systems were also developed. US submarines attached sensors to Soviet undersea cables. Electronic pins, the size of golf tees, activated by satellites, placed in walls and in the earth, could pick up conversations and evidence of Soviet nuclear tests. The *Glomar Explorer* deep sea rescue ship, built by the agency, retrieved half of a Soviet nuclear weapon submarine from over 16,000 feet in the mid-Pacific in March 1968. Satellite monitoring devices penetrated Soviet communications cables.

Establishing factual intelligence on the Soviet Union, however, is not the same as gauging Soviet intentions, and the continuing argument about technical versus human intelligence flares up whenever there is disagreement about US security and foreign policies.

# 12
# ESTIMATES
## *1967–1976*

*S*ome months after the Cuban missile crisis, the Deputy Soviet Foreign Minister, Vasily Kuznetsov, visited John McCloy, presidential adviser on disarmament, at his home in Connecticut. The two men discussed the removal of Soviet IL-28 bombers still remaining in Cuba after the withdrawal of the Soviet missiles there. McCloy insisted that all long-range Soviet military capability should be withdrawn from Cuba. Kuznetsov turned to him, angrily, 'All right, Mr McCloy, we will get the IL-28s out as we have taken the missiles out. But I want to tell you something, Mr McCloy. The Soviet Union is not going to find itself in a position like this ever again.'[1]

The consequence of America's superior nuclear strength was a Soviet determination to match, if not exceed, that strength. This was not anticipated in the USA at the time. Few people, in either the Kennedy or the Johnson administrations, believed that the Soviets would go all out for a nuclear force that was larger than that of the USA because it did not make sense to do so. It only took a certain number of missiles for deterrence as long as neither side was strong enough to launch a first strike so powerful that all its opponent's missiles were destroyed. Nevertheless, as Richard Helms later acknowledged, building more nuclear warheads and missiles was precisely what the Soviets did. US failure to appreciate the Soviet build-up at the time, said Helms, 'probably wasn't a golden moment for American foreign policy'.[2]

Technical intelligence for several years after 1961 showed that while the Soviets were building and testing a number of different missiles, they were inaccurate and plagued by teething problems. In all, the evidence gathered by CIA analysts suggested that despite its best efforts, the USSR was far behind the USA, both quantitatively and qualitatively.

By 1967, however, it was clear that the Soviet rate of missile and warhead construction was faster than anticipated. There was the prospect of a real missile

Randy Cordes in his Langley office in SOVA, the Soviet Analysis section of the CIA's Directorate of Intelligence, in the summer of 1991. With the collapse of the USSR and its replacement by the Commonwealth of Independent States, these offices and their specializations were reorganized.

gap. The analysts' view now was that the Soviets would construct enough missiles to give them parity with the USA. At most, they considered, the Soviets might build a few more missiles than were necessary in order to claim superiority for prestige purposes.

They were wrong. The Soviet missile programme had developed an awesome institutional momentum which swept away previous restraints. The escalation was only checked with the successful negotiation of the first Strategic Arms Limitation Treaty (SALT I) in 1972. After 1967 the CIA estimate of Soviet strength was continually revised upward (see table).

| | Actual numbers | | CIA estimates of Soviet numbers for: | | | | |
|------|------|------|------|------|------|------|------|
| Year | USA | USSR | 1967 | 1968 | 1969 | 1970 | 1971 |

| Intercontinental ballistic missiles (ICBMs) | | | | | | | |
|------|------|------|------|------|------|------|------|
| 1966 | 904 | 292 | 420–426 | 514–582 | 505–695 | 509–792 | 499–844 |
| 1967 | 1054 | 570 | 423–484 | 670–764 | 805–1010 | 775–1027 | 805–1079 |
| 1968 | 1054 | 858 | 536–566 | 848–924 | 946–1038 | 949–1154 | 939–1190 |
| 1969 | 1054 | 1028 | 570 | 858 | 1038–1112 | 1158–1207 | 1181–1270 |
| 1970 | 1054 | 1299 | 570 | 858 | 1028 | 1262–1312 | 1360–1439 |

| Submarine-launched ballistic missiles (SLBMs) | | | | | | | |
|------|------|------|------|------|------|------|------|
| 1966 | 590 | 27 | 24–30 | 24–32 | 24–78 | 24–114 | 30–138 |
| 1967 | 628 | 27 | 21 | 29 | 37–53 | 61–85 | 85–117 |
| 1968 | 656 | 43 | 24–27 | 43–46 | 75–94 | 123–158 | 187–238 |
| 1969 | 656 | 120 | 27 | 43 | 94–110 | 158–238 | 222–366 |
| 1970 | 656 | 232 | 27 | 43 | 110–126 | 184–248 | 296–376 |

By 1972, while the number of US ICBMs remained at 1054 and SLBMs at 656, Soviet ICBMs totalled 1527 and SLBMs 440.

Sources: John Prados, *The Soviet Estimate: U.S. Intelligence Analysis and the Soviet Military Threat* (New York, Dial Press, 1982), pp. 183–199; Lawrence Freedman, *U.S. Intelligence and the Soviet Strategic Threat* (London, Macmillan, 1978), pp. 107–108.

Richard Nixon, in the White House from January 1969, and his Special Assistant for National Security, Henry Kissinger, had an avid interest in intelligence and were determined to mould the intelligence community to their own ends. Nixon was already deeply wary of the CIA and what he termed its Georgetown-liberal ethos (Georgetown being the fashionable part of Washington DC). This attitude was to permeate not only his dealings with the CIA but also those of other senior members of the administration.

The agency's underestimation of the Soviet threat in the mid 1960s was to play straight into the hands of the military, although with hindsight the military was seen to have overestimated the extent of the threat. Nixon and his powerful Secretary of Defense, Melvin Laird, chose to regard military estimates as being more accurate than the CIA on Soviet missile strength. As a result, Laird was able to disregard CIA estimates and rely instead on his own Defense Intelligence Agency (DIA) analysis.

## THE MIRV DEBATE

The conflict between the agency and the military came to a head in 1969 over the Soviet SS-9 ICBM. They disagreed over whether the SS-9 had a multiple independently targeted reentry vehicle (MIRV) capability. In effect, 'MIRVing' a missile turned it into several missiles as each re-entry vehicle could be programmed to strike a separate target. For example, the result of MIRVing the US ICBM force increased the number of re-entry vehicles from 1054 ICBMs and 656 SLBMs to a total of 7274 warheads.

In the mid-1960s MIRVing was clearly the next step in the arms technology race and the first successful MIRVs were developed for the US Minuteman III missile in 1968. It was expected, therefore, that the Soviets would MIRV the SS-9. This view was enthusiastically endorsed by the Pentagon, which wanted a larger US MIRV programme and improved anti-missile defences.

The question was whether the Soviets had the necessary skills and technology to develop a MIRV system comparable to the USA's. Initially, the CIA thought that they had but, by 1968, satellite reconnaissance and telemetry (deciphering the electronic signals from missiles, planes, and warheads) intelligence proved that they did not yet have the capability to MIRV the SS-9. This conclusion was set out in a National Intelligence Estimate of October 1968, in the last weeks of the Johnson presidency.

When the new administration took office, Nixon, Laird, the Air Force and the DIA strongly opposed this estimate and argued that the SS-9 was being MIRVed after all. In their view the Soviets might be able to inflict a first-strike attack on US missile sites, and steps had to be taken to meet this threat. A first-strike capability, by definition, had to be so devastating that no retaliation was possible. By increasing their missile production so much, the Soviets were bouncing the United States into a major missile building effort in order to maintain deterrence.

At stake in the debate over the SS-9 was a vast budget, vast patronage, and important decisions about the next stage in US offensive nuclear capability.

There was now a real missile gap and the CIA knew that it would incur considerable hostility if it persisted in arguing that the SS-9 was not MIRVed. Congress was debating the ratification of the Nuclear Non-Proliferation Treaty and both the Senate Armed Services Committee and the Foreign Relations Committee were holding hearings on the nature of the Soviet nuclear threat and the measures needed to counter it. Thus the agency came under considerable pressure to modify its conclusions. Nixon publicly stated that the 1968 estimate was wrong, while Laird declassified and released detailed intelligence findings on the SS-9, which predictably alarmed Congress and supported his claims for more sophisticated anti-ballistic missile systems.

The agency analysts stuck to their guns, in effect arguing that the request for increased military spending and the anxieties which prompted it were premature. In order to forestall an unseemly public quarrel, the DCI, Richard Helms, decided to prepare a new estimate which would go over all arguments and evidence again.

When Helms' new estimate was presented to the US Intelligence Board in August 1969, most of the other agencies, having carefully reviewed all the evidence, now agreed with the CIA's conclusion that the Soviets, on economic, military and technological grounds, were unlikely to attempt strategic superiority over the USA. Laird was furious and demanded that this conclusion be deleted, claiming that it subverted administration policy. Helms bowed to the pressure and excised the offending section. His decision was bitterly resented within the DDI.

However, there was sympathy for his predicament particularly since the Vietnam estimates battles were still fresh, and Helms was fighting for the agency's position on the inside of the new administration. Helms had gone far enough in the Senate in disagreeing with Laird: it would have been a tactical mistake in terms of Washington politics for him to have angered Laird any more. Laird almost personified the Republican party. He was well-respected and vastly influential – so much so that Nixon always refused to fight with him. John Huizenga, head of the Board of National Estimates and involved in writing the estimate, said that despite Laird's intervention, 'by and large the impact of the paper was pretty much the same'.[3] In 1978 Helms expressed what was probably his view when he told the Senate Intelligence Committee that when the Director of Central Intelligence 'clashes with the Secretary of Defense, he isn't a big enough fellow on the block'.[4]

When evidence of actual Soviet MIRV development became clear in 1972, the CIA's position was vindicated. The SS-9 was never MIRVed, and when the Soviets eventually designed their MIRV system at the end of 1974 it was with the much smaller SS-19 missile.

## SALT I

The MIRV debate coincided with another contentious issue in US-Soviet relations: an arms limitation agreement. After eight years of the Vietnam war, the expense of the arms race in addition was an increasingly heavy burden. The US economy was feeling the strain of both, and Nixon hoped that an arms agreement would defuse the increasingly bitter anti-war feeling. An agreement might also help to quantify the differences between the US and Soviet capabilities and thus achieve some kind of parity of forces.

The question was how to monitor any agreement. The Soviets had always refused to accept on-site inspections because they knew they would reveal Soviet weaknesses. Satellite and aerial surveillance made the verification of arms agreement theoretically possible, but were they enough? By the 1970s the Soviets had improved their camouflage techniques which afforded their new weapons systems some measure of protection against US spy satellites. So, could US security safely depend upon technical intelligence?

In June 1969, Helms told the National Security Council that the CIA was confident that technical intelligence methods could, in fact, successfully verify a treaty. Kissinger thought Helms had reached this conclusion in order to further the CIA's power and influence. This was also the view of the Joint Chiefs of Staff who were equally suspicious of Helms' claims about verification. In the event, Kissinger and Nixon used Helms' testimony, bypassed the NSC, the CIA and the Joint Chiefs completely in the SALT negotiations and agreed a treaty with Moscow through a personal, secret 'backchannel' with the Soviet Ambassador in Washington, Anatoly Dobrynin.

The SALT I treaty was signed in May 1972 amidst considerable fanfare. The presidential election was only a few months away and Nixon and Kissinger were anxious to sell the agreement to the US electorate. The fact that the CIA considered it could monitor the treaty without on-site inspection carried great weight in Congress. In the cold light of day, however, the terms seemed more advantageous to the Soviets. Because of the differences of opinion about America's ability to verify, Nixon and Kissinger had decided that they would confine verification to quantitative matters – numbers of missiles and so on – rather than to qualitative ones such as missile accuracy and MIRV development. The advantage of this plan was that all parties agreed that quantitative verification was possible. The major drawback was that by agreeing to a large quantity, the Soviets could stay within the agreement while simultaneously developing, testing and deploying new weapons systems. But this was glossed over, leaving the impression that SALT I was a comprehensive treaty.

A few weeks after the signing of the agreement, Helms became chairman of a steering group set up to monitor SALT I and which consisted of officials from the DIA, National Security Council, the service intelligence departments, and the CIA. Their reports soon confirmed that Soviet weapons development was continuing in apparent contravention of the limitations which SALT was supposed to have established. That Kissinger was aware of the political significance of these reports was evident from his subsequent actions: he ordered Helms to send the steering group's reports only to the National Security Council which would then decide what information to release and whether the Soviets were adhering to SALT I or not. In addition, all SALT intelligence was to be highly classified and was not to be distributed. This meant, in effect, that the White House was trying to hold back information in order to keep secret the fact that SALT did not stop the Soviet arms build-up.

This Gilbert and Sullivan situation was essentially a short-term arrangement to see Nixon through the election. But by the time Nixon resigned in August 1974, criticisms of SALT in Congress and the press had begun to mount. There was more and more pressure for the facts of Soviet military and economic capability to be established for all to see. It was a matter of some moment in 1974–5 because the new President, Gerald Ford, hoped to conclude a second arms limitation agreement, SALT II, in time for the 1976 presidential election.

At the beginning of 1975 the Senate and the House both set up select committees on intelligence and the evidence given to them on SALT gave a damaging impression of muddle and secrecy. William Hyland, a senior CIA analyst who was later Kissinger's deputy on the NSC, was questioned by the House Committee about the backchannel procedures between the White House and Dobrynin. If the Russians were told of violations, he was asked, then why was this information kept secret in Washington? 'We are keeping a hold item secret from people who might read the Central Intelligence Bulletin that is disseminated in several hundred copies', explained Hyland to a bemused committee.[5]

## SOVIET ESTIMATES

The controversy over the monitoring of SALT I coincided with, and in many ways helped to accelerate, attempts to reduce the CIA's power and influence on the estimates. Jealousy and concern about the CIA's position in the intelligence community, and about CIA estimates, particularly the agency's low-key view of Soviet capabilities, had been building up for several years. Admiral Stansfield Turner, President Carter's DCI from 1977 to 1981, gave expression to some military resentment of the agency by his habit of writing some estimates himself. Although he had every right to do so, this led to considerable anger among the agency's analytical staff who saw Turner as effectively questioning their ability. But there was widespread feeling that the CIA's analysis had been defective in several key instances and that reform was necessary.

One man who shared this view was General George Keegan, Assistant Chief of Staff for Air Force intelligence, who had over thirty years' experience in military intelligence. Keegan believed that in concluding SALT I the Soviets were simply manipulating US public opinion while they strengthened their military forces. In the drive for détente, he argued, the intelligence community, led by the CIA, had refused to acknowledge the imbalance. The USA must enjoy superiority over the Soviets in every military area.

In response to pressure from Keegan and from the Ford administration, in 1975 the agency tried to reach a consensus within the intelligence community on Soviet objectives. A report entitled *Understanding Soviet Strategic Policy* was written by Fritz Ermath, National Intelligence Officer for the Soviet Union, but consensus was impossible. Ermath argued that there were three broad views of Soviet policy within the intelligence community: the Keegan view; the CIA view that the Soviets were not aiming for world domination but were engaged in a standoff battle with the USA, constantly seeking to maintain and improve their existing interests; and the State Department view that the Soviets wanted military parity with, but not superiority over, the USA, and would be opportunistic expansionists. By pointing out these differences, Ermath appeared to be arguing that the USA had no idea what the Soviets' real intentions were.

The Ermath report was seen as a confession of analytical weakness and confusion but one can easily argue that Ermath's description of the different US attitudes also accurately mirrored the arguments and conflicts within the Soviet leadership about US aims and intentions.

In 1975, an error in the CIA's calculation of Soviet military expenditure led

President Jimmy Carter and President Leonid Brezhnev in Vienna on 18 June 1979 having just signed the second US–USSR Strategic Arms Limitation Treaty – SALT II. After the December 1979 Soviet invasion of Afghanistan, Carter asked the US Senate to defer ratification of the Treaty, saying that Brezhnev had 'lied' to him about Soviet intentions.

to a concerted attack by its Washington opponents which considerably reduced the agency's power and influence on the estimates. There were also enormous differences in estimates of efficiency and costs which were very hard to quantify in bald statistics. It was virtually impossible to set a true value on the rouble in dollar terms and no one believed the Soviets' own estimates, least of all the Soviets themselves.

The CIA's Office of Economic Research developed a 'building block' method in which actual Soviet economic output was costed in US terms. For example, if the USSR produced 100 tanks, they were counted at what it would cost the USA to produce 100 comparable tanks. This US cost would then be projected in roubles to assess the impact on the entire Soviet economy.

The building block method was strongly criticized by the DIA which since 1974 had been headed by Major General Daniel Graham, a zealous anti-communist who had a highly political view of the struggle with the Soviets. Since 1970 DIA analysts had used a different method for costing the Soviet military and had come up with consistently higher figures for Soviet military spending than the CIA. The costs of the different weapons systems, the DIA argued, were not in fact comparable because fundamentally the two economies were not comparable.

By the middle of 1975 the challenge to the CIA as *the* estimator of the Soviet Union had crystallized. William Colby, DCI in 1973–6, decided that he had to reach a consensus or else every estimate would become controversial and would be ineffective. He appointed a joint CIA-DIA study group, giving for the first time a non-CIA team of analysts equal weight with the agency's own. The CIA analysts were forced to accept that their estimates of Soviet spending had been about half of what the Soviets had actually spent. In February 1976 the agency's estimate was revised upward: the Soviet Union was spending much more than had previously been estimated on its military, with 10–15 per cent of Soviet GNP consumed by military spending as opposed to the 6–8 per cent previously thought by the CIA. The alarm about violations of SALT I seemed suddenly much more serious.

As a result of the manifest success of the DIA in forcing a CIA revision of Soviet expenditure, the agency's monopoly of the National Intelligence Estimates was weakened. When Colby dissolved the Board of National Estimates in 1973 this meant that all the final assessors of CIA estimates were outside the agency. Other intelligence agencies and groupings began to press for more influence. Among the prime movers was the President's Foreign Intelligence Advisory Board (PFIAB), the civilian overseers of the intelligence community, which independently reviewed estimates and made recommendations about intelligence organizations and activities.

In August 1975 the chairman of the PFIAB, George W. Anderson, suggested to President Ford that there should be 'competitive analysis' of the CIA's Soviet estimate. As Anderson well knew, this suggestion, by promoting a rival of equal status to the CIA's Soviet analysis, would give the PFIAB considerable power over the Director of Central Intelligence. Colby fought off this encroachment but the following year, after the 1976 estimate had to be revised, Ford agreed to Anderson's renewed request. It was a milestone decision. Now the CIA was no longer *primus inter pares*, but was just one of several competing agencies.

## TEAM A / TEAM B

Two teams were set up under the National Security Council. The A Team was a group of CIA analysts while the B Team was a group of outside experts headed by Professor Richard Pipes of Harvard which contained a preponderance of critics of both SALT and the building block method. The resulting reports held no surprises. The A Team adopted the traditional containment view. Although they amended the estimate of Soviet military spending, they maintained the CIA's view that the Soviets, while all the time improving their weapons systems, were less efficient than the USA. The B Team took a more hardline attitude: the Soviets were intent on a first-strike, war-winning capability against the USA and were pursuing a policy geared towards achieving global domination for which thus far the USA had failed to prepare.

Both teams presented their report to PFIAB and argued their respective cases. The 1976 estimate was sent back to the CIA three times for redrafting and was not finally approved until January 1977.

There is some doubt as to how much the B Team report actually influenced the estimate, but there is also some puzzlement as to why the exercise was conducted in this way since the B Team was composed of known hawks and thus its conclusions were predictable. But although its immediate effects were short-lived, the whole Team A/Team B debate was an event of crucial significance to the agency. Thirty years of policy, of strategic plans, of politics, depended on the CIA's assessment. The agency was being challenged in the area of its most precious and important expertise: the Soviet estimate.

Was the agency wilfully closing its eyes and sticking to a preconception that the Soviets could not afford truly vast military expenditure? Or was the agency right? The answer was that both teams were half right, and an outcome that neither team had envisaged: the end of the Cold War.

The irrationality and riskiness of Soviet policy put both teams off the scent. The Soviets took a colossal and conscious risk that their economy might collapse under the burden of military spending, and this was not appreciated by either party.

## DECLINE

The change in the agency's position and authority between 1974 (the start of Team A/Team B) and 1981 when President Reagan entered the White House was dramatic. In many respects, the agency's height of power and weight was 1965–74 when it held its own over Vietnam. Then, from 1974, there was a succession of troubles: the fall of Saigon and the end of people-intensive CIA operations in South East Asia; the general shift in the country's attitude on foreign policy and especially secret policy in the wake of Watergate and Vietnam;

the mistaken assumptions about CIA involvement in Watergate; Jimmy Carter campaigning and winning in 1976 partly on the grounds that the CIA was 'evil'. And finally the Team A/Team B affair, effectively challenging the agency's analysis.

Between 1974 and 1981 the country was half persuaded that the CIA was a rogue elephant. There were Congressional committees of inquiry into its operations and history. There were newspaper stories and revelations about its activities. Admiral Stansfield Turner, DCI for four years from 1977, convinced people that he was hostile to the agency. Jimmy Carter spoke of the agency in his 1976 presidential campaign in the most disparaging terms.

If pundits had attacked the agency in 1970–1, they would almost certainly have been brushed off. In the days when Henry Kissinger was roaming through Washington selling SALT I, Team B would have had short shrift. The fact that the debate took place was a sign of the agency's diminished position.

For a generation the agency had been a calming voice at a time of great tension. It did not go along with Kennedy over the 'missile gap'. It published a landmark report in 1960 on the deep inefficiencies of the Soviet economy, a salutary reminder that although sputnik had gone up first, the Soviets were not economic giants. It did not go along with alarmist projections that the Soviets would intervene in Vietnam. It was probably the least enthused – because best informed – observer of the China *démarche*.

The CIA managed to stay apart from the corruption of military estimates being tied to military budgets. It stood up to McCarthy. Its overall view was not swayed dramatically by political blandishments to tailor its estimate of the Soviet threat one way or another: that is why Nixon and Kissinger tried to keep the agency out of the White House, and why in the mid-1970s it faced the Team A/Team B examination.

From the start the agency brought the good news that the Soviets were weaker than many thought. Agency people generally were not alarmists. This gave the agency its standing in the foreign policy establishment, and made it political and military enemies. The agency's separateness from the military consensus was an aspect of its civilian tone. It is the least military major intelligence agency in the world both in terms of its institutional structure and in terms of its thinking. It has a general counsel, a public relations branch, a congressional liaison, a congressionally appointed inspector general. It is not nicknamed the 'company' for nothing: it resembles a multinational corporation and not a military outfit.

# 13
# NIXON

## 1969–1974

' *T* o this day', wrote General Vernon Walters in 1978, 'I believe Mr
Nixon harbours the idea that someone in the CIA tried to do him
in, or acted in some way against him.'[1] Walters had been Deputy
Director of Central Intelligence, 1972–6, during the Watergate scandal. He did
not share Nixon's view of the CIA that was to dog his relationship with the
agency for the five and a half turbulent years of his presidency.

Nixon was different from his immediate predecessors: he was not part of the
governing consensus. His non-collegiality alienated insiders. He was a president
who exercised to the full the prerogatives of his office, thrilled with power,
determined to mould a Nixonian élite which he hoped would displace the old
east coast, Ivy League, liberal establishment, the Washington 'fat cats'. He was
passionately antagonistic to the Washington power structure:

> I won the 1968 election as a Washington insider, but with an outsider's
> prejudices. The behind-the-scenes power structure in Washington is often
> called the iron triangle: a three-sided set of relationships composed of
> Congressional lobbyists, Congressional committee and subcommittee
> members and their staffs, and the bureaucrats in the various federal depart-
> ments and agencies. These people tend to work with each other year after
> year regardless of changes in administration: they form personal professional
> associations and generally act in concert.[2]

Nixon urged his cabinet members not to recruit their staffs solely from eastern
schools and companies but to look to the south, the west and the midwest:

> We can't depend on people who believe in another philosophy of govern-
> ment to give us their undivided loyalty or their best work ... If we don't

get rid of those people, they will either sabotage us from within, or they'll just sit back on their well-paid asses and wait for the next election to bring back their old bosses.[3]

This was the siege mentality which faced the CIA Director, Richard Helms. Helms was lucky to escape the purge. But he was an effective administrator and he was well thought of in Congress. The touchstone of Helms' *modus operandi* was that he was there to serve policy, not to make it, and this self-effacement enabled Nixon, grudgingly, to accept him.

Unlike Johnson, Nixon was not gregarious. He was a loner who preferred to work and to think in comparative solitude. Rather than deal directly with the heads of agencies and departments, he used trusted aides like John Ehrlichman and H. R. Haldeman. He also relied a great deal on Henry Kissinger who served first as his National Security Adviser and then as his Secretary of State as well. Helms dealt almost entirely with Kissinger and his deputy, Alexander Haig, and not with Nixon who preferred to remain removed from direct contact.

## KISSINGER

Nixon made it clear that he wanted Kissinger to take charge of intelligence and that the National Security Council staff in the White House under Kissinger would control the intelligence community. This was the beginning of a shift of power away from the CIA to the NSC. It was both a personal shift of power by the President in his own interests and an institutional shift. From this point on, under successive presidents, the agency began to lose influence to the NSC staff and the President's National Security Adviser, who in turn has paralleled and at times challenged the Director of Central Intelligence for the *de facto* position of the President's chief intelligence officer.

R. Jack Smith, Deputy Director of Intelligence, 1966–71, gave a vivid description of the change in atmosphere when Nixon came in to the White House:

It was just as though the shades in the White House were pulled down all of a sudden. They came in with the assumption that everybody outside the White House was partisan to one degree or another, on one side or another, and was trying to grab a slice of the White House power. They were antagonistic right from the outset. If the CIA has any work to do at all, it is work on behalf of the President. The President is the man the agency serves. If the President feels that we are just another of the contenders out there with policy axes to grind, then it is hard for the agency to do its work. We suddenly had to work in this chill compared to what we had had before.[4]

Helms felt this chill right away. It was customary for the DCI to open NSC meetings with a briefing on the subject being discussed and then to attend the rest of the meeting to answer questions or deal with points as they came up. In December 1968, before Nixon's inauguration, Helms was told by Kissinger that in future he would have to leave the NSC meetings after his initial briefing. This was a major threat to the agency's position in the intelligence bureaucracy. The NSC was the preeminent policy organization in intelligence and foreign policy matters. The exclusion of the DCI from NSC meetings would severely limit the agency's influence and status in the Washington scheme of things.

Helms raised the matter with the new Defense Secretary, Melvin Laird. The President would be vulnerable from a statutory point of view to criticisms that he was making strategic decisions without the advice of his chief intelligence officer. Laird agreed that the DCI should not be excluded from NSC meetings, and Helms stayed. But it was a taste of things to come. Similar proposals were made to other heads of agencies, all designed to concentrate power and authority in the White House.

Kissinger, who was Nixon's right hand man when it came to cutting out the agency (and the State Department and the military), employed an oblique approach. He would never say directly what he or the President wanted but instead demanded general analysis. 'Send me what you've got, and I'll know what I like when I get it', was the Kissinger line. Backed by the President, Kissinger insisted on being given the raw material of intelligence analysis – the cables, agents' reports, communications' intercepts, photographs and technical intelligence. With the NSC staff, he made his own interpretation of the material separately from the CIA, and briefed the President accordingly. Nixon, who prided himself on his grasp of foreign policy and his knowledge of other countries, always read the detailed briefings that circulated before NSC meetings. This meant that Helms was dealing with a President and a National Security Adviser who were unusually well-informed.

This state of affairs directly affected the agency's ability to perform in two ways. First, being knowledgeable, Nixon and Kissinger kept the CIA on the

*Overleaf* Left to right: President Richard Nixon; Bob Haldeman, chief of staff; Henry Kissinger, National Security Adviser, and John Ehrlichman, assistant to the President for domestic affairs, in the Oval Office. This was Nixon's inner circle of advisers.

defensive. Secondly, with the exclusion of outsiders from the policymaking process, the CIA, along with other agencies and departments, was often in the dark as to just what policy was being followed.

The secrecy with which Nixon and Kissinger surrounded their policy objectives and their efforts to achieve them had a dangerously isolating effect on the White House. Every major department and agency in the Washington bureaucracy resorted to intrigue to find out what was going on. The chairman of the Joint Chiefs of Staff instructed a Navy yeoman working in the Joint Chiefs liaison office in the White House to obtain copies of Kissinger's cables and other secret documents. A naval officer monitored telephone calls between Nixon, Kissinger and Haig. From these, as one of the Joint Chiefs of Staff recalled:

> It was clear that Haig was running to Nixon and shooting down Kissinger. Kissinger was running to Nixon and shooting down Haig. Nixon from time to time would cut Kissinger off totally and not see him, whereupon Kissinger would become totally paranoid. It all made it totally impossible to carry out structured policies.[5]

This situation affected the State Department as well as the CIA and the military. Ray Cline, who left the CIA in 1969 to become director of the State Department's intelligence and research bureau, resigned in disgust in 1973:

> The White House almost totally disregarded the State Department in the Nixon era. Crucial intelligence was often suppressed to insure that only Nixon and Kissinger had the full body of information on which to make broad judgements. The whole interagency bureaucracy was emasculated to provide a monopoly of power for the White House.[6]

## BUREAUCRATIC IN-FIGHTING

Although the initial attempt to exclude Helms from the NSC meetings had failed, Nixon was still determined to bend the intelligence community to his will. In December 1970, he ordered James Schlesinger, Assistant Director of the Bureau of the Budget, to review the agencies and organization of American intelligence. Three months later Schlesinger produced his report, 'A Review of the Intelligence Community', in which he criticized the estimates as tending to be anodyne in their attempt to reach a consensus and argued that the role of the Director of Central Intelligence was a fiction. Intelligence, the report stated, cost a great deal more than was realized by Congress, but the big expense – technical intelligence collection – was worthwhile and produced far better information than old-fashioned political intelligence.

Schlesinger's report did scant justice to the effective coordinating system within the intelligence community which Helms had helped set up. Helms had overseen the development of the United States Intelligence Board Committee structure and the CIA procedures for rationalizing resource allocations within the intelligence community. Helms had also established the National Intelligence Resources Board which reviewed and controlled intelligence budgets. This coordinating system worked because it enabled differences between the various intelligence agencies to be resolved without too much friction. Schlesinger's report, by encouraging bureaucratic challenges to the status quo, undermined it.

In November 1971 Nixon issued a presidential directive implementing Schlesinger's recommendations. A subcommittee of the NSC, the National Intelligence Committee, chaired by Kissinger, was set up to coordinate and review the activities of the intelligence community. The DCI retained responsibility only for the overall intelligence budget. These moves relegated to the sidelines both the NSC and the DCI, and the DCI's role as head of the intelligence community. Ray Cline, with the advantage of having worked both in the CIA and the State Department, summed up the problems which Helms faced during his tenure as DCI:

A Vietnam-obsessed President Johnson and a secretive President Nixon never gave Dick Helms much of a chance to be the kind of DCI that Dulles was for Eisenhower and McCone was for Kennedy. They both viewed Helms and the CIA primarily as an instrument for the execution of White House wishes by secret methods. They neither seemed to understand nor to care about the carefully structured functions of central intelligence as a whole, and increasingly under Nixon and his principal assistant, Dr Kissinger, disregarded analytical intelligence except for what was convenient ... in support of Nixon-Kissinger policies. Incoming intelligence was closely monitored and its distribution controlled by Kissinger's staff to keep it from embarrassing the White House, and the national estimates function fell into comparative disrepute and neglect. I doubt that any could have done better than Helms in the circumstances. One thing is clear, however: the CIA was deteriorating in its influence and its capability to influence policymaking by objective analysis.[7]

# CHILE

A similar deterioration was evident in the area of covert operations. In retrospect it can be seen that up to the mid-1960s the agency was blessed with an extraordinary run of good luck. There was an assumption that no matter what happened anywhere in the world, the CIA would be ready and able to deal with it at a moment's notice. The history of the agency was dotted with brilliant, rapid operations that contained or forestalled problems.

The Cuban missile crisis, while enhancing the CIA's reputation, was a watershed. Nothing was so intense afterwards. The world was settling down; deterrence was working; the old empires were gone. The CIA began to see its role in more long-range terms. It would no longer simply respond to events but would seek to control and direct them. It was no longer possible to run the kind of low-profile, low-key operation that toppled Mussadegh, and the agency began quietly withdrawing from the subversion emphasis of the 1940s and 1950s.

In 1970, when it looked as if the Marxist Salvador Allende would win the Chilean presidential election, Nixon ordered the CIA to mount a covert operation to prevent Allende from winning. Old agency hands were appalled: there was only a matter of weeks in which to operate and the agency had wound down its operations in Chile. The CIA station chief in Santiago, Henry Heckscher, fired off a volley of objections until finally told to stop. He was ordered to return to Langley where he was rebuked by the DDP, Thomas Karamessines, for failing to understand that this was something the CIA had to do even though it did not want to. 'Nobody', said Karamessines, 'was going to go into the Oval Office, bang his fist on the table and say we *won't* do it.'

The CIA had a history of successful political manipulation in Chile. In 1962 and 1964, when Allende had previously sought election, the agency had spent $4 million supporting the Christian Democrats led by Eduardo Frei. As the 1970 election approached, Allende made another bid for the presidency, arguing that Frei's policies of land reforms and wealth redistribution were half-hearted and that an Allende government would be more vigorous, particularly in its pursuit of nationalizing industry. The CIA was consistently doubtful about its ability to influence the outcome of the 1970 elections: a 1968 National Intelligence Estimate on Latin America concluded that the forces for social reform were running too strongly to be manipulated from outside.

The 40 Committee was the interdepartmental group established by the NSC to review CIA covert operations. In March 1970, six months before the elections,

Fidel Castro and President Allende of Chile standing together in November 1971 on a balcony at La Moneda, the presidential palace in Santiago de Chile. Allende was the first Marxist to be democratically elected in Latin America, and was the target of a CIA destabilization campaign.

it approved the first anti-Allende propaganda campaign. Henry Kissinger chaired the committee. 'I don't see why we need to stand by and watch a country go Communist due to the irresponsibility of its own people,' he declared.[8] But despite another propaganda campaign against him, Allende won the September 1970 election.

Allende's victory alarmed a number of big US corporations which had substantial interests and investments in Chile, particularly Anaconda Copper, and the International Telephone and Telegraph Corporation (ITT) on whose board John McCone now sat. A joint CIA-ITT effort was developed to prevent Allende from coming to power. The chairman of Anaconda had offered the State Department $500,000 in corporate funds to be used against Allende. Helms, sceptical of success, simply provided the names of useful contacts. The corporations, and some military circles within Chile itself, expressed fears to Kissinger and the Attorney General, John Mitchell, that Chile would become a Soviet client state. Nixon then ordered the CIA to try to thwart Allende's confirmation as President by the Chilean Congress. If Allende was confirmed, then the Chilean economy was to be made to 'scream'.

What evolved was a two-track approach. The first, Track I, was overtly diplomatic and economic in character. The second, Track II, was ultra secret and involved plans for a military coup. Despite expenditure of $250,000, Track I failed to prevent the confirmation of Allende's election and soon petered out. Track II also ran into serious difficulties, chief of which was the lack of any serious alternative to Allende. In addition, the commander of the Chilean armed forces, General René Schneider, was known to be a strong democrat who would firmly reject any military plotting against the new government and his influence carried weight within the highest levels in the Chilean army.

Despite this, the US military attaché in Santiago and the Defense Intelligence Agency came up with the names of two army officers who would be helpful in organizing a coup: retired General Robert Viaux and General Camilo Valenzuela, commander of the Santiago garrison. Viaux began to make plans but soon realized that Schneider would have to be removed if there was to be any chance of success. Helms, however, had made it clear that assassination was out of the question so when Heckscher, the CIA station chief, cabled Langley that Viaux intended to kidnap Schneider and his deputy, there was considerable alarm. The agency had given some small arms to the plotters, but revolvers and rifles are assassination, not coup weapons, and the dangers of being connected to a killing loomed large. Karamessines met Kissinger and Haig at the White House and it was decided to warn Viaux against any precipitate action.

The situation became dangerously confused when Valenzuela informed the CIA that he too was planning a coup, also beginning with the kidnapping of Schneider. Although Viaux and Valenzuela knew of each other's plans, neither was willing to collaborate with the other. On 19 October, six days before the Chilean Congress met to confirm Allende's election, Valenzuela made an unsuccessful attempt to kidnap Schneider. At this point the CIA tried to discourage the plotters. However, Viaux went ahead with his coup attempt on 22 October. Schneider was stopped on his way to work and was mortally wounded in the ensuing struggle. The following day Helms, after reviewing the singular lack of success of Track II, reported that 'now only the Chileans themselves can manage a successful coup. The Chileans have been guided to a point where a military solution is at least open to them.'[9]

Track I and Track II continued the effort to subvert Allende's government. Between Allende's inauguration as President in November 1970 and his death in September 1973, the CIA spent $8 million focused, the agency later acknowledged, on stimulating 'the military coup groups into a strong unified move against the government' and gathering intelligence on Allende's plans in the event of a military uprising. If Allende was to be otherthrown, the CIA was determined that Chileans should do it. Some of the lesson that Kermit Roosevelt had tried to teach twenty years earlier had seeped through; the Bay of Pigs had finally shown Washington policymakers that direct US involvement in coups was politically counterproductive. When the coup which finally toppled Allende took place in 1973, the agency was not directly involved although it knew the details of the plot and had encouraged the plotters.

The overthrow of Allende coincided with the growing furore over Watergate. The atmosphere of suspicion which raged over the activities of the Nixon administration also spread to the CIA whose connection to the coup plotters quickly became known. It mattered little that the agency had been against the operation from the start. The end result, as far as most commentators were concerned, was that one of the few countries in Latin America with a functioning democracy was delivered by the CIA into the hands of a military dictatorship that rapidly demonstrated great brutality.

## WATERGATE

The obsessive secrecy with which the Nixon White House had shrouded itself found its logical conclusion in the Watergate saga. Paranoia and intrigue had run riot and the result was a conspiracy, in parts resembling a farce, which gradually smothered the Nixon administration. The secrecy evaporated into the most public humiliation ever of a US president.

Within hours of a break-in at the Democratic national headquarters in the Watergate building on 17 June 1972, four and a half months before the presidential election, Howard Osborn, head of the CIA's office of security, telephoned Helms at home and told him that a former CIA employee, James McCord, was one of the five men arrested, and that the other four were Cuban-American exiles from Miami who had had contact with the agency in the past. McCord had been a senior officer in Osborn's office until his retirement in 1970. Furthermore, Osborn continued, another ex-agency man, Howard Hunt, was also implicated in the break-in since his name was in the notebooks of two of the intruders.

On 19 June, Helms had his usual morning meeting with his deputy directors and they discussed the break-in and the involvement of McCord and Hunt. It was the latter's connection which caused particular anxiety because the CIA had helped him with equipment and disguises while he was working for Nixon.

In the summer of 1971 Hunt had been hired by John Ehrlichman, Nixon's Special Assistant for Domestic Affairs, as a consultant to the White House on security matters. At Ehrlichman's request, the Deputy Director of Central Intelligence, General Robert Cushman, agreed to see Hunt. Hunt asked the agency to give him an office and a monitored telephone system and answering service in New York. Cushman felt strongly that since this request probably involved domestic surveillance of US citizens from which the agency was banned by law, he could not agree. Subsequent requests by Hunt for recording and camera equipment and disguises were granted. After Daniel Ellsberg, an analyst with the Rand Corporation, leaked *The Pentagon Papers* in 1971 revealing top-level US policy discussions during the Vietnam war, Hunt probably used a CIA-supplied disguise in his burglary of the office of Ellsberg's psychiatrist. Nixon had been determined that Ellsberg should be prosecuted, and Hunt was seeking evidence to damage Ellsberg's reputation but failed to do so. A CIA psychiatric profile of Ellsberg – the first ever carried out by the agency on a US citizen – was also done.

Hunt's requests caused considerable unease at the agency. Thomas Karamessines even took Hunt out to lunch in an attempt to find out what was going on but Hunt just replied that he was engaged in 'political work'. Helms had vetoed any further assistance to Hunt, but it was obvious to everyone present on 19 June that the agency was facing a potentially enormous scandal. William Colby, now number three at the CIA as executive director-comptroller, was put in charge of dealing with Watergate and protecting the agency. There was, Helms told him, one fundamental strategy: to distance the agency from the scandal as far as possible – 'just stay away from the whole damn thing'.

Nixon, however, had different ideas. On 20 June 1972, only three days after the burglary, he and Bob Haldeman, Special Assistant to the President, had fastened on the idea of getting the CIA to ask the FBI to drop their investigations on the grounds that the burglary was part of a CIA operation. J. Edgar Hoover had just died and there was a new FBI director-designate, L. Patrick Gray. Gray was happy to accept that the CIA was possibly involved in the break-in, an impression the White House was anxious to foster. Nixon and Haldeman also intended using a little blackmail on Helms by intimating that the Cuban connections of four of the Watergate burglars might lead to the exposure of some nasty CIA skeletons. On 23 June, Haldeman summoned Helms and the deputy DCI, Vernon Walters, to the White House where he met them with Ehrlichman. Haldeman asked Helms whether there was a CIA connection with Watergate.

Howard Hunt (left, back to camera, conferring with his attorney) on 29 September 1973 testifying before the Senate Select Committee on Presidential Campaign Activities – the Watergate Hearings. Hunt was an ex-CIA officer who spearheaded the Nixon White House 'Plumbers' unit responsible for several illegal activities including the attempted break-in to the Democratic National Headquarters in the Watergate building in Washington DC.

Helms said there was not. Haldeman next suggested that FBI investigations in Mexico were throwing up connections with the Bay of Pigs. Helms replied that he had no idea what Haldeman was talking about, and said, 'I had no interest in the Bay of Pigs that many years later, that everything in connection with that had been dealt with and liquidated as far as I was aware and I did not care what they ran into in connection with that.'[10]

Haldeman persisted. He wanted Walters to call Gray at the FBI and tell him that the Bureau's investigations into Watergate might interfere with CIA operations in Mexico and that therefore they should be 'tapered off, reduced or something'.

Helms agreed that Walters would speak to Gray. When Walters saw Gray, he confined himself to reminding the new FBI director that the CIA and the FBI had an understanding that if they ran into each other's agents they would notify each other. In the meantime Helms tried to find out whether there was some connection between the Watergate intruders and a CIA operation in Mexico or with the Bay of Pigs. There was not. On 26 June, John Dean, counsel to the President, summoned Walters to the White House for another meeting about

Watergate. Walters was a Nixon appointee, the President's eyes and ears in the agency, or so it was hoped. But Walters held out no hope for Dean and told him in straight terms that the CIA could not intervene with the FBI and that there was no CIA operation in Mexico that might conflict with FBI investigations. He advised Dean to fire everyone connected with the break-in because otherwise 'what is now a small conventional painful explosion will become a multi-weapon hydrogen bomb'.[11]

Gray had come to the same conclusion but, unlike Helms and Walters, he was still willing to try to protect Nixon and his staff from the consequences of being involved in the burglary and subsequent cover-up attempt. This was eventually his undoing and he was forced to resign from the FBI in April 1973, after it emerged that he had burned some files containing cables forged by Hunt implicating Kennedy and the CIA in Diem's assassination.

In August 1972, James McCord, awaiting trial for his part in the break-in, warned an old friend at the CIA office of security that pressure was being put on the defendants to admit that they had been part of a CIA operation. Dean had also passed on to Walters Howard Hunt's suggestion that the agency should pay off the burglars since they were indicating that they would take complete responsibility for the break-in if they were paid handsomely to do so. Walters pointed out that any such expenditures from secret funds would have to be reported to the Congressional oversight committees, a procedure Dean did not welcome. The CIA also had copies of photographs that Hunt had asked the agency to develop. They featured the Los Angeles building in which Daniel Ellsberg's psychiatrist had his offices, and were given to the FBI team investigating the burglary. This caused another alarm at the White House and in February 1973, John Dean suggested to the CIA that it ask the FBI to return all the photographs and CIA memos concerning Watergate. 'The only result,' said Vernon Walters, 'would be to leave an arrow in the Department of Justice files pointing directly at the CIA.'[12] Once again the agency said no to Dean.

Even the CIA's most hostile critics acknowledged that in the agency were the only people in Washington who were prepared to say 'No' to the Nixon White House. But for Helms there was a price to pay. In November 1972, Nixon summoned him to Camp David and fired him. In his farewell speech delivered in the main entrance hall at Langley, Helms stressed that the agency had no involvement in Watergate. His people believed him but were, understandably, anxious about their future.

# 14
# TROUBLE
## *1973–1975*

J ames Schlesinger, author of the critical 1971 review of the intelligence
community, succeeded Richard Helms as DCI. Although he was only
Director for five months (February-May 1973), he was seen as Nixon's
revenge on the agency and was unpopular. William Colby was one of the
few people within the agency who expressed any admiration for Schlesinger:

> He had developed some strong ideas about what was wrong with [the
> agency] and some positive ideas as to how to go about righting those
> wrongs. So he arrived at Langley running, his shirt tails flying, determined,
> with that bulldog, abrasive temperament of his, to implement those ideas
> and set off a wave of change both in the practice of intelligence generally
> and in the organization and operation of the CIA specifically.[1]

Schlesinger was the agency's first political director and his job was to restore the
CIA as a secret presidential arm. 'The trouble with you fellows,' said one of
Schlesinger's aides to John Huizenga, head of the Board of National Estimates,
'is that you're not on the team.' He meant, of course, on the Nixon team. Nixon
was not interested in the CIA as an established bureaucracy carrying out objective
professional jobs: he wanted it to do his will.

Schlesinger was working for the Rand Corporation when his managerial
expertise came to the attention of Nixon. In 1971, Nixon appointed him chairman
of the Atomic Energy Commission which he completely reorganized. Schlesinger
applied the same managerial ruthlessness to the CIA. About seven per cent of
the CIA's total staff were either fired or forced to take early retirement. Most
departures occurred in the Directorate of Plans. It was a painful process but
many believed that it was long overdue.

Schlesinger, like Bissell before him, believed that the day of clandestine operations had been overtaken, and that technical intelligence should now be at the forefront of agency activities. Schlesinger was also determined to tie analytical procedures to technical intelligence. The Board and the Office of National Estimates were reviewed with the intention of abolishing them (a move effected by Schlesinger's successor, William Colby), and in the meantime they lost their right to decide what to analyse. Schlesinger told the analysts that their main function was to write papers to order for the White House. This meant that estimates could more easily be controlled by Kissinger and Nixon.

These changes hit the agency like a whirlwind and there was no respite when the White House announced on 11 May that Schlesinger would be the next Defense Secretary and that William Colby would succeed him as DCI. Schlesinger's and Colby's new appointments were part of a reconstruction designed to win more support for the administration in Congress as it became more enmeshed in the coils of Watergate. Schlesinger was a respected administrator who could be expected to control the military and especially military spending. By taking him out of Langley, Nixon was signalling that he would no longer seek to dynamize the secret world. By appointing Colby as DCI, Nixon was also signalling to the agency that he would cease harrying it and, since Colby was a long-time agency hand, that the agency would be well-placed to reassert itself within the Washington power structure. Colby, faced with an agency unsettled by the Schlesinger reforms, and with a public opinion restive over misdeeds in high places, knew that his tenure as DCI would be tricky.

## WHISTLEBLOWERS

Distrust of government and politicians was one of the great changes in attitude of the 1960s and it was intensified by the divisiveness of the Vietnam war and the unsavoury intrigues of Watergate. There was a widespread belief that the CIA's shadowy hand was involved in a range of illegal activities. This led to a greater scrutiny of the agency in the press and to the emergence of whistleblowers from within the agency itself.

In 1967, a series of articles in the magazine *Ramparts* revealed the CIA's connection with the National Student Association. These exposés were followed by articles in the *New York Times* and other newspapers revealing CIA connections with corporations, trusts, individuals, research centres and universities. Journalists David Wise and Thomas B. Ross had been the first to give accurate details of some CIA operations in their book, *The Invisible Government* (1964), while Alfred W. McCoy's book, *The Politics of Heroin in Southeast Asia* (1972), linked the CIA with the heroin trade in Indochina.

In 1973 there was a spate of hostile press articles. In January, the *New York Times* ran an unflattering profile of Cord Meyer, one of the agency's leading officers on the clandestine side. A month later the same paper revealed in a blaze of publicity that the CIA had trained police from twelve domestic agencies. Critics regarded this as a breach of the CIA's charter not to operate inside the United States and demanded a Congressional investigation. In April a book by David Wise, *The Politics of Lying*, revealed that between 1958 and 1961 the CIA had trained Tibetan guerrillas at a base in Colorado, again with the implication that the agency had broken its charter. On 11 May, at the trial of Daniel Ellsberg for leaking *The Pentagon Papers*, the judge, furious at White House interference (Ehrlichman had telephoned the judge during the trial and offered him the post of Director of the FBI) and Hunt's burglary of Ellsberg's psychiatrist's office, declared a mis-trial and dismissed all charges against Ellsberg.

These books and articles and publicity about the Ellsberg trial were bad enough. Much worse, from the agent's point of view, was to come. Two books published in 1974 by former agency employees, Philip Agee and Victor Marchetti, attracted worldwide attention.

Victor Marchetti had resigned from the CIA in 1969 after fourteen years' service, 'disenchanted and disagreeing with many of the agency's policies and practices, and, for that matter, with those of the intelligence community and the US government'. As an analyst specializing in Soviet military affairs, and then in 1966–9 a staff officer in the office of the DCI, Marchetti knew some of the agency's top secrets. Marchetti wrote his whistleblowing book *The CIA and the Cult of Intelligence* in collaboration with John D. Marks, a former officer at the State Department's intelligence and research bureau, so it carried authority. Marks had resigned in 1970 in protest at US policy in South East Asia and particularly the invasion of Cambodia.

The agency was determined to fight Marchetti and Marks. When Marchetti had joined the CIA in 1955 he had signed the standard contract promising that he would not reveal anything he had learned in his job. Thus the book was in breach of contract. The agency was not claiming that Marchetti did not have the right to publish the book, only that he could not use the classified information to which he had access while working for the CIA. The CIA's general counsel, Lawrence Houston, suggested that Marchetti be prosecuted. Helms concurred and asked Nixon for his support which would be crucial once the case came to court. Nixon agreed and for two years the agency pursued Marchetti through the courts and eventually won. It was a considerable victory because there was a major constitutional issue involved: first amendment rights to freedom of speech. In the Marchetti case the agency effectively won the right of pre-publication suppression.

Marchetti and Marks were required to drop 168 passages from their book. The first excision, on the grounds of endangering national security, was made on the eleventh page of the typescript. It was Henry Kissinger's comment to the 40 Committee in 1970 that 'I don't see why we need stand by and watch a country go Communist due to the irresponsibility of its own people'. This was followed by other cuts ranging from whole paragraphs to one word.

Over the next six years many of the passages originally cut were reinstated as the information became public through Congressional hearings and investigations, as well as the Freedom of Information Act introduced in 1974. But this still did not diminish the sensitivity of the book as far as the CIA was concerned. One officer involved with the case said:

> There were breaches of security in the book which would have turned your hair gray. The naming of principal agents in six or seven cases, for example; the naming of one head of government who helped us; the relationship with another government. The least that would have happened apart from blowing agents and getting some of them killed, was certainly our ouster from a number of countries. Possibly the overturning of a couple of governments. It was dynamite.[2]

There was little the agency could do about the other book published in 1974. Philip Agee's *Inside the Company: CIA Diary*, written with the help of the Cuban government, was published in England outside the reach of the American courts. Agee, who had served in Latin America in 1969, became sympathetic to Marxist ideals. This was successfully exploited by Cuban agents who persuaded him to name everyone he knew in, and everyone he knew who was associated with, the CIA. The book named several hundred CIA officers and identified cover organizations and relationships with governments and companies. Names of agents were also revealed in *CounterSpy*, an anti-CIA newsletter published by radical American journalists.

In one edition of *CounterSpy* the name and address of the CIA station chief in Athens, Richard Welch, was published. It was reprinted in the English language

*Athens News* on 25 November 1975 and a month later Welch was murdered on his own doorstep. In the edition of *CounterSpy* that had identified Welch, Agee had written: 'The most effective and important systematic efforts to combat the CIA that can be taken right now are, I think, the identification, exposure and neutralization of its people working abroad.'

Agee always vehemently denied that his revelations had anything to do with Welch's murder, pointing out that Welch had been identified in an East German publication as a CIA officer in 1967, and that the Athens house he lived in was well known as the CIA station chief's, but within the agency there was very real bitterness and anger against Agee, as well as the belief that he was, as the CIA in-house journal *Studies in Intelligence* put it, 'the first real defector in the classic sense of the word'. The publication of his book and other subsequent articles led to a worldwide reshuffle of personnel and inflicted considerable damage on the agency's Latin American programme. In 1981 the US Supreme Court deprived Agee of his passport.

Marchetti and Agee were both products of a disaffected and disillusioned era. Books 'exposing' the CIA, revealing political plots and covert actions – the news behind the news, America's secret policies – sold well. Neither author, however, knew the darkest secrets – the assassination plots known as the 'Skeletons' or 'The Family Jewels'.

## SKELETONS

After the spate of hostile books in the spring of 1973 Schlesinger, just two days before he was due to leave the agency, issued a directive ordering all the senior operating officials in the agency to 'report to me immediately on any activities now going on, or that have gone on in the past, which might be construed to be outside the legislative charter of this agency ... I invite all ex-employees to do the same.' It was Schlesinger's successor, William Colby, who had to take responsibility for this task.

Colby had been a dedicated cold warrior. A brave and resourceful OSS officer, he had parachuted twice into Nazi-occupied Europe, once in France and once in

*Overleaf* The body of Richard Welch, CIA chief of station in Athens, arrives at Andrews Air Force Base on 30 December 1975. Next to William Colby, then DCI, stands Welch's daughter, Molly, and next to her his ex-wife, Patricia. Welch's son, Patrick, a Marine lieutenant, salutes at right. On 23 December Welch had been assassinated by terrorists, becoming the thirty-fourth star on Langley's wall.

Norway. He joined the CIA in 1950 and went to Frank Wisner's Office of Policy Coordination. Apart from his temporary assignment to the Phoenix programme in Vietnam in the late 1960s, he had worked continuously on the clandestine side of the agency. When Colby's appointment as DCI was announced the press homed in on his association with Phoenix, a programme by then associated in the public mind with systematic murder and torture.

Colby had believed in America's policy in Vietnam and he had given his best there. The Colby who had run Phoenix, however, was not the same man who became DCI in May 1973. A colleague who worked with him in the 1960s remembered the difference: 'He was a lot meaner and nastier then, and a lot dirtier. A prick. Colby changed quite a bit. The Colby today is a different Colby. The Colby I knew in the agency was a real sonofabitch. Very intense. Very hardworking.'[3]

Like many other people, Colby had been affected by the mood of disillusionment and dissent that developed as the Vietnam war progressed and, after the death of his daughter in April 1973, he was thought by colleagues to have become more religious (he was a Catholic) and reflective.

Colby's confirmation hearings in the Senate were protracted and difficult – a sign of things to come. In the period between Schlesinger's departure and Colby's swearing-in on 4 September 1973, it was decided that Colby should inform the chairmen of the Congressional committees to which the agency reported about the grey-area operations that had been revealed following Schlesinger's directive.

'The Skeletons' report (as it was called in the agency) was a closely typed 693 pages and covered everything that could be construed as CIA dirty tricks. It opened with a summary of CIA contacts with Egil Krogh, John Ehrlichman's assistant at the White House and head of the White House special investigation unit, the 'plumbers' who were behind the Watergate break-in. Krogh was also secretary of the cabinet committee on international narcotics control. The CIA had contact with Krogh in all these capacities and, although they were in no sense illegal, they could certainly be embarrassing in the aftermath of Watergate. CIA employees working in other government agencies and departments were also listed, for although again this was perfectly legal, it was potentially embarrassing because the suggestion could be made (and was) that the agency through its officers detailed to other departments was spying on the White House and on the Washington bureaucracy.

Other items on the list included 'contacts with Watergate figures' and 'activities directed at US citizens', in particular the surveillance of various anti-war and dissident groups, as well as several newspaper columnists suspected of obtaining sensitive information. The list also gave details of a long-standing intercept programme of Soviet mail: there was information about the agency's involvement with the Bureau of Narcotics and Dangerous Drugs. Details were also given about the various domestic police support programmes and the polygraphing of employees of other government agencies. Last, but by no means least, were the accounts of the assassination plots, not just against Castro, but against the Congolese leader Patrice Lumumba, Abdul Kassem of Iraq and the Dominican dictator Rafael Trujillo. Lumumba, Kassem and Trujillo were all killed by domestic enemies before CIA plans were implemented, although the men who killed Trujillo used weapons supplied by the CIA.

On 18 December 1975, Seymour Hersh, a leading investigative reporter from the *New York Times*, telephoned Colby and told him that he had information about the CIA's surveillance of anti-war and dissident groups in the USA, surveillance which Hersh believed to be in breach of the agency's charter. Colby acknowledged that 'on some few occasions' in the past the CIA had conducted such surveillance which might have been in breach of its charter. He stressed, however, that the agency had reviewed such activities in 1973 and that as a result clear directives had been issued which made it plain that henceforth the agency would operate firmly within the law. Hersh's story appeared on 22 December and was front-page news. It was a turning point for the CIA and for the American public, and it signalled the start of an intense public scrutiny of the agency.

## COLBY'S FIGHT

After he had spoken to Hersh, Colby had warned President Gerald Ford, who succeeded Nixon on 9 August 1974, that a difficult story was about to break. In the 1950s and 1960s Ford had been one of the twelve Congressmen involved in the Congressional informal arrangements for oversight of the CIA and he had ensured that the understandings between Congress and the agency worked well. Although he strongly supported the principle of Congressional oversight, in practice he was content for the agency to tell him what it thought he should know. Ford had been happy to operate in that pre-Watergate system built on the understanding that the agency would not embarrass the President or other elected representatives with unpleasant knowledge. It was the old idea of plausible deniability and practically it had a lot to recommend it. But after Watergate, and with Ford as President, all this changed.

Ford was spending Christmas 1974 at Vail, in Colorado, and as vacation reading for him Colby compiled the Vail report, produced from the earliest 'Skeletons' survey in an unclassified form so that it could be released by the White House. He had already shown both documents to Henry Kissinger who had vehemently opposed Colby's view that the secrets should be made public. However, Colby recalled that when Kissinger reached the section on assassinations, he became noticeably more thoughtful and said, 'When Hersh's story first came out I thought you should have flatly denied it as totally wrong, but now I see why you couldn't.' Colby had been ahead of everyone in realizing that the agency's dirty secrets would come out sooner or later given the atmosphere of the time. He also realized ahead of most others that the existence of the agency was in question, and that the best hope for its future was for him to be the agent of revelation rather than to fight a rearguard action against disclosure.

Matters took a serious turn for Colby when the acting Attorney General, Larry Silberman, asked him whether he had given the 'Skeletons' list to the Justice Department. When Colby replied that he had not, Silberman told him that in withholding evidence of illegal actions for eighteen months, he himself was possibly guilty of a crime. The Justice Department now began to take action on the allegations in Hersh's article.

Colby's decision to recommend that the President should reveal the 'Skeletons' caused consternation inside and outside the agency. Nobody was more bitter than Richard Helms who had been, in succession, Deputy to the Director of Plans, Director of Plans, Deputy DCI and finally DCI when most of the 'Skeletons' were being buried. Helms knew that the disclosures would reflect adversely on the agency and he strongly opposed Colby's decision. 'Helms never forgave Colby for the disclosures,' said one retired clandestine service chief. 'Helms could never have done what Colby did. There are two camps among CIA people: pro-Colby and anti-Helms and vice-versa, and they'll never really come together.'[4]

In strategic terms Colby was making a planned evacuation from an exposed position, but he refused to let the agency be presented as a kind of rogue elephant, rampaging around the world without let or hindrance. If there were actions which were now condemned, he intended to demonstrate that the agency had acted under orders. To that end he involved the political leadership in both the White House and the Congress, by showing their approval and knowledge of operations, and thus their complicity, regarding this as the best hope for the agency's survival.

The investigations and suspicions brought to a head by Watergate revealed the paradoxes of the CIA's operations and in a typically American way, commented Colby, this was resolved messily and in public:

> We were under attack. I had to be responsive to the committees on the larger question in order to protect the real secrets. The real secrets are the sources, the people ... I took the position very strongly that we should protect the secrets, the people and some of the technology, and that we should try not to stonewall on anything else. That's the argument and it's a good argument.[5]

## PUBLIC SECRETS

As revelations of questionable activities began to mushroom in Congress and the press, the possibility that agency officers might be prosecuted caused an uproar within the CIA. David Atlee Phillips described the atmosphere of that fraught 1974 Christmas:

> Overnight the CIA became a sinister shadow organization in the minds of the American people. Visions of a CIA payroll swollen with zealous and ubiquitous cloak-and-dagger villains impervious to good judgment and outside control arose throughout the country. CIA was seen as what the detractors had been so long claiming: unprincipled spooks threatening American society. That was not the CIA I knew, but I realized that any image less sinister would never really be believed by Americans still stunned by Watergate ... The Hersh story, I found on returning to Langley after the Christmas holidays, had produced massive cracks in what had been up to that time a fairly monolithic intelligence establishment.[6]

Such was the anxiety that five days after Christmas Colby called a meeting of the agency's officers in the main auditorium at Langley. He tried to reassure them that he was protecting the agency which would survive, in his judgement, if it could get the true story across. He believed that CIA officers would not be convicted by any fair jury for activities which took place so long ago and under different circumstances.

Despite Colby's attempts at reassurance, most of those present disagreed with him, believing that if the principle of agency secrecy was broken, the agency would be effectively destroyed.

Was Colby right? Was it his job to save the agency? If the agency was a presidential instrument, wasn't it up to the President to save it? As a presidential appointee shouldn't Colby have checked with the President to make sure that it was all right to confirm stories to journalists? Shouldn't he have checked with his own general counsel before admitting to Hersh that the agency had acted illegally? In reply Colby argued:

> I think that in our society, not just in our government, if you take a number of people and put them in a career position, they'll fight to maintain it. They'll differ as to how to maintain it, but they'll fight to maintain it. Everybody will fight to maintain the integrity of the career they've adopted, and in that sense if the President wanted to get rid of it, yes, he could do it ... I think the people in the White House for a long time were delighted that I was doing it and keeping it out of the White House. I certainly didn't get any criticism from them along that line. What I got was some criticism that I was being too generous with some of the information. I had a sense that they wished it wouldn't happen – I wished it wouldn't happen myself. I was the head of the organization and took the rap for it.[7]

The imperatives of the organization had taken over. At stake now was the integrity of careers and of the CIA as an institution, rather than the job it was meant to do. By 1973 the CIA was no longer close to the President or the President's men. Symptomatic of this was the fact that Colby saw the President alone only three times in the two years and five months he was Director. The old certainties of the tripartite relationship between the agency, the President and Congress had vanished after Watergate.

## THE ROCKEFELLER COMMISSION

When Ford returned from Colorado after Christmas 1974, he announced on 4 January that he was setting up a blue-ribbon commission on CIA activities within the USA which would look into allegations of CIA wrongdoing, determine whether the agency had exceeded its authority and make recommendations to prevent abuses in the future. 'It is essential,' Ford declared, 'that we meet our security requirements and at the same time avoid impairing our democratic institutions and fundamental freedoms. Intelligence activities must be conducted consistently with both objectives.'[8]

Ford's statement was ambivalent to say the least. There was no hint that the agency had acted on behalf of the President: he wanted the country to think that the agency was somehow acting on its own. Ford sought to remake the presidency by turning the office into a people's tribune against Washington, against the government. But at the same time he did not want a deep investigation into the executive branch, hence the fairly limited terms of reference of the commission which conducted its investigations in private and reported directly to the President. Ford's Vice-President, Nelson Rockefeller, was appointed to head the commission, but it was soon clear Congress did not intend to be ignored. On 21 January, the Senate voted to create a select committee to study governmental operations with respect to intelligence activities chaired by Senator Frank Church. A month later, the House of Representatives followed suit with the establishment of a Select Committee on Intelligence, chaired by Representative Otis Pike. For the next two years the CIA was in the full glare of public scrutiny. Colby saw the Rockefeller Commission as an ambivalent attempt by Ford to meet public demands for an investigation while at the same time protecting as many embarrassing secrets as it could:

> I discovered that I was being somewhat too open and candid for some people's tastes. After my second or third appearance, the Commission's chairman, Vice President Rockefeller, drew me aside into his office at the Executive Office Building and said in his most charming manner, 'Bill, do you really have to present all this material to us? We realize that there are secrets that you fellows need to keep and so nobody here is going to take it amiss if you feel that there are some questions you can't answer quite as fully as you seem to feel you have to.' I got the message quite unmistakably, and I didn't like it. The Vice President of the United States was letting me know that he didn't approve of my approach to the CIA's troubles, that he would much prefer me to take the traditional stance of fending off investigation by drawing the cloak of secrecy around the agency in the name of national security. So I mumbled something appropriate and went on to give the commission what it needed to get a fair picture of CIA's history.[9]

Colby was taking an enormous risk, not just with his career, but with the agency. His judgement was that the shield of national security would not protect the agency from investigation; that if such investigation was resisted the agency

William Colby, Director of Central Intelligence 1973–6, testifying before the Senate Intelligence Committee (the Church Committee) on 4 August 1975. Colby successfully fought for the CIA's survival by making explicit the hitherto secret involvement of presidents and Congress in CIA actions.

could be blown open by Congress with really damaging consequences, and that therefore the best hope was for the agency to reveal itself. He wanted 'an American service', he said to a senior clandestine service officer who argued that he should not reveal the agency's skeletons; by this he meant that the CIA, if it was to survive, had to find a place within the American political system that carried Congressional and public support. If this meant that the agency could have few secrets, or could not undertake certain types of activity, so be it. 'Colby drove the White House, and in particular three senior people, Ford, Rockefeller, and Kissinger, straight up the wall,' observed one CIA man observing him from the wings.

As a result of forcing the commission to hear what he wanted it to hear, Colby effectively determined the shape of the Rockefeller report. It emphasized the dangers the USA faced from an estimated 500,000 or more communist-bloc intelligence officers, nearly 2000 communist-bloc diplomats in the USA, and the technical intelligence of the Soviet Union and its allies. With this combination of the threat without and the threat within, the report fundamentally exculpated the agency of wrongdoing. Some of the dubious activities which deserved criticism and should not be permitted to happen again were, as the report acknowledged, initiated or ordered by presidents, while others were in the grey area between responsibilities delegated to the CIA by Congress and the NSC, and activities specifically prohibited to the agency. In any event, said Rockefeller, the agency itself had taken appropriate steps in 1973 and 1974 to check these activities.

On the most controversial question of all, the assassination plots, the report adopted a noticeably ginger approach, noting that this information only came to the attention of the commission after its inquiries were underway and that as a result time did not permit a full investigation before the report was due: 'The President therefore requested that the materials in the possession of the Commission which bear on these allegations be turned over to him. This has been done.'

It was a conclusion that begged for a sequel.

# 15

# INVESTIGATION

## 1975–1976

*P*ublication of the fact that the CIA had been involved in assassination plots meant that Congressional investigation of the agency was inevitable. In the wake of Watergate, it seemed to confirm the darkest fears of Americans that the agency was an undemocratic, unanswerable secret police.

For the first thirty years of its existence the agency's relationship with Congress was informal. In essence, the DCI and his close colleagues dealt personally with the chairmen of the relevant Senate and House committees (foreign affairs, appropriations, armed services), and other senators and representatives who were 'friends' or who had significant political influence in areas important to the agency. This relationship worked because the agency was trusted, DCIs were respected, and the CIA was seen as one of America's principal barriers to the communist world's ambitions and subversion.

In 1954 these assumptions were threatened when the Hoover Commission studying the executive branch of government recommended, with regard to the CIA, not only a Congressional oversight committee drawn from both the House and the Senate, but also an advisory board of the great and the good to take an overview of the agency's work and make recommendations to the President. The advisory board proposal was implemented by Eisenhower with the establishment of the President's board of consultants on foreign intelligence activities, but the Congressional oversight proposal was firmly rejected. In 1955, when Senator Mike Mansfield attempted to introduce a bill implementing Hoover's recommendations, he met with fierce opposition from Senators Russell, Hayden and Saltonstall of the Armed Services and Appropriations Committees who were reluctant to see their privileged relationship with the agency watered down. Dulles had convinced senior Senators of the security dangers involved in formal oversight: too many people would know secrets; committee staff would share information. However, a compromise was reached whereby CIA subcommittees were created in the Senate Armed Services and Appropriations Committees, and in the House Armed Services Committee.

In 1961, after the Bay of Pigs, Senator Eugene McCarthy tried to introduce formal oversight of the CIA, but the proposal was again defeated. In the mid-1960s, as the Vietnam war intensified and as nuclear proliferation, space technology and increased international tension diverted Congressional attention away from domestic affairs, demand for inside knowledge of world affairs increased. Richard Helms responded by increasing the number of CIA briefings to committees. In 1967, seventeen Congressional committees were receiving detailed briefings from the agency. By the mid-1970s the DCI, or his deputy, was averaging thirty to thirty-five committee appearances annually.

The agency still had its powerful friends in Congress, notably Senator Russell and Senator Henry Jackson who could be trusted to keep information to themselves and not to use it for political advantage. As a result, the agency had a much easier ride in Congress and enjoyed a much greater financial flexibility than other agencies and the armed services. While General Curtis LeMay had to account for every penny spent on the Strategic Air Command and the B-52, the CIA did not have to account in the same detail for the money it spent on the U-2, the satellites, the SR-71, or the covert operations conducted in the 1960s.

Richard Helms was the last DCI to experience this freedom and flexibility, and to maintain it he had to work harder at cultivating Congress than any of his immediate predecessors. He had to contend with ever stronger criticism, especially from Senator William Fulbright of the Senate Foreign Relations Committee who disliked the secretive relationship between the agency and its friends in Congress. Fulbright pressed the agency on such sensitive issues as the number of agency personnel in embassy posts abroad and agency involvement with multinational corporations in Latin America.

## CONGRESS

By the beginning of the 1970s a sea change had taken place in Congress. Senator Russell's death in 1971 marked the effective end of the heyday of the all-powerful committee chairmen. The mid-term elections of 1974, just after Watergate, produced a large influx of new, thrusting Senators and Representatives who were impatient with the traditions of seniority and who blamed the old guard, in part, for the collapse of political standards that Watergate represented. They wanted to make their reputations quickly and they wanted to know what was going on.

Senator Frank Church, chairman of the Senate Intelligence Committee, holds up a poison dart gun developed by the US Army as Senator John Tower looks on. The Committee was inquiring into CIA assassination plots at the time – 17 September 1975 – and learned that the agency had thirty-seven lethal poisons in its laboratories.

The results of the change in Congress were evident in the Congressional investigations into the CIA. Frank Church, the chairman of the Senate Select Committee investigating the CIA, had ambitions to be the Democratic presidential candidate in 1976. He saw his committee as providing him with national exposure and a major plank in his campaign. For his part, Otis Pike, the chairman of the equivalent House committee, also regarded investigating the CIA as a useful rung on the political ladder. Both committees wanted to know everything about the CIA. The issue they immediately homed in on was the Rockefeller Commission report's acknowledgement of assassination plots about which President Ford had retained the evidence.

The extent of the CIA's archive (by October 1980 it amounted to 470 million pages) meant that the investigations were necessarily selective and thus the resulting reports were fundamentally impressionistic in their portraits of the agency. They focused on the drama, not the nature or purpose of the CIA.

As with the Rockefeller Commission, Colby once again managed to dictate the agenda of the investigations in his effort to save the CIA from disbandment or emasculation by Congress. He telephoned Frank Church and offered him and his staff full cooperation, saying, 'I was fully available for discussion on how we could go about assisting in the comprehensive investigation he had in mind while at the same time protecting the necessary secrets of intelligence work.'[1]

As a result, Church received all the information that had been given to Rockefeller. Church also questioned DCIs and CIA officers, past and present, but despite intense media pressure he showed a keen awareness that operational secrets needed to be kept.

It was in the area of necessary secrets that Otis Pike's committee ultimately failed. It operated in a politically partisan manner and had clearly made up its mind that the agency was in the wrong before it had heard the evidence. Relations with the agency and the White House were frosty and on several occasions Ford and the Attorney General rejected Pike's requests for particular documents and information. The Pike Committee finally broke up after internal wrangling before it had completed its work. Its unfinished report was leaked to the press at the beginning of 1976.

By this time the intense fascination with intelligence was beginning to wear off. The murder of Richard Welch in Athens in December 1975 had brought home the damaging consequences of constant leaks and uncensored information about the nation's secrets. At a press conference in February 1976, Ford declared:

> It is essential that the irresponsible and dangerous exposure of our nation's intelligence secrets be stopped. Openness is a hallmark of our democratic society but the American people have never believed it necessary to reveal secret war plans of the Department of Defense, and I do not think they wish to have the true intelligence secrets revealed either.

But while secrets were accepted as a necessity, assassinations were a different matter, and profoundly shocking to public opinion.

## ASSASSINATION PLOTS

The key publication of the Church Committee was its report on the assassination plots. This confirmed that the CIA had tried to assassinate Patrice Lumumba and Fidel Castro, but had not planned the deaths of General René Schneider in Chile, Ngo Dinh Diem and his brother Nhu in Vietnam, or President Rafael Trujillo of the Dominican Republic. The Committee could not satisfactorily establish whether the plots were authorized by American presidents or other senior governmental officials above the CIA, but found that successive administrations had clearly not ruled out assassination as an acceptable course of action. The CIA had not tried to assassinate foreign leaders on its own initiative, Church declared. The most that could be said against the agency and its senior officers was that they had misunderstood presidential orders, or orders issued in a president's name. In all these cases there was a good ground for mis-understanding – ambiguity was a consistent hallmark – but not enough to blame the president concerned.

It was interesting, however, that the Committee itself did not rule out assassination in certain cases. In his preface to the report, Frank Church wrote:

> It is sometimes asked whether assassination should be ruled out absolutely, such as in a time of truly grave national emergency. Adolf Hitler is often cited as an example. Of course, the cases which the committee investigated were not of that character at all. Tragically, they related to Latin leaders and black leaders of little countries that could not have possibly constituted a threat to the security of the United States.
>
> The only time when Fidel Castro permitted his island to become a base for Russian missiles, the only time during which it might have been said that he had become a threat to the security of the American people, was the one time when all assassination activity, plans, and plots against his life were stood down.

When John McCone and William Colby were questioned about their attitude to assassination, they both firmly stated that in their view it was wrong. Richard Helms took the view that it was not only morally wrong but inefficient as well: it just didn't work. Helms cited the example of Diem in Vietnam whose assassination resulted, he pointed out, in 'a revolving door of prime ministers ... for quite some period of time, during which the Vietnamese government at a time in its history when it should have been strong was nothing but a caretaker government.' Helms simply did not believe that political assassination was a 'viable option in the United States of America these days'.

Besides the assassinations report, the Church Committee published others on mail opening, on the performance of the intelligence agencies generally, and on intelligence activities and the rights of Americans. These reports basically agreed with the findings of the Rockefeller Commission. The Church Committee also published two surveys of the history of American intelligence development, one of them on the CIA itself.

Richard Helms, Director of Central Intelligence 1966–73, testifying to the Church Committee. Helms defended his record and argued, in partial contrast to Colby, that secrecy was essential to the conduct of effective intelligence operations.

## COLBY'S FEAT

William Colby was the DCI who had to deal with Rockefeller, Pike, Church, the high-point of press interest, and the fall-out of each new revelation of CIA activity over the years. He knew that the extensive house cleaning that was involved because of the investigations would change the relationship between Congress and the agency on the one hand, and Congress and the President on the other. He therefore sought to achieve democratic sanction for the agency, and for secrets.

While nearly every skeleton in the agency was revealed, no real operational changes were effected by the revelations. Nearly all the secrets were 'dead'. It was a very in-house debate and the big questions were never really addressed, such as: should the United States have a secret, centralized intelligence service? When should the USA break international law and the laws of other countries? Should there be an area, within a democracy, of absolute secrecy where only experts and a few public representatives were in the know?

The reluctance to define these questions accurately reflected ambivalent American public opinion on the murky subject of intelligence. It was an ambivalence that exasperated CIA people. Vernon Walters reflected: 'Americans have always had an ambivalent attitude toward intelligence. When they feel threatened they want a lot of it, and when they don't they tend to regard the whole thing as immoral.'[2]

R. Jack Smith was more detailed:

> How does a secret espionage agency operate in what is an open society? I think Americans in our era have gone childish about the question of an open society. The values they have are those of a kindergarten – I'll be fair to you: you be fair to me. It's banal. The ethics of personal relationships do not apply to international affairs. And I don't think Bill [Colby] recognizes that if you follow his argument to its conclusion, you cannot have an intelligence service. You've got to allow room for it somehow, as the British have done for centuries as the business of the Crown. The Crown has its rights, and people in Britain know that it needs to do certain things in certain ways, and they do not question it. You've got to have some sort of sanctuary in a society's set of values in which secret things take place. America has never grown up in its thinking about it.[3]

Colby was fired in November 1975 in what became known as the 'Halloween Massacre', when President Ford dismissed Kissinger as his National Security Adviser (though he remained Secretary of State), and James Schlesinger as Defense Secretary. Colby's departure was intended to signal the end of the CIA revelations which were damaging confidence in US secrecy at home and abroad. His successor was George Bush.

## BUSH

Bush was the first politician to become DCI. He served for fifty weeks and four days. His job was to put a lid on revelations, to restore CIA morale, to secure Congressional acceptance of the agency and its work, and to ensure that President Ford suffered no surprises from the intelligence sector in a presidential election year. Vietnam, Cambodia, Watergate, CIA revelations, the fall of Saigon in April 1975, had all been media stampedes. Both Ford and the agency needed a DCI who would not be fazed by press attention.

As chairman of the Republican party during Watergate, Bush had impressed

George Bush is sworn in as the eleventh Director of Central Intelligence on 30 January 1976. Behind him stands General Vernon Walters, Deputy DCI. Supreme Court Justice Potter Stewart administers the oath, while Barbara Bush and President Gerald Ford look on.

people by not panicking and by acting firmly in the party's interests. He was the party's troubleshooter. With the broad collapse of the acceptance of secrecy in the democracy, the agency, the DCI, and the President were all suddenly vulnerable in unexpected ways. Bush was put in to shield that vulnerability, not to politicize the agency. His appointment was a recognition that the agency's position had already become political because of the revelations and investigations. When the Democrat Jimmy Carter won the 1976 presidential race, Bush offered to stay on as DCI in an effort to demonstrate that the post should be de-politicized as much as possible, but Carter preferred to appoint his own man. When Bush left on 20 January 1977, he was the first DCI to go because of a change in the White House.

Despite Bush's attempts to be non-political, old hands in Congress saw his appointment as being a potential step to the presidency. In order to secure his appointment by Congress, Ford had to announce that Bush would not be his running-mate in 1976. Bush accepted this, although it was an undemocratic limitation on him. 'Give Frank Church a call,' he said, echoing the Senator's remark that the agency was a 'rogue elephant'. 'Tell him I'm a tame elephant.'

One of Bush's first acts as DCI was to change the agency's most senior staff. There was a general agreement that the effective way to underline the end of revelations was to put new people in, so that the agency itself would be seen to pay for its revealed past. Within six months of his arrival at Langley, eleven of the top fourteen agency department heads were replaced. The changes were done with care. Bush appointed E. Hank Knoche, a long-term agency officer, as his deputy, signalling his confidence in the agency and its people. The A Team/B Team debate, set in motion under Colby, took place during Bush's watch. Bush always backed the CIA team. He rapidly developed a reputation for listening to the professionals, and acting on their advice. As an ex-member of Congress (he had been a Republican Representative for Texas, 1966–70), he used his friendships in Congress effectively, reassuring everyone that the agency was acting sensibly and properly. He appeared in front of Congressional committees fifty-one times as DCI – more than once a week.

Bush also addressed the loss of confidence abroad in the CIA that had flowed from the investigations. Four Latin American secret services had broken their connections with the agency, fearful that their secrets would be exposed. Bush met these fears by demonstrating the value to foreign services of cooperation with the agency. He gave the British access to US satellite intelligence, showing that despite the investigations and media attention, effective intelligence work was continuing.

After the November 1976 elections, Bush briefed President-elect Carter and his team. There was a particular problem about satellite intelligence due to come to a head around 1985: investment needed to be made in new satellite systems if the USA was to maintain its coverage of the USSR. Carter held up his hand: 'I don't need to worry about that,' he said, looking at Bush. 'By then George will be President and he can take care of it.'

## CONGRESS AND COVERT OPERATIONS

Besides the glare of publicity from the Congressional investigations, the agency also found itself fettered with new and highly unwelcome legislation. The 1974 Hughes-Ryan Amendment to the Foreign Assistance Act of 1961 was passed in the wake of revelations about the CIA's role in toppling Allende. It required the DCI to brief no fewer than eight separate Congressional committees in advance of any CIA action apart from intelligence collection.

The amendment meant that for the first time Congress had given legislative recognition to the CIA's covert action function and, while limiting it, was accepting it. Secret operations were not prohibited: Congress simply wanted to know about them. This provision resulted in wholesale leaks of information given to the committees by the CIA, either through the members of the committees or their staffs. It also signalled a much tougher attitude towards alleged wrongdoers, as Richard Helms found to his cost.

During the confirmation hearings for his nomination as Ambassador to Iran in February and March 1973, Richard Helms had testified that the CIA had not tried to overthrow the Allende government in Chile. However, the Track I and Track II plans to remove Allende were revealed by Colby to the House Subcommittee on Inter-American affairs. This contradicted Helms' testimony and led to Helms being prosecuted on misdemeanour charges. When he appeared in court in October 1977, Helms, as part of a deal he had made with the Justice Department, pleaded *nolo contendere*, not admitting his guilt though being subject to conviction. He was fined $2000 and given a two-year suspended sentence. After he left the court, he went to the Kenwood Country Club, in Bethesda, Maryland, where four hundred retired CIA officers gave him a standing ovation and within minutes collected cheques and cash to pay the fine: to them Helms was a hero for having kept the secrets.

The result of increased Congressional oversight meant that very few covert operations were proposed and the agency retreated more and more into its analytical work. Ford disliked this development, and blamed the revelations and Congressional inquiries for an emasculation of the US intelligence capability:

Anytime you tell some 200 people in Washington DC the details of a 'secret' operation, the odds are overwhelming that they'll be in the media soon. Rather than risk exposure and embarrassment, the intelligence agency will simply decide not to undertake the operation it planned. That's what happened to the CIA.[4]

# 16
# CARTER

J immy Carter was a complex, insecure man whose personal virtues rapidly became vices in a presidency dogged by major international problems. He was naïve. As the small-town peanut farmer from Plains, Georgia, he won the 1976 election on an anti-Washington platform, the Washington of what he called the three national disgraces: 'Watergate, Vietnam and the CIA'. He emphasized political purity and openness in the face of sordid compromises and hucksterism. He was also quite ignorant about important areas of US policy, notably international affairs, seeking to remedy gaps in his knowledge by swotting up vast quantities of facts and data. His ignorance made him insecure and he was reluctant to delegate, thus increasing his workload.

The strain soon told. The presidency is a wearing enough job at the best of times but Carter aged more rapidly than most. He was hardworking and well-meaning but these qualities were not enough to meet the crises of his presidency.

The early 1970s witnessed a series of intelligence failures – failure to predict the 1973 Yom Kippur war, the 1973 OPEC oil embargo, the nature of the 1974 Portuguese revolution, to monitor effectively India's testing of a nuclear device in 1974, and the 1974 Turkish invasion of Cyprus. Such failures mushroomed during the Carter administration, partly because of the shocks the agency had endured since 1974, partly because of Carter's distrust of the agency which in turn seriously affected morale, and partly because of divisions in Carter's approach to foreign policy and intelligence.

Carter did not understand intelligence and saw its product in the strictly narrow terms of order-of-battle detail. His first choice as DCI was Theodore Sorensen, a Kennedy aide who did not impress Congress. Sorensen withdrew his nomination, and Carter's next choice was Admiral Stansfield Turner who had been in Carter's class at Annapolis Naval Academy.

## TURNER

Turner had come to Washington in the 1950s. He had been a liaison officer between the Navy and the State Department. He loved the whole milieu and caught what he called 'Potomac fever', determined to return to Washington to become an insider in the circles which so fascinated him.

From the start Turner's relations with the CIA were antagonistic. One of his first and most urgent concerns, he announced, was 'to put the CIA's much criticized past behind us', thus ignoring the work of Colby, Church, Ford and Bush. He took a critical view of Bush:

> He was tops for CIA people. They loved him. He was just the kind of director they want. He did exactly what they wanted him to do. They run the agency. That's what I came up against. But I can't run anything without being in charge. The place was a shambles in administration and needed somebody to take charge of it, and they didn't want that.[1]

Turner did take charge, bringing with him a number of naval aides. A White House adviser at the time recalled:

> One of Turner's problems was that he was a military man and didn't like anybody looking over his shoulder. I often said to him, 'Stan, you've never run an operation. I have, and let me tell you, when somebody gives orders that don't make any sense you have to do what's best for the operation. It's important to have people who know about the business.'[2]

Within the CIA, Turner soon became the most unpopular DCI in memory, easily overtaking James Schlesinger. He made it clear to the agency in no uncertain terms that not only was it a shambles organizationally, but that in his view it was a disgrace. Every CIA officer who dealt with him felt that he made up his mind without paying attention to anything they said or what the consequences might be. He concentrated on technical intelligence and dismantled what was left of the clandestine service: 820 positions were abolished, including those of approximately 200 experienced covert operations officers and more than 600 back-up officers and staff in covert action and espionage.

While it was true that the agency had become bloated because of Vietnam, and that reductions were necessary, Turner's managerial style made the dismissals

Three former DCIs – Richard Helms, George Bush and James Schlesinger – attend Admiral Stansfield Turner's swearing-in as director on 9 March 1977. Bush had pressed Carter to keep him on as DCI, arguing that the post should be depoliticized and not change with a new president, but Carter disagreed.

President Carter's National Security Adviser Zbigniew Brzezinski (left) and Stansfield Turner, Director of Central Intelligence (1977–81), laugh together following a 24 January 1978 presidential decision giving Turner control of the US intelligence budget. Behind the scenes, Brzezinski and Turner did not get on.

extremely bruising to those concerned.

Turner's emphasis on technical intelligence meant that during his directorship the technical experts were pre-eminent. He believed that those on the clandestine side, who relied on human intelligence, were living in the past and had simply never come to terms with change, explaining:

> The 'human' people have not understood the revolution in intelligence collection brought on by the technical systems. It means they have got to change. You can't have this enormous flow of data coming into the system without it changing the way you go about all your intelligence. One, you never send a spy when you can get the information you want by technical means. Two, you now focus the human collector on the missing pieces: there's always going to be an element that isn't obtainable by the technical systems. But that means that you recruit differently and that you target differently, and they're not willing to do that.[3]

The tensions within the agency were exacerbated by Turner's extensive use of the polygraph or lie detector which he regarded as 'the most important specific tool of counterintelligence'. It was used for screening applicants seeking employment in the CIA as well as for periodic, unscheduled retesting of employees. But Turner also attempted to have the use of the polygraph applied to civilian contractors and to certain other government personnel. While the value of the polygraph was recognized by agency officers, Turner's over-reliance on it had a very unsettling effect on agency morale. One officer who left during Turner's time as DCI found that polygraph information from his CIA file was leaked to the *New York Times*.

There was a fundamental weakness in Turner's approach. The issue was not human versus technical intelligence: what was needed in the aftershocks of Watergate, Vietnam and the OPEC embargo was clear-eyed assessment of an unsettled world and the US role in it. What happened instead during the Carter administration was a retreat into neo-isolationism in a search for old certainties. Turner's systems and machines seemed to provide a kind of certainty. Time would show how fragile it was.

## NATIONAL INTELLIGENCE OFFICERS

When intelligence producers have a general feeling that they are working in a hostile climate, what really happens is not so much that they tailor the product to please, although that's not been unknown, but more likely, they avoid the treatment of difficult issues.[4]

This comment was made by John Huizenga, the last director of the Office of National Estimates. It was an accurate reflection of the difficulties faced by the analytical side of the agency during the 1970s.

There was a complete overhaul of the estimating side of the CIA while Colby was DCI. By June 1973, the membership of the Board of National Estimates had dropped from an average of twelve to six. Colby felt that the process of estimates by committee had become increasingly unwieldy, inflexible, and inexact. He wanted to make the agency's analysis more immediate, faster and less academically conscious. He decided to replace the board with specialist national intelligence officers who would enjoy a free run of the agency's information.

National intelligence officers would be familiar with all aspects of their area of responsibility. Thus the NIO for the Soviet Union would deal with the Soviet economy and with Soviet military capabilities, whereas previously at least two officers would have been responsible, one for the economy, and one for military matters.

An important result of the new NIO system was that there was far less emphasis on achieving consensus. Dissent was incorporated in the text rather than footnoted. Each NIO had a strong interest in maintaining his reputation by writing clear and effective estimates. And since NIOs were not hamstrung by committees, they could respond to events more quickly.

## IRAN

There was a painful symmetry about the fact that the event which sealed the fate of the Carter administration was the Iranian revolution of 1979. In 1953, the CIA had overthrown Mussadegh and replaced him with the Shah. In 1973 the Shah was one of the leaders of the OPEC embargo, yet he was supposed to be America's friend with a CIA man, Richard Helms, as US Ambassador in Tehran.

Both the CIA and the State Department were slow to realize the extent of domestic opposition to the Shah's ruthless economic and social modernization programme. Most of the agency's activity in Iran was concerned with monitoring Soviet missiles and communications. It paid little attention to reporting the domestic situation, which was left to US diplomats. By late 1978, it was clear that the Shah was facing a revolution, and the Carter administration had been caught on the hop. It was an intelligence failure of epic proportions and was aggravated by vacillation on the part of the White House.

Carter had a see-sawing relationship with his Secretary of State, Cyrus Vance, his National Security Adviser, Zbigniew Brzezinski, and his DCI, Stansfield Turner. Vance and Brzezinski were often at odds, Vance taking a softly-softly approach and Brzezinski adopting a resolutely hard-line approach towards the Soviet Union. Carter veered from one to the other, never deciding between the two. Turner, for his part, concentrated on technical intelligence development and on rooting out secrets that had not been revealed during the Rockefeller, Church and Pike period. He was also faced with Brzezinski as a major bureaucratic rival. These disagreements and lack of coordination permeated the handling of crises in the Carter administration.

When revolution broke out in Iran at the end of 1978, culminating in the return of the Islamic fundamentalist Ayatollah Khomeini in February 1979, Carter could not decide whether to support the Shah or the new leader. One of the reasons for his indecision was the lack of intelligence about the situation in the country. Gary Sick, the Iran specialist on the NSC, declared as the crisis broke:

> The most fundamental problem at the moment is the astonishing lack of hard information we are getting about events in Iran ... This has been an intelligence disaster of the first order. Our information has been extremely meagre, our resources were not positioned to report accurately on the opposition forces [or] on external penetration.[5]

The consequences of the investigations and of Turner's emphasis on technical intelligence and the agency's and State Department's taking too much on trust from the Shah were coming home to roost, encouraged by a nervous White House. On 11 November 1978 Carter sent a note to Vance, Brzezinski and Turner, indicating his dissatisfaction with the standard of political intelligence:

> To Cy, Zbig, Stan: I am not satisfied with the quality of our political intelligence. Assess our assets and as soon as possible give me a report concerning our abilities in the most important areas of the world. Make a joint recommendation on what we should do to improve your ability to give me political information and advice. J.C.[6]

Supporters of Ayatollah Khomeini occupied the US Embassy in Tehran on 4 November 1979, blindfolded and shackled the sixty-nine diplomats, Marines and staff, and separated the women (here being led out of the embassy). They demanded the extradition of the Shah, then in the United States receiving treatment for the cancer that killed him, in exchange for the hostages.

The consequence of depending on machines and thus not hearing the tone of voice and the nuances of information was at last slowly being recognized by Carter. Turner, however, suspected that the note was aimed at making him and the CIA a scapegoat for the intelligence failure.

In November 1979, eight months after the Ayatollah established a virulently anti-American, anti-communist Islamic revolutionary state, the exiled Shah was allowed to enter the United States for cancer treatment. Islamic militants reacted by occupying the US Embassy in Tehran, holding hostage sixty-nine diplomats, marines and staff. Although Khomeini released sixteen women and blacks, the remaining fifty-three, including three CIA officers, were confined for 444 days.

The agency was criticized for not seeing the danger of the embassy being occupied. The CIA station chief in Tehran, Thomas Ahern, successfully managed to destroy CIA files when the militants invaded the embassy. However, most of the military attaché's papers were captured, some of them naming sources within Iran, and the shredding machine used by Ahern made it possible for his files to

Sheikh Sadegh Khalkhali, Iranian Islamic Revolutionary judge, inspecting the remains of the US Special Forces C-130 transport and one of the helicopters that crashed in the Great Salt Desert 190 miles south-east of Tehran in April 1980. The crash forced the abandonment of a mission to rescue the embassy officials being kept hostage in Tehran.

be painstakingly reconstructed.

In April 1980, six months after the embassy was seized, Carter authorized a secret military rescue mission to release the prisoners. The CIA was only peripherally involved. All the weaknesses of technical intelligence were evident in this mission. There was no CIA network of agents in Tehran, and this meant that information gathering at a very basic level was slow and difficult. The USA was forced to rely on reports from British and Canadian diplomats. They played an instrumental part in the intelligence side of the crisis. It was only at the end of December 1979 that a former CIA agent was brought out of retirement and sent to Tehran.

No room was allowed for error or loss in the rescue mission. Carter, who insisted that the rescue mission be as small as possible, did not realize that by insisting on accuracy he was increasing risk. If one element failed, the whole mission would be in danger – which is exactly what happened. Two helicopters crashed into a transport plane, killing eight soldiers and the mission was aborted.

# COMING TO TERMS WITH SECRECY

To many, Iran, the change to the NIO system and the hostility of the President were symptoms of the inexorable decline of the agency. Bureaucratically, the agency was no longer preeminent in the intelligence community either at home or abroad. The DCI was only nominally the President's chief intelligence officer: the real power now lay with the National Security Adviser and the NSC. The creation of the NIOs was an implicit slight on the CIA's analytic performance.

The decline of the agency's power and influence was compounded by attitudes within the administration. Carter's adoption of a noisy human rights policy was all froth and no substance, while Turner's dependence on technical intelligence meant that the element of human surprise and fallibility was dangerously discounted.

There was a very strong feeling in governing circles, by the late 1970s, that all the disclosures and revelations about the CIA had gone far enough. Carter and Turner confused temporary disaffection with the CIA with a settled popular determination not to have secrecy. In Congress, many senators and representatives were concerned by Carter's ineffectiveness and his emasculation of the CIA and once again special care was taken in appointing qualified chairmen of the relevant committees. It was a sign that Congress wanted to come to terms with the CIA and with secrecy.

The Iranian crisis ultimately consumed the Carter presidency. By a combination of bad luck, bad judgement, vacillation, pushing the CIA to the edge of the administration, and lack of clear objectives, the President and his advisers were seen to have brought the USA to a position of international weakness. What had actually happened was different. Carter had come in with an idealistic view of the United States, of its world role, and of the possibilities of détente with the Soviet Union. He found that much of what he had thought of as wrong and 'evil' was not. By the end of his administration he had completed a policy U-turn, approving major increases in military spending and approving more CIA covert action than had Ford. But politically he had missed the boat. The seizure of the embassy in Tehran and the failure of the rescue mission sealed his fate as a one-term President.

# 17
# REAGAN
## *1981–1988*

T he filmstar, John Wayne, died in 1979. In October that year the *Reader's Digest* published an article, 'The Unforgettable John Wayne':

Who can forget the climax of [*True Grit*]? The grizzled old marshal confronts the four outlaws and calls out: 'I mean to kill you or see you hanged at Judge Parker's convenience. Which will it be?'

'Bold talk for a one-eyed fat man,' their leader sneers.

Then Duke cries, 'Fill your hand, you sonofabitch,' and, reins in his teeth, charges at them firing with both guns. Four villains did not live to menace another day.

Ronald Reagan was recalling this evocative scene from *True Grit* in a tribute to his old friend. A year later, Reagan was elected president of the United States.

The tribute encapsulated Reagan's own gut feelings. After the disasters of the 1970s there were many Americans who felt that the USA was pitted against a world of jeering outlaws. Reagan felt that during the 1970s his country had lost its way and its sense of purpose. Like his old friend Duke Wayne he would prove that America could find itself, and its purpose, again.

For all his campaign statements about making America great again, Ronald Reagan was actually far less belligerent and activist than he sounded. It was not that he did not mean what he said – he did – but when he came into office he found that the world, and America's role in it, was far more circumscribed and complicated than the black-and-white years of the early Cold War which had a formative influence on him.

Reagan believed strongly that the foreign policy disasters of the Carter years were due to mismanagement and weakness at the highest levels. The poor performance of the agency had become a focal issue for Reagan supporters, in a way quite different from Jimmy Carter's views four years earlier. The Committee on Present Danger, formed by Paul Nitze and other members of the Team B group which had reviewed CIA analysis of Soviet strategic forces in 1976, and the Madison Group of young Washington insiders, felt that the CIA needed support rather than criticism. They considered that its operational effectiveness had been impaired by Carter and Turner. Some Reaganites also thought that the agency had lost its objectivity and become too partisan on the Soviet question in the late 1970s, but this was a separate issue.

When Reagan took office in January 1981, he had two objectives with regard to the CIA: to restore its morale and operational ability, and to make it once again a can-do, energetic organization.

## TRANSITION TEAM REPORT

During the change of administration hand-over teams were at work in all government agencies and departments. They consisted of new administration advisers who consulted with the outgoing leadership and senior staffers. Because the CIA was the focus of so much concern, the Reagan transition team dealing with the agency was considered to be especially important. The head of the team was a Reagan loyalist, Bill Middendorf, but most of the work devolved on Lieutenant General Edward Rowny who had resigned from the Army over the SALT II negotiations. The other members of the team included Ed Hennelly of Mobil Oil, a friend of Reagan's DCI-designate William Casey; three former CIA officers – John A. Bross, Walter Pforzheimer and George Carver; and three staff members from the Senate Intelligence Committee who were all supporters of the Madison Group and the Committee on Present Danger – Angelo Codevilla, Mark Schneider and Kenneth deGraffenreid. Casey also sat in on some of the team's deliberations.

The final report of the transition team proved so sensitive that the CIA sent its only copy to the White House for safekeeping. It was a lengthy, thorough and at times tendentious critique, firmly placing responsibility for the CIA with the policymakers. Drafts of its arguments included the observation that:

> The fundamental problem confronting American security is the current dangerous condition of the Central Intelligence Agency and of national intelligence collection generally ... [This is] at the heart of faulty defense planning and a vacillating and misdirected foreign policy.

The decades-old rivalry between the State Department and the CIA, and the Nixon-Kissinger détente policy, were two key elements that had determined the CIA's performance. It was emphasized that decisive action at the CIA was 'the keystone in achieving a reversal of the unwise policies of the past decade'.

Reagan's people were looking for failures. Twelve major intelligence failures were identified by a member of the team: (1) the failure to predict the size of the Soviet military effort and military sector of the Russian GNP; (2) the 'consistent gross misstatement' of Soviet global objectives; (3) the failure to predict the massive Soviet build-up of ICBMs and SLBMs; (4) the failure to understand Soviet missile development prior to SALT I; (5) the failure to predict the improvements in Soviet ICBMs in the late 1970s; (6) the general failure to explain the characteristics of Soviet conventional weapon systems and vessels – for example, the Soviet T-64 and T-72 tanks and the new Russian guided missile cruisers; (7) the wholesale failure to understand or attempt to counteract Soviet disinformation and propaganda; (8) the failure to detect the presence of a Soviet brigade in Cuba; (9) the apparent internal failure of counterintelligence generally; (10) Iran; (11) the failure to predict the nature of the 'so-called wars of national liberation' in Africa and Central and South America, and (12) the 'consistent miscalculation' regarding the effect of the massive technology transfer from the West to the East. Some of these alleged failures were debatable and were regarded as legitimate disagreements and matters of opinion.

Much of the transition team's dissatisfaction with the agency's handling of Soviet policy was centred on the Soviet Russia division in the Directorate for Intelligence. Many of its officers could not speak Russian and it was felt that its analysis was poor. Eventually, after much discussion between the CIA and the new administration, the 250-strong division was moved from Langley to a satellite office in Virginia and some of its officers were reassigned.

When it came to technical intelligence collection, particularly satellite photo-reconnaissance, the transition team estimated that the USA was so far behind that the satellite effort required an annual $1.5 billion increase for the next five years to make up lost ground. One of the reasons for this state of affairs was cuts initiated during the Carter presidency, but far more serious was the information disclosed to the Soviets by William Kampiles, Christopher Boyce and Andrew Lee.

## MONEY SPIES

Kampiles, Boyce and Lee spied for money, not ideology. The particular vulnerability of US security lies in the deep-rooted isolationist instinct of the
country. Too many Americans are functionally unaware of the outside world,
seeing everything from a US perspective. Most of the spies who have really
damaged US security have done so for money, often on the assumption that the
USA is so unendangered, so rich and powerful that their spying would not make
any real difference. The Walker family spy ring, exposed in 1985, which provided
Moscow with billions of dollars worth of information about US naval security,
was a case in point.

William Kampiles joined the agency in March 1977, resigning eight months
later after his request to join the clandestine service was rejected. He took with
him a copy of the manual of the *KH-11* satellite and sold it to the Soviets for
$3000. Kampiles was arrested, tried, found guilty of espionage and sentenced to
forty years. Also in 1977, Christopher Boyce, a twenty-two-year-old college drop-
out working as a $140 a week clerk with TRW Corporation, the builder of the
*KH-11* satellites, and a friend, Andrew Daulton Lee, were arrested for selling
secrets to the Soviets. Boyce was sentenced to forty years and Lee to life.

In June 1985, a clerk at Langley was arrested for spying for Ghana: money
and love were her motives. Another case involved Edward Lee Howard, an
agency officer who used drugs and stole money, and failed lie-detector tests when
questioned. He was forced to resign from the agency. He then sold information
to Moscow. He escaped to the USSR in October 1985 just as the FBI was about
to arrest him, and in the opinion of the KGB became one of their most valuable
defectors. He gave away details of the CIA's Moscow station and the names of
several agents, who were interrogated and shot.

## CASEY

William Casey had been one of Reagan's chief campaign managers. He had
wanted to be Secretary of State or of Defense, but those posts went to Alexander
Haig and Caspar Weinberger. At the CIA, having been baulked of his initial
choices for government appointments, he did not want to preside over an
emasculated agency. When he became DCI in January 1981 he was, at sixty-
seven, the oldest man to hold the post. He was also the first (and only) DCI to
be given cabinet rank: a step Reagan took to make up for Casey's disappointment

President Reagan and William Casey, Director of Central Intelligence (1981–7), in the Oval Office. Casey secured improved budgets for the CIA, and set up intra-agency task forces to deal with drugs and terrorists. He was implicated in the Iran-Contra affair, but died before Congressional investigations were completed.

at not being at State or Defense. However, by giving Casey cabinet status Reagan added to his authority as DCI and to the position of the CIA within the intelligence community.

Casey had served with the OSS in London during the war, managing espionage penetration of Germany. Like William Donovan, he came from an Irish-American Catholic background and was a New York Republican lawyer. He was tough and effective, unhaunted by ideals. Though he was intelligent, he was also narrow and conventional in his judgements of people. He wanted to make the CIA a can-do agency, like the OSS of his youth, and he poured resources into the operations side of the house. He was convinced of the need for the CIA, and was a great supporter of the agency. He thought that reducing the effectiveness of the nation's chief intelligence agency had been a prime cause of the trouble America had had with Iran. As a result, Casey made clear that there would be no far-reaching sackings at the agency: it had already endured enough.

Reagan let Casey run the agency much as he wanted. Casey succeeded in gaining Reagan's approval of Executive Order 12333 which allowed the CIA to operate domestically, for the first time, in order to collect 'significant' foreign intelligence as long as it did not involve spying on the domestic operations of US corporations and on US citizens. The order also empowered the CIA to conduct 'special activities' within the USA as long as they were approved by the President and did not involve efforts to influence US political processes, the media, or public opinion. With this order, Reagan was demonstrating that he trusted the agency.

While it was a fillip to agency morale to have a DCI in the cabinet after a decade of friction with the White House, there were mixed feelings about Casey himself. One senior ex-CIA officer who had also been an OSS colleague commented that, 'we pay lip service to the idea of support, for the sake of the agency. In fact Casey is regarded as a bad choice.'

Casey was attended by controversy right from the beginning. During his confirmation hearings his business interests had come under fire. In June 1981, as Reagan's campaign manager, he was suspected of being involved in securing the briefing papers prepared for President Carter for one of the televised presidential election debates. Casey always denied the allegation. When he appointed another Reagan campaign manager, Max Hugel, as Director of Operations, there was huge opposition within the agency since Hugel had no intelligence experience whatever. After a press campaign which alleged improper stock-trading practices on his part, Hugel resigned as DDO. In the middle of these difficulties, several senators made it clear that they would prefer to see Casey's able Deputy Director, Admiral Bobby Ray Inman, as DCI. Reagan, however, remained loyal to Casey. Inman, who was widely credited with securing sizeable increases in intelligence appropriations from Congress, resigned from the CIA in June 1982.

Casey was not comfortable with Congress. He made it clear that he regarded senators and representatives as mere politicians. He read out long statements and made a bad witness. The Senate committees preferred dealing with Casey's deputy, John McMahon, who succeeded Inman.

Because of the Hughes-Ryan Amendment of 1974, Casey had to notify both the Senate and House intelligence committees about covert action. He also had to notify them of any intelligence failures. This was in contrast to the position of the National Security Council which was not dependent on Congress for financial appropriations and whose internal decision-making process was, with the exception of covert action, kept secret from Congress because of executive privilege. This meant that in Reagan's administrations the NSC became the preferred conduit for secret activities since the CIA was too exposed to Congressional and public scrutiny to be used as a really secret presidential instrument.

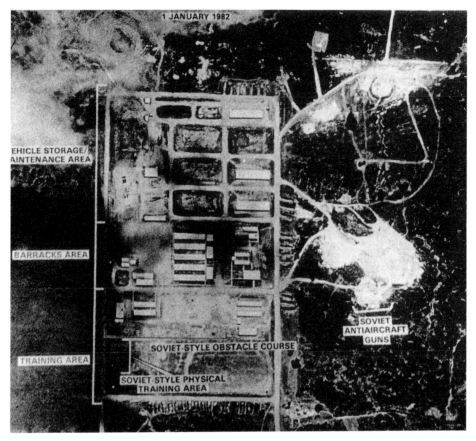

In the 1980s, intelligence was more and more used to secure political and propaganda gains. This CIA aerial photograph of a barracks in Villa-Nueva, Nicaragua, in March 1982, reveals the extraordinary detail available through US spy technology. The release of such photographs was strenuously opposed by the agency, but ordered by the President.

## CENTRAL AMERICA AND AFGHANISTAN

Central America and Afghanistan revealed the limits of the CIA's role in covert operations. Within months of the Marxist Sandinista movement overthrowing the government of Nicaragua in 1979, it looked as if another Cuba had appeared on the US doorstep. Indeed, thousands of Cuban military advisers and technicians began flooding into Nicaragua, followed by Soviet economic and military aid. When the Sandinistas began advising and supporting rebels in nearby El Salvador, Reagan decided to act against them.

Within Congress, however, there was strong resistance to covert action. The Sandinistas had defeated the greedy and corrupt Somoza regime which had bled

223

Eugene Hasenfus, a freelance contract pilot flying supplies to the Contra guerrillas in Nicaragua, being led away to captivity on 7 October 1986 having been shot down by Sandinista forces. At the time it was assumed by the press that Hasenfus was employed by the CIA. Later it became clear that he was not.

the country dry for decades. El Salvador had one of the most brutal and repressive military dictatorships in the history of Central America. The case for US intervention against Nicaragua, despite the Sandinista's links with Cuba and the Soviets, was by no means clear-cut. In December 1982, Congress passed the Boland Amendment forbidding the CIA or the Department of Defense to fund military equipment, training, advice or any other support for operations aimed at overthrowing the Sandinista government.

Reagan fought against the Boland Amendment. He managed to secure substantial aid packages from Congress, including CIA advisers and bases in Honduras and Costa Rica for the anti-Sandinista 'Contras'. But Congress always prevented the direct use of the CIA in Nicaragua itself. Reagan recognized the widespread public reluctance to risk another Vietnam (the fear of which generated support for the Boland Amendment) and he also wished to avoid a fight with Congress since he needed congressional goodwill elsewhere. To avoid public scrutiny, Reagan's approach was to use the NSC staff in the White House secretly to support the Contra movement against the Sandinistas. The furthest the agency could go was to develop proxy operations, where it worked with guerrillas outside Nicaragua, or with the forces of other countries, notably Argentina and Israel.

Afghanistan became the focus for the CIA's largest covert operation since Vietnam although, as in Central America, very few CIA people were actually involved. In 1979 Soviet forces invaded the country in order to prevent the fall of a Soviet puppet regime there. Under Carter, the CIA went into action in support of the Afghan guerrillas fighting the regime. Reagan and Casey ratcheted up the support. Unlike the case with Nicaragua, Congress also supported the Afghan guerrillas and voted $250 million a year in their support.

As a result, not hemmed in by Congressional restrictions and parsimony, the CIA's Afghan operation provided a welcome boost to morale. Although long and gruelling, the Afghan guerrilla war became the Soviet's Vietnam and ultimately played a role in the dissolution of the Soviet empire.

## CHANGING ANALYSIS

The importance of the CIA's analytical work was not neglected by Casey. Within the agency itself, there was criticism of the cumbersome procedures and inertia of the estimating system. One former analyst observed that very few people on the analytical side had military or foreign experience, nor did they understand Washington politics:

> We were babes in the wood out there. Ivory-towered ... We were so far removed from the realities of the world that we looked through rosy glasses. Our analytical record, I am afraid, speaks for itself on this. All too often we underestimated Soviet capabilities and intentions right across the board.[1]

Casey tried to improve the whole process in part by revitalizing the Directorate of Intelligence, and in part by reorganizing the analytical side of the agency on a geographical basis with each area covering the whole gamut of subjects. It was a logical step forward from the basis of Colby's NIO system. Thus area divisions and country and theme desks were amalgamated to conform with NIO subject responsibilities, whereas before there had been a difference between NIO areas and CIA divisions and desks.

There were, however, fears within the agency that Casey, who had been Reagan's election campaign manager, would try to politicize the estimates in line with administration policy. In 1984, the NIO for Latin America, John Horton, a senior and respected analyst, resigned from the agency in protest over what he considered to be Casey's political interference with an estimate on Mexico. What galled Horton, as he later explained, was that it was not the policymakers who were putting pressure on the DCI, but Casey himself who was putting pressure on his own officers to produce reports that accorded with administration wishes. Horton's criticism was taken very seriously in Washington. Casey argued that as DCI the estimates were *his* estimates, and that therefore they should say what he thought.

In general, however, most analysts felt that Casey did not politicize the estimates to any great extent. He was more flexible about including well-argued alternative views, and this was popular with other intelligence agencies. General Daniel Graham, who in the 1960s had worked on Soviet analysis in the CIA, and had then become director of the Defense Intelligence Agency, thought that Casey had 'really lowered the boom on arrogant treatment of other points of view. CIA people now feel that if they've got a point, Casey will take it. It's very encouraging.'

## SPY TRAP

During the 1980s the intelligence community was rocked by a bewildering series of defections, arrests and re-defections which exposed both successes and failures in counterintelligence. In 1981 Ronald Pelton, an employee of the National Security Agency, was arrested for giving away one of the most important US intercept operations, codenamed 'Ivy Bells', which placed listening pods over Soviet underwater cables. He was sentenced to three consecutive life terms plus ten years. In 1984 in Norway, Arne Treholt, the son of a leading socialist ex-cabinet minister and politician, was arrested and later convicted of spying for the Soviet Union. He had been under suspicion since 1979. He was sentenced to twenty years.

The year 1985 was an *annus mirabilis* which left intelligence professionals reeling. In May of that year the Walker family Navy spy ring was arrested. The following month, the CIA clerk who spied for Ghana was arrested. In October, Edward Lee Howard escaped to Moscow. In November, Jonathan Jay Pollard of the Naval Investigative Service was arrested for spying for the Israelis, an act which American public opinion found particularly shocking. Also in November, Larry Wu-Tai Chin was arrested for spying for China since the 1950s. This was the only long-term penetration of the CIA that has ever been uncovered.

In the same month a Soviet defector, Vitali Yurchenko of the KGB, caused a sensation when he decided to go back to the Soviet Union, and this led to considerable criticism of the CIA that they had mishandled Yurchenko's debriefing. Before his re-defection, however, Yurchenko had pointed the finger at Edward Lee Howard.

In addition to Soviet spies inside the US intelligence community, security at the US Embassy in Moscow was causing considerable concern. The building was so riddled with bugs and listening devices that it would either have to be torn down or undergo an overhaul which would cost millions of dollars. In the spring of 1987 at least one of the marine guards at the embassy fell for the time-honoured 'honey-trap': seduced by female KGB agents.

The British fared rather better in 1985 with Oleg Gordievsky, a senior KGB official who was acting resident in London. He defected in June to the British as KGB counterintelligence closed in on him.

Gordievsky had been working for the British since the early 1970s and had held top positions within the KGB both in Moscow and abroad. He had detailed knowledge of KGB operations in Western Europe and North America and of KGB headquarters in Moscow. He was one of the most important spies ever recruited by Western intelligence.

Towards the end of this memorable year Casey pointed out that once the screaming headlines about Pollard and Howard and Yurchenko were set aside, the West was well ahead. During the previous three years, he observed, the Soviets had lost 200 of their intelligence officers who were either arrested or expelled from over twenty countries. They also lost a number of senior officers through defection. 'What rating do you give that combination of factors? I wouldn't mark it very high,' he said. A CIA station chief agreed:

> Two hundred of their officers exposed is an intelligence disaster of major proportions. It means they can never operate in the West again ... All their experience and training has become a waste – they might be able to operate in Third World countries, but that's it. It will take years for the Soviets to replace them.[2]

## TERRORISM

During the 1980s there was a dramatic increase in the range of subjects which US intelligence was expected to address. Of these none was more momentous than the growth of international terrorism, a subject of major concern to the Reagan administration. It was not just that the ethnic diversity of the United States meant that it had links with every country in the world, it was also a fact that Americans and American interests were scattered across the globe and were vulnerable to attack.

Irish, German, Italian, and Palestinian terrorism were facts of life by the time Reagan took office, but the 1980s also witnessed the emergence of overtly terrorist states such as Qaddafi's Libya. One of the first estimates Casey drew up as DCI was on terrorism.

One of the main problems which faced those who drafted and reviewed the estimate was how to define terrorism. Ambassador Lincoln Gordon, to whom Casey eventually went for a decisive estimate, decided to work from what the man in the street thought terrorism was – kidnapping, assassination, blowing up airplanes, hijacking, the bombing of public places, etc. Gordon concluded that while some particular terrorist groups had links with Moscow, these were ambiguous, and it could not be said that Moscow was behind international terrorism.

Casey volunteered the agency for a lead role in counterterrorism, but the reality was always limited. These limitations were never sufficiently recognized by Casey, and this caused a level of anxiety within the agency which was borne out by subsequent events. Counterterrorism was a police or special military function which the CIA could support but not engage in itself without changing its character. The parasitic relationship between terrorists and their host states meant that more than one US agency was required to deal with them. There would also have to be close cooperation with the police and intelligence agencies of other countries, even those of unfriendly countries. The Lebanon was to provide graphic and terrible illustrations of all these difficulties.

The Lebanon was a daunting prospect in 1983, riven by an eight-year civil war involving Maronite Christians, Muslims and Palestinians which gradually sucked in other countries in the Middle East – Syria, Israel and, later, Iran. The USA had become directly involved in 1982 when Reagan sent US forces to supervise the evacuation from Beirut of over 10,000 Palestinian men, but they were unable to prevent Israeli-backed Lebanese forces from massacring thousands of Palestinian women and children left behind in the Beirut camps. In April 1983, the US Embassy in Beirut was destroyed by a suicide bomber from the Islamic Jihad terrorist group, resulting in the deaths of sixty-three people. The bomber had hit the central section of the embassy where a high level meeting of the

CIA's Beirut station was taking place. Not only was the Beirut station annihilated but also several high-ranking officers from neighbouring Middle East stations were killed. Six months later, on 23 October 1983, two car bomb attacks killed 241 US marines and fifty-eight French paratroopers at their headquarters in Beirut.

With the help of Mossad, the Israeli intelligence service, the terrorists responsible for these attacks were traced back to Syria and Iran. For Casey, it was vital to re-establish the CIA's Beirut station and to discover as much about these groups as possible so that effective action could be taken against them. Beirut was the most dangerous posting in the world and Casey needed a highly experienced man. His choice was William Buckley, who had been involved in Phoenix in Vietnam and who had also served important tours of duty in Egypt and Pakistan. Buckley had scarcely started his job before he was kidnapped by Islamic Jihad in March 1984. A photograph of Buckley, taken just before he died under torture, was subsequently released by his captors. Terry Anderson, the bureau chief of Associated Press who was kidnapped just a year after Buckley, was forced to carry Buckley's body from his basement cell after the final torture.

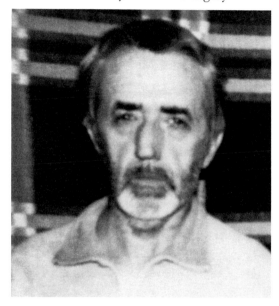

A still of William Buckley, CIA chief of station in Beirut, taken from a video released in October 1985 by his Islamic Jihad captors. Buckley was kidnapped on 18 March 1984, severely tortured, and died in captivity, probably before this video was distributed.

Buckley's kidnapping and murder intensified Casey's desire to hit back at the terrorists. After an attempt to train Lebanese hit squads failed, Casey arranged with a Saudi middle man to carry out a reprisal against Sheikh Mohamed Hussein Fadlallah, a fundamentalist Shia cleric who was believed to have been involved in a number of terrorist attacks. In March 1985, a massive car bomb exploded near Fadlallah's office and killed eighty people, most of them civilians. Fadlallah survived. He hung a banner over the ruined buildings and the human remains: 'The work of the United States.'

The involvement with the murderous world of Lebanese terrorism proved disastrous for the agency. The CIA lost more senior officers, chiefs and deputy chiefs of station there than it had during thirty years in Indochina. Lebanon revealed the dangers of a purely reflexive response to a complex political situation in which terrorism was an important, but not the only, element.

The same was true of the capture of the Palestinian terrorists who hijacked the cruise ship *Achille Lauro* and murdered an elderly Jewish passenger in October 1985. The airplane flying the terrorists out of Egypt was intercepted over the Mediterranean and forced to land in Italy. This was a dramatic and highly public action, demonstrating the depth of intelligence the agency actually had on terrorists, but it also caused the fall of the Italian government and serious domestic problems for Egypt, one of America's closest allies in the Middle East.

Similar problems arose in April 1986 when Reagan ordered air raids on Libya as retaliation against Qaddafi's support for terrorist groups. The raids were opposed by Egypt and US allies in Europe (with the exception of Britain) who feared that they might not only generate sympathy for Qaddafi in the Middle East, but also lead to more ugly terrorist attacks in Europe.

The CIA was not involved in carrying out either of these operations. Significantly, they had been managed by members of the National Security Council staff, in particular Lieutenant Colonel Oliver North of the Marine Corps, who was an assistant to the National Security Adviser, Robert McFarlane. North had played a vital role in the major covert operations of the early 1980s: supplying the Contras, mining Nicaraguan sea lanes, combating death squads in El Salvador, preparing plans for the release by force of the TWA passengers and crew taken hostage by Arab terrorists in 1986.

In the media, the CIA was the focus of attention as far as these covert operations were concerned. People thought that despite all denials to the contrary, and despite the Boland Amendment, the agency was responsible. In fact, this was a smokescreen for the NSC which, unsuspected by Congress or the media, now had an extensive operational capability. This was blown apart by the Iran-Contra scandal.

## IRAN-CONTRA

The Byzantine intrigues of Iran-Contra exposed an administration that was floundering and grotesquely out of its depth in Middle East politics. Senior members of the administration – the Secretary of State George Shultz, and Defense Secretary Caspar Weinberger – had from the start condemned the plan to trade arms with Iran in return for Iranian help in securing the release of people kidnapped in Lebanon, but Reagan and North went ahead. As negotiations with the Iranians became ever more complicated, Robert McFarlane and his successor as National Security Adviser, Admiral John Poindexter, became increasingly nervous and unhappy.

The raison d'être of Iran-Contra was the great feeling of frustration felt by Reagan. By 1985 he had no major foreign policy successes to his credit except the invasion of Grenada and the capture of the *Achille Lauro* hijackers. He had won a second term in 1984 and he was determined to have a glowing foreign policy success to show for it by the end. The proposal to exchange arms for hostages offered a number of dazzling prospects: the release of the hostages, opening up a channel to Iran and developing a pro-American faction there, and last, but by no means least, a way to circumvent Congress by using the money the Iranians paid for the arms to support the Contras.

Because of the high-level opposition to the deal, the CIA, the State Department and Department of Defense were never told the full story. McFarlane kept it within the NSC staff with his assistant, North, in charge. This secrecy within the administration was already working against coordination and control. With the involvement of the Israelis as cut-outs in the arms deals, a further layer of intrigue was added. The middleman to the Iranians, arms dealer Manuchar Ghorbanifar, was devious and unreliable. North and McFarlane never really knew with whom they were dealing in Tehran and whether they could deliver all the hostages. But once the deal-making started, it developed a momentum of its own which blinded the NSC to the mess they were getting into. Some hostages were released, but also new hostages were taken. It was clear that the Iranians and their terrorist friends were using the scheme to blackmail the US government, playing upon the real concern in the White House for the hostages.

How far were Casey and the CIA involved? It is a question that has continued to be asked since the story broke in November 1986. Casey later stated that he was never told the full story and did not know many of the details:

> I don't know everything that occurred on the Iranian side among and between the people who were working with the Iranians. I don't know everything the NSC did. The NSC was operating this thing: we were in a support mode.[3]

This was basically correct. The CIA supplied the planes which transported the arms to Israel. CIA communications networks were used and the agency helped to set up the Swiss bank account into which the Iranians paid money for the arms.

In November 1985 Casey had asked the President to sign a retrospective authorization for any 'prior actions taken by government officials' in the affair. He was anxious that the use of the CIA airplanes might have been illegal. Reagan was reluctant to sign Casey's draft, but eventually signed an authorization for the CIA to support the NSC operation to continue the arms sales. He ordered Casey not to tell Congress about this.

The main question was, when did Casey know about the diversion of the arms money to the Contras? The plan was apparently hatched at the beginning of 1986 but, according to Casey, the first he knew about it was when a former legal client of his, Roy Furmark, who had a financial interest in the arms deals, came to see him on 7 October 1986. Furmark told him that he suspected a Contra connection to the arms sales and advised Casey to check the Swiss bank account of Lake Resources, a CIA front company, into which money from arms sales had been paid. Furmark also said that since the Iranians had withheld payment for the last shipment of arms, leaving Furmark and other underwriters in debt, they intended to take action against the US government to recover their money.

NSC INTELLIGENCE DOCUMENT

Lt. Col. Oliver North testifying to the Congressional Committee investigating the Iran-Contra affair. During the hearings it emerged that many of the activities thought to have been the CIA's were, in fact, North's, operating out of the NSC staff in the White House.

Casey phoned Poindexter the next day to tell him of the conversation, and to warn him that Furmark and his associates were trying to get their money back. He suggested that it might be necessary for Poindexter to prepare some kind of statement for public consumption. Poindexter refused, saying that they were still hoping that some hostages would be released. Casey also contacted North and asked him if any CIA people had been involved in the Contra funding. North assured him that this was not the case.

To be forced to ask North for such information showed clearly that Casey was acknowledging the reality of the diminished responsibility of the agency and the DCI. Either he thought that Reagan's White House people might have asked CIA staff to keep him in the dark, or he thought that it would be too dangerous to ask people in the agency what was going on because they might not know and, in finding out, would leak their findings to Congress and the press.

The operation finally disintegrated in November 1986 when the Iranians leaked the story of US arms for hostages to a Beirut magazine. They had what they wanted – the arms – and by leaking the story there was the added bonus of a propaganda victory against the 'Big Satan', the United States. US allies in Europe were appalled not just by the damage which Iran-Contra did to US interests, but also by the vistas of hypocrisy, naïveté and incompetence with which the transactions were handled. The crafty mullahs in Tehran had outwitted Reagan and his associates with consummate ease.

No one involved emerged with any credit in the subsequent investigations. Reagan came through as lazy and downright mendacious; Poindexter and North were fired, and when they appeared before the Senate intelligence committee, unprecedentedly for US serving officers, they invoked the Fifth Amendment, which enables individuals to refuse to give evidence that might incriminate them.

It was ironic, therefore, that so much suspicion surrounded the role of Casey and the CIA. The two were by no means identical, but some Congressmen were convinced that the operation was the CIA's and that the agency had broken the law. They ridiculed Casey's assertion that the agency's role had merely been one of support. They were ascribing a degree of power and influence to the agency that it had lost over ten years before, after the Church Committee investigations.

The CIA was a victim of its own legend. Shortly after testifying to the House Foreign Affairs Committee in December 1986, Casey collapsed at his desk in Langley. He died five months later of a brain tumour.

Casey's deputy, Robert Gates, was nominated to succeed him. Gates had been promoted by Casey. He came from the analytical side of the agency. He was cautious, professional, institutional, and safe – qualities needed after the amateurs and ideologues of Iran-Contra. But this was not enough for the Senate when his confirmation hearings came up. Republicans controlled the Senate, but they were insulted at the lack of confidence in Congress evident in the Reagan administration. As a mark of displeasure they joined the Democrats and indicated that Gates would not be confirmed. He withdrew his nomination. Two days later, Reagan nominated William Webster, director of the FBI, as DCI.

Webster's brief was to bring the agency on to an even keel. He did not want to be a policymaker like Casey, nor did he believe that the DCI should have cabinet rank. He was solely an adviser. The wheel had come full circle.

# 18

# PAX AMERICANA?

## 1988–

*I*n October 1985 Robert Gates, then the forty-two-year-old Deputy Director of Intelligence, gave a paper to the eleventh convention of the Association of Former Intelligence Officers. The paper was entitled 'The future of the intelligence community' and it examined ten major areas of concern that Gates considered would dominate intelligence to the year 2000. The trends in these areas were, he argued, going to be a mixture of new, specific problems, and a greater complexity of existing ones.

Gates' first trend was the revolution in the way intelligence is communicated to policymakers, particularly electronic dissemination by computer. The second was the increasing difficulty of obtaining necessary data. Soviet camouflage techniques were already reducing the effectiveness of monitoring missile tests and sites. The third trend identified by Gates was the problem of recruitment. There was a decline in the number of suitable potential recruits who could pass the polygraph, the main reason for which being that so many young men and women used or had used drugs. However, once people joined the agency they tended to stay. The attrition rate was less than four per cent, the lowest anywhere in either government or industry. The fourth trend was a revolution in relations with Congress which was playing, and would continue to play, a much larger role in foreign policy. The fifth trend was the use by the executive branch of intelligence for the purpose of public education. Under the Reagan administration, intelligence was published to help win support for presidential policies in the press and in Congress.

The sixth trend, a corollary of the fifth, was the increasing dissemination of intelligence to US allies and others. The seventh prospect already discernible was the dramatic increase in the diversity of subjects which the intelligence community was expected to address, including foreign technology developments; genetic engineering; trends in worldwide food and population resources; religion;

Robert Gates being sworn in at the start of the controversial October-November 1991 Senate hearings into his appointment as Director of Central Intelligence. Gates had been nominated as DCI once before – in 1987 – but had withdrawn when it became clear he would not be approved by the Senate. In 1991 he was successful, with the Senate voting 2:1 for him.

human rights; drugs; terrorism, and high-technology transfers. This also led to a wider range in the users of intelligence right across the Washington bureaucracy. Gates' ninth trend was the growing centrality of intelligence to the foreign policy process of the government. In certain areas, Gates suggested, notably technology transfer, drugs and terrorism, there would be no effective policy without intelligence.

The tenth and final trend was that 'intelligence is the only arm of government looking to the future'. As the world became more complex and as policymakers needed more information, the intelligence community was the only sector of the government which was looking ahead. The community was faced with the constant uphill struggle of trying to convince a policymaker to do something which would benefit the future. It was a problem of democracy's short horizons and brief attention spans which had faced Gates' predecessors and would prove no less pressing to his successors.

Gates defined these new trends in terms of a bureaucracy seeking to identify with the other important government democracies. His imagination was reserved for methodology, not objectives or opportunities.

## CHANGE

Since 1985, the old certainties on which the CIA was founded have shattered. Gates' trends are still valid, but they will operate in a radically different context. The 1991 Gulf War; the withdrawal by the Soviet Union from Eastern and Central Europe; the demise of the Soviet Communist party and communist system; the complete discrediting of totalitarianism of the right and left; time running out for the oligarchs in Red China, and the failed coup in the Soviet Union in August 1991 that led to radical internal reform, were all changes that no one had foreseen even in 1988. The USA is now the only superpower and most of its former enemies are competing for its friendship.

In America, government is more accountable to Congress than it was a decade ago. There has been a sharp decline in the ideal of secrecy, a growing refusal to accept a world of secrets upon which intelligence operations depend. In consequence, an intelligence agency needs to think imaginatively about the future, largely because the complexity of events, and of technology, means that imagination is the most effective tool left to the human brain trying to comprehend developments and possibilities.

## NEW PROBLEMS

The Gulf War capped a string of post-Cold War changes – in Europe, the Middle East, South America, Africa, and the Far East – that have confirmed the United States as ascendant in the world. In turn, this has required a redefinition of US security objectives, and thus intelligence objectives.

Instead of America going home, and the expressions of US power therefore ebbing with the Cold War's end, a Pax Americana – with the support of the Soviet Union and the Gulf allies – has developed. And this has cut across the NATO alliance and the European Community.

In Europe, Germany, labouring under the burden of assimilating its new eastern third, has been totally absent from the Western security debate. Poland and Britain, with strong support from France and the USSR, are endeavouring to consolidate US power in Europe in NATO as the best way of securing the containment of a united Germany.

In the Soviet Union, both Mikhail Gorbachev and Boris Yeltsin have courted the United States as the best friend of their country's future. In Africa there has been a simple capitulation to the reality of Soviet withdrawal. In the Far East, US power is seen as preventing any Japanese military resurgence. Smaller states see US power as a protection against economic domination by larger regional neighbours. In contrast to the Vietnam war, US performance in the Gulf 'has left a very deep impression of competence' according to Lee Kwan Yew, Singapore's elder statesman. Bob Hawke, former Prime Minister of Australia, has said that since 1945 the USA has seen its security commitment in Asia 'primarily as a contribution to its global containment of communism and of Soviet military power', but that this has now changed to a peacekeeping stance.

## MIDDLE EAST

In the Middle East, perhaps the most critical region, the Gulf War jolted every country in the area to compete for US friendship. Now, even Iran seems to accept what Egypt and Israel have long accepted: that the key to the region's future is in Washington. In turn, Washington has encouraged France and the Soviet Union to act as go-betweens in the region. France deals with the PLO because Washington refuses to have official contacts with the organization, and the USSR has brought its influence to bear on its clients in the region, notably Iraq and Syria, to reduce terrorism and hostility to Israel.

The Gulf War demonstrated that US mid-east policy was distorted by the idea that 'my enemy's enemy is my friend'. Iraq had limited US support in the Iran-Iraq war, and it was clearly hoped in Washington that Saddam Hussein would make Iraq an effective mid-east counterweight to Iranian disturbance. Senator Alan Simpson, in April 1990, apologized to Saddam for the way the US media was treating him. It was an example of the US tendency to treat every client as a friend. Iraq, after all, was also a substantial enemy of America's particular friends in the region: Israel, Saudi Arabia, and Kuwait.

The geopolitics of the region involve the world – and Washington politics – today more than ever. The Israeli lobby in Washington is of prime significance, especially given Israeli intelligence's historical ties with the CIA. Before 1967, US oil companies offset Israeli influence in Washington; since then, Israel has dominated US policymaking in the region. This was the real significance of the Iran-Contra affair: conflict between Arab states is of direct benefit to Israel, and Israel's role as a middleman in the arms-for-hostages deals needs to be seen in this light.

The Soviet Union's desire – shared with Czarist Russia – for a warm water port was a cardinal feature of the 1970s and early 1980s, leading Moscow to bid for regional power with its invasion of Afghanistan, its massive military support for Iraq, the Yemen, and Syria, and its attempt to mollify the mullahs in Iran.

Historically, the mid-east is a revolutionary area. One of the central themes of CIA activity in the region was the fear that revolutions (against secular governments; against monarchies; against democratic regimes) would be taken over by the USSR. The fact that this did not take place to any great degree displayed both the incompetence of the USSR, and the strength of local feelings. But the prospect was a US fixation, and it was strongly supported by the Soviet Union's geographic proximity, and its claims and activities which constantly threatened to secure a beach-head in the area. The CIA's (and State Department's) analysis of the region was filtered by these perspectives; its awareness of regional power-play consequences was blunted by Cold War assumptions. As a result, there was a failure to predict the 1990 Iraqi invasion of Kuwait.

It is in this context that the US alliance with Israel needs to be seen. The Israeli connection met the US preoccupation with acquiring a presence in the area in order to prevent the Soviet Union securing regional strength during the early Cold War period when the European empires were vanishing. Subsequently, the US objective of securing oil supplies and preventing Soviet advances, and the Israeli objective of preventing Arab unity against Israel, were both met by playing-off Arab states and securing Israeli power.

The 1990s have witnessed the end of the post-1945 Cold War, but cold war is the ordinary state of mankind, and new cold wars have already commenced. Accountability to the President or to Congress is still an issue for the agency. In 1990 Congress appointed its own Inspector General to investigate the agency from within. But the President still gives the agency its orders.

The CIA predicts the shape of the future with the interests of the United States in mind. The questions for the future include many that have been addressed in the past. Just because there are more democracies in the world today than there were five years ago does not mean that US national security is necessarily more assured. So the agency should be expected to continue to keep its eye on the rest of the world. But new subjects, and new emphases, are already demanding attention.

The Japanese economic and technological challenge has direct security effects. If Japan becomes the sole manufacturer of certain computer chips required for airplanes or rockets, for example, this would impinge upon US security. The question of the Federal government becoming involved in combating commercial espionage is another matter that the behaviour of some Japanese firms has raised. And this, in turn, comes back to the place of secrecy in a democracy: should US taxpayers' money be used by the CIA (or the FBI) to protect commercial secrets of direct value not simply to the country, but to a small number of shareholders? Whether the agency becomes so involved or not, however, President Bush has made clear to it that political, economic and commercial intelligence on Japan is now of utmost importance to the USA, and has imposed this task on the agency as a collection and analytical priority.

Energy supplies; the future of the Commonwealth of Independent States; the likely development of intelligence-enhancing drugs; genetic engineering prospects; secure computer systems; the greenhouse effect (will the sea level rise? Will there be more deserts?); changes in population patterns and the likely consequences; new diseases, particularly AIDS, are some of the new questions. What is manifestly clear is that future shocks are going to be largely economic: commercial competition between nations; international financial transactions; and the supply of raw materials, oil and food.

## NEW WORLDS

Judge William Webster, William Casey's successor as DCI in 1987, resigned to return to private law practice in August 1991. His main tasks had been to reassure Congress that the agency had not been responsible for the arms-for-hostages deals and that it had not broken US law.

Webster succeeded in both these undertakings, but in the process implicitly made clear that DCI was not synonymous wih CIA (William Casey personally, rather than the CIA, was shown to be intimately involved in Iran-Contra), and that the agency was no longer so close to the presidency: Casey's deputy, Robert Gates, observed in 1986 that the CIA was mid-way between the White House and Congress when it came to accountability. The appointment of a congressional Inspector General, and regular congressional scrutiny of agency activity to make sure that the agency was acting within the law had made this the case. In consequence, when a president wanted a covert operation, such as Iran-Contra, or to teach a lesson to the Libyan leader Muammar Qaddafi, he no longer could expect the agency to undertake it.

Recognition of the changing world gave Robert Gates, President Bush's nominee as Webster's replacement, severe problems. Gates had also been Reagan's first choice to replace Casey in 1987. Four years later, once it was plain that Casey had operated largely outside agency channels and that Gates had not been instrumental in any of the arms-for-hostages deals, Bush considered that the way was open for Gates' nomination a second time.

Gates was young – aged 48 in 1991 – and had an impressive career: National Intelligence Officer for the Soviet Union, 1981–2; Deputy Director of Intelligence, 1982–6; Deputy Director of Central Intelligence, 1986–9; Deputy National Security Adviser, 1989–91. He had impressed Bill Casey with his hard Cold War view of the Soviet threat, and his willingness to pursue topics of interest to President Reagan, such as counterterrorism, in ways that also appealed to reigning political sensibilities. He had also impressed George Bush. Bush, who had the politician's desire to advance younger men who would then be dependent on his patronage, found in Gates not only political sensitivity and bureaucratic mastery, but also a desire to have the President as patron.

The backdrop to the 1991 Senate hearings on Gates' nomination was the collapse of communism in the USSR and the disintegration of the Soviet empire following the failed August 1991 coup attempt by hard-liners in Moscow. These elements combined to make the hearings in September and October 1991 the most fraught and revealing ever for a DCI nomination. The world on which Gates had commented in the 1980s had passed away far more completely than had been apparent just weeks previously.

The hearings turned into a battle over old sores in the CIA's analytical side. Casey and Gates had been self-avowed protagonists of a stronger voice for the CIA in US policymaking circles and had also shared classic Cold War views. But many analysts in the DDI, and especially in its Soviet division, took the CIA's traditionally low-key attitude to the USSR. As the A Team/B Team debate in the mid-1970s had shown, they tended to suspect the strength of the Soviet economy and its military capabilities. They were also more positive about the wind of change that Mikhail Gorbachev seemed to usher in during the mid-1980s. Under Casey and Gates, however, their views had often been rejected and ridiculed, and many thought their careers had suffered because of honest analyses. After the failed coup attempt in Moscow, with its signal that the Soviet system had really collapsed, a settling of scores took place in Washington.

Several serving and retired CIA analysts gave evidence that as DDI and then DDCI in the 1980s, Gates had trimmed estimates to serve prevailing political wishes. In particular, he was accused of presenting harsher estimates of the Soviet threat than CIA analysts did in order to please President Reagan and William Casey. Cited in particular was the analysis of the Soviet Union in the mid-1980s, when both the CIA and the Reagan administration depicted Moscow as being dangerously expansionist, and Mikhail Gorbachev as being a flash in the pan, unlikely to have a long-term effect on Soviet society or policy.

Melvin A. Goodman, a former division chief in the CIA's Office of Soviet Analysis with twenty-four years' service in the agency, considered that the review process, whereby divergent views could be accommodated in an estimate, had been subverted. He testified that:

> There were two primary targets for politicization. First, nearly all intelligence issues connected to covert action. That is, the operational commitments that Casey had made regarding Iran, Nicaragua, and Afghanistan. All those issues were politicized. The second area concerned Casey's other major concern, his world view of the Soviet Union. That is, the Soviet Union as the source of all US problems in the international arena. Casey seized on every opportunity to exaggerate the Soviet threat. ... Gates' role in this activity was to corrupt the process and the ethics of intelligence on all these issues. He was Casey's filter in the Directorate of Intelligence. ...

He pandered to Casey's agenda. ... Gates' other contribution was to ignore and suppress signs of the Soviet strategic retreat, including the collapse of the Soviet empire, even the Soviet Union itself.[1]

Harold Ford, a respected thirty-year veteran of agency analysis, concurred, saying that Gates lacked 'integrity of judgment' and that he 'ignored or scorned the views of others whose assessments did not accord with his own'.[2] Jennifer L. Glaudemans, a young analyst who in 1989 resigned from the CIA in disgust at what she saw as slanted analysis, went further:

There was, and apparently still is, an atmosphere of intimidation within the Office of Soviet Analysis. Many, including myself, hold the view that Mr Gates had certain people removed because of their consistent unwillingness to comply with his analytical line ... The only answer I have heard to this perception problem was from Mr Gates himself a few days ago to this committee. He said that when he was a junior analyst, and his views were not accepted, that he too thought this was politicization. Senators, I think that answer is the most smug, condescending, and callous answer to such a sensitive question I could possibly imagine.[3]

Gates successfully fought back, providing chapter and verse to refute specific charges, demonstrating an impressive ability to recall events and to marshal evidence. 'There were a number of unhappy analysts early in my tenure,' he stated, acknowledging the testimony of those opposing his nomination, 'unhappy about too much change from a comfortable, familiar past.'[4] He admitted mistakes:

I think we overestimated statistically how big the Soviet GNP was, giving a false impression of the economic strength they had and their ability to sustain this military competition as far into the future as anybody could see. It was not by trying to underplay Soviet strength but by overestimating it that we erred.[5]

But he could also claim substantial strengths. He had been responsible for a 1983 estimate that said the rate of growth in Soviet military procurement had levelled off and was at zero. This had resulted in a tense battle with Reagan's Secretary of Defense, Caspar Weinberger, who at the time was pressing for a major US military build-up. 'It was not a fun time,' said Gates. It emerged that in 1986 he had convened a group of specialists outside the agency to provide a dispassionate estimate of Soviet capabilities and intentions; that they had reported that in their estimation the Soviet Union was tottering, and that Gates had presented that finding directly to President Reagan. This showed that Gates had not suppressed 'soft' views, and went some way to counter testimony to the contrary. In sum, Gates justified his conduct by constant reference to the record:

> A careful review of the actual record of what was published and sent to policy makers demonstrates that the integrity of the process was preserved. We were wrong at times, but our judgments were honest and unaffected by a desire to please or to slant. Our review process wasn't easy, but it was far from closed ... I was demanding and blunt, probably sometimes too much so. I had, and have, strong views, but ... I am open to argumentation, and there was a lot of that, and I never distorted intelligence to support policy or please a policy maker.[6]

He committed himself to maintaining the integrity and objectivity of CIA analysis. He conceded that there was and had been an atmosphere of fear and suspicion of politicization within the DDI in which he had played an unpopular role, and undertook to try to change this. 'The selection of the head of American intelligence is not a popularity contest', he remarked. 'I sure as hell wouldn't win one at CIA.'[7]

On 5 November 1991, the Senate confirmed Gates as the fifteenth Director of Central Intelligence. He was the first DCI to come from the analytical side of the agency. Under oath he promised to become part of a new beginning in American intelligence, citing his long working relationship with George Bush (dating back to 1976 when Bush had been DCI), acknowledging his position as a presidential favourite, and echoing his stated view that Congress had a strong role in directing the agency:

> The President thinks I'm the right man for the job ... This uncommon relationship between us and his expectations, having himself been Director, offer a unique opportunity to remake American intelligence, and to do so while preserving and promoting the integrity of the intelligence process in a strong and positive relationship with Congress.[8]

For the future, Gates held, a new world order required new approaches that

A morning staff meeting in the Langley Operations Center of the CIA Directorate of Intelligence's Office of Current Production, together with staff from the White House, State Department and the Pentagon, comparing notes on analytical work and research under way.

should be set by 'the President, his senior advisers, and, with some appropriate involvement in the process, the Congress'.[9] He recommended some changes immediately: that the CIA should stop investigating Soviet conventional forces and leave it to the Defense Intelligence Agency to handle; that the resources so released within the agency should be redirected to look at political, social and economic issues in the republics of the Commonwealth of Independent States; that bureaucratic streamlining should occur in those areas where the agency duplicated work being done by others. The 'biggest immediate threat to American security', he declared, was the proliferation of nuclear, chemical and biological weapons, and of ballistic missile technology. Allied to this was the need to keep a close eye on Soviet nuclear forces 'both in connection with the arms-control agreements that have been signed, but also in terms of assuring ourselves that what they are telling us about control of these weapons to the extent that we can determine is in fact true'.[10]

'The Director of the CIA is supposed to keep the game honest', said former DCI Richard Helms about the Gates hearings.[11] This was the real issue. Whatever the intelligence priorities set in the future, it was of the utmost importance to the agency that its analyses should be presented to the President and to policymakers fearlessly and honestly. This was more important than accurately predicting revolution, war and peace around the world.

William Donovan had highlighted the importance of accurate research and analysis to policymaking. The CIA had fought to maintain objectivity, especially during the Johnson and Nixon years. The evidence of Gates' nomination hearings was that in the 1980s, Casey and Gates had made analysis their prisoner, shaping it to support presidential perceptions, with which they generally concurred. If the agency was going to be respected and influential in governing circles in the future, Gates would have to demonstrate that he was immune to political pressure. 'I think if you look at the overall picture of production on the Soviet Union by the agency during this entire period', he said during his nomination hearings, 'it is a period where we got a lot right, we got some important things wrong, but people were basically calling them as they saw them.'[12] In other words, his professional judgement was that mistakes, both his and others', were honest ones. Previous DCIs had been able to manipulate estimates. Gates, as DCI, because of the storm over his past judgements, would have to present agency analyses without any obvious manipulation, keeping his own views carefully separate and not seeking to promote his own beliefs or those of the President. In consequence, he would be in effect a prisoner of the agency.

# US Presidents since 1933

ROOSEVELT, Franklin Delano (1882–1945)  Democrat  1933–7  1937–41
                                         1941–5  Jan–April 1945
TRUMAN, Harry S (1884–1972)[2]           Democrat  1945–9  1949–53
EISENHOWER, Dwight David (1890–1969)     Republican 1953–7  1957–61
KENNEDY, John Fitzgerald (1917–63)*      Democrat  1961–3
JOHNSON, Lyndon Baines (1908–73)[2]      Democrat  1963–5  1965–9
NIXON, Richard Milhous (1913–)[1]        Republican 1969–73 1973–4
FORD, Gerald Rudolph (1913–)[2]          Republican 1974–7
CARTER, Jimmy (James Earl) (1924–)       Democrat  1977–81
REAGAN, Ronald Wilson (1911–)            Republican 1981–4  1984–9
BUSH, George Herbert Walker (1924–)      Republican 1989–92

\* Assassinated   1. Resigned
2. Vice Presidents who took office by succession and not election

# Select Bibliography

PHILIP AGEE, *Inside the Company: CIA Diary*, Penguin, Harmondsworth, 1975.

DALE ANDRADE, *Ashes To Ashes: The Phoenix Program and the Vietnam War*, Lexington Books, Lexington, Mass., 1990.

JAMES BAMFORD, *The Puzzle Palace: A Report on America's Most Secret Agency*, Houghton Mifflin, Boston, 1982, and Sidgwick & Jackson, London, 1983.

MICHAEL R. BESCHLOSS, *May-Day: Eisenhower, Khrushchev and the U-2 Affair*, Harper & Row, New York, and Faber, London, 1986.

MICHAEL CHARLTON AND ANTHONY MONCRIEFF, *Many Reasons Why: The American Involvement in Vietnam*, Hill and Wang, New York, 1978.

MICHAEL CHARLTON, *From Deterrence to Defense: The Inside Story of Strategic Policy*, Harvard University Press, Cambridge, Mass., 1987.

RAY S. CLINE, *The CIA Under Reagan, Bush and Casey*, Acropolis Books, Washington DC, 1981.

WILLIAM COLBY AND PETER FORBATH, *Honorable Men: My Life in the CIA*, Simon & Schuster, New York, and Hutchison, London, 1978.

WILLIAM COLBY AND JAMES MCCARGAR, *Lost Victory*, Contemporary Books, Chicago, 1989.

PETER COLEMAN, *The Liberal Conspiracy: The Congress for Cultural Freedom and the Struggle for the Mind of Postwar Europe*, The Free Press, New York, 1989.

GEORGE C. CONSTANTINIDES, *Intelligence and Espionage: An Analytical Bibliography*, Westview Press, Boulder, Co., 1983.

MILES COPELAND, *The Game of Nations*, Simon & Schuster, New York, and Weidenfeld & Nicolson, London, 1969.

EDWARD J. EPSTEIN, *Legend: The Secret World of Lee Harvey Oswald*, Hutchison, London, 1978, and Ballantine Books, New York, 1979.

WILBUR CRANE EVELAND, *Ropes of Sand: America's Failure in the Middle East*, W. W. Norton, New York, 1980.

LAWRENCE FREEDMAN, *US Intelligence and the Soviet Strategic Threat*, Macmillan, London, 1977.

JOHN LEWIS GADDIS, *Strategies and Containment: A Critical Appraisal of Postwar American National Security Policy*, Oxford University Press, New York, 1982.

JOHN LEWIS GADDIS, *The United States and the Origins of the Cold War, 1941–1947*, Columbia University Press, New York, 1972.

JOSEPH C. GOULDEN, *Korea: The Untold Story of the War*, McGraw-Hill, New York, 1983.

ZALIN GRANT, *Facing the Phoenix: The CIA and the Political Defeat of the United States in Vietnam*, W. W. Norton, New York, 1991.

DAVID HALBERSTAM, *The Best and the Brightest*, Barrie & Jenkins, London, 1972.

SEYMOUR HERSH, *The Price of Power: Kissinger in the Nixon White House*, Summit Books, New York, and Faber, London, 1983.

WILLIAM J. HOOD, *Mole: The True Story of the First Russian Intelligence Officer Recruited by the CIA*, Weidenfeld & Nicolson, London, 1982.

RHODRI JEFFREYS-JONES, *The CIA & American Democracy*, Yale University Press, New Haven, 1989.

WALTER LAFEBER, *America, Russia and the Cold War 1945–71*, John Wiley, New York, 1971.

ERNEST W. LEFEVER AND ROY GODSON, *The CIA and the American Ethic*, Ethics and Policy Center, Georgetown University, Washington DC, 1979.

ALFRED W. McCOY WITH CATHLEEN B. READ AND LEONARD P. ADAMS, *The Politics of Heroin in Southeast Asia*, Harper Torchbooks, New York, 1972.

VICTOR MARCHETTI AND JOHN D. MARKS, *The CIA and the Cult of Intelligence*, Jonathan Cape, London, 1974, and Dell, New York, 1975.

DAVID C. MARTIN, *Wilderness of Mirrors*, Ballantine Books, New York, 1981.

CORD MEYER, *Facing Reality: From World Federalism to the CIA*, Harper & Row, New York, 1980.

JOSEPH E. PERSICO, *Casey*, Viking, New York, 1990.

DAVID ATLEE PHILLIPS, *The Night Watch: 25 Years of Peculiar Service*, Atheneum, New York, 1977.

THOMAS POWERS, *The Man Who Kept the Secrets: Richard Helms and the CIA*, Weidenfeld & Nicolson, London 1980.

JOHN PRADOS, *The Soviet Estimate: US Intelligence Analysis and Russian Military Strength*, The Dial Press, New York, 1982.

JOHN RANELAGH, *The Agency: The Rise and Decline of the CIA*, Weidenfeld & Nicolson, London, 1986, and Touchstone, New York, 1987.

JEFFREY RICHELSON, *American Espionage and the Soviet Target*, William Morrow, New York, 1988.

FELIX I. RODRIGUEZ AND JOHN WEISMAN, *Shadow Warrior*, Simon & Schuster, New York, 1989, and W. H. Allen, London, 1990.

KERMIT ROOSEVELT, *Countercoup: The Struggle for the Control of Iran*, McGraw-Hill, New York, 1979.

JOSEPH B. SMITH, *Portrait of a Cold Warrior*, Ballantine, New York, 1976.

JOHN STOCKWELL, *In Search of Enemies: A CIA Story*, W. W. Norton, New York, 1978.

JOHN TAFT, *American Power: The Rise and Decline of US Globalism*, Harper & Row, New York, 1989.

ROBIN W. WINKS, *Cloak & Gown: Scholars in the Secret War, 1939–1961*, William Morrow, New York, 1987.

DAVID WISE AND THOMAS B. ROSS, *The Invisible Government*, Jonathan Cape, London, 1965, and Vintage Books, New York, 1974.

BOB WOODWARD, *Veil: The Secret Wars of the CIA 1981–1987*, Simon & Schuster, New York, 1987, and Headline, London, 1988.

PETER WYDEN, *Bay of Pigs: The Untold Story*, Jonathan Cape, London, 1979.

DANIEL YERGIN, *Shattered Peace: The Origins of the Cold War and the National Security State*, Penguin Books, Harmondsworth, 1980.

# Notes

## Introduction

1 Ray Cline, *The CIA Under Reagan, Bush and Casey*, Acropolis, Washington DC, 1981, p 141.

2 William Colby and Peter Forbath, *Honorable Men: My Life in the CIA*, Simon & Schuster, New York, 1978, p 87.

3 Victor Marchetti and John D. Marks, *The CIA and the Cult of Intelligence*, Laurel, New York, 1980, pp 237–8.

4 *Sunday Times*, 3 January 1982.

5 *Newsweek*, 26 November 1983.

6 *Daily Express*, 29 March 1985.

## Chapter 1 – **CREATION**

1 In all, there were eight battleships at Pearl Harbor. One, the *USS Pennsylvania*, was in dry dock and was damaged. Another, the *USS Utah*, was a US Navy target ship for naval and air manoeuvres, and was sunk by the Japanese.

2 Interview, Richard Helms.

3 David Bruce, 'The National Intelligence Authority', *Virginia Quarterly Review*, July 1946.

4 Lieutenant General Hoyt S. Vandenberg, Statement before the Armed Services Committee of the US Senate, 27 April 1947.

5 Thomas Troy, *Donovan and the CIA*, University Publications of America, Frederick, Maryland, 1981, p 574.

6 H. Montgomery Hyde, *The Quiet Canadian: The Secret Service Story of Sir William Stephenson*, Hamish Hamilton, London, 1962.

7 Troy, op cit, p 40.

8 Troy, op cit, pp 44–51.

9 Anthony Cave Brown, *Wild Bill Donovan: The Last Hero*, Times Books, New York, 1982, p 161.

10 Bruce, op cit.

11 Interview, Herschel Williams.

12 Interview, James R. Murphy.

## Chapter 2 – **LEGACY**

1 Bruce, op cit.

2 John Ranelagh, *The Agency: The Rise and Decline of the CIA*, Touchstone, New York, 1987, pp 61–4.

3 Joseph F. Lash, *Franklin and Eleanor*, W. W. Norton, New York, 1971, p 666.

4 Richard Harris Smith, *OSS: The Secret History of America's First Central Intelligence Agency*, University of California Press, Berkeley, California, 1972, pp 6–7.

5 Bradley F. Smith, *The Shadow Warriors*, Basic Books, New York, 1983, pp 100–3.

6 Interview, James R. Murphy.

7 Ray S. Cline, *Secrets, Spies and Scholars: Blueprint of the Essential CIA*, Acropolis Books, Washington DC, 1976, p 76.

8 Cave Brown, op cit, pp 271–3; Kim Philby, *My Silent War*, MacGibbon & Kee, London, 1968, pp 61–2.

9 Interview, Gerhard van Arkel.

10 Vandenberg, op cit.

## Chapter 3 – **DIRECTORS**

1 Interview, Lawrence Houston.

2 Cline, *The CIA*, pp 130–1.

3 Interview, Richard M. Bissell, Jr.

4 CIA, 'Policy Governing Concurrences in National Intelligence Reports and Estimates' directive, 13 September 1948.

5 Interview, William Bundy.

6 US Congress, Senate Select Committee to Study Government Operations with Respect to Intelligence Activities (hereafter referred to as Church Committee), *Final Report*, Vol. I, p 257.

7 Interview, Richard M. Bissell, Jr.

8 Interview, John Blake.

## Chapter 4 – **FRIENDS?**

1 George F. Kennan, *Memoirs 1925–50*, Pantheon, New York, 1967, pp 547–59.

2 Dean Acheson, *Present at the Creation*, W. W. Norton, New York, 1969, p 219.

3 Interview, Tom Braden.

4 Interview, Tom Braden, *World in Action: The Rise and Fall of the CIA*, Granada Television, June 1975.

5 Cord Meyer, *Facing Reality: From World Federalism to the CIA*, Harper & Row, New York, 1980, pp 99–101.

6 *Time*, 7 May 1956.

7 Quoted in Richard Deacon, *'C' – A*

*Biography of Sir Maurice Oldfield*, Macdonald, London, 1985, p 119.

8 Interview, Ray S. Cline.

### Chapter 5 – **COUPS**

1 John Taft, *American Power: The Rise and Decline of US Globalism*, Harper & Row, New York, 1989, pp 152–7.
2 Interview, R. Jack Smith.
3 Church Committee, *Final Report*, IV, p 62.
4 Tom Braden, *World in Action: The Rise and Fall of the CIA*, Granada Television, June 1975.
5 Interview, Richard M. Bissell, Jr.
6 Thomas Powers, *The Man Who Kept the Secrets*, Knopf, New York, 1979, p 31.
7 Joseph B. Smith, *Portrait of a Cold Warrior*, Ballantine Books, New York, 1976, p 95.
8 Kermit Roosevelt, *Countercoup: The Struggle for the Control of Iran*, McGraw-Hill, New York, 1981, p 18.
9 Interview, Kermit Roosevelt.
10 Interview, Victor Marchetti.
11 Walter LaFeber, *Inevitable Revolutions*, W. W. Norton, New York, 1983, p 107.
12 Leonard Mosley, *Dulles: A Biography of Eleanor, Allen and John Foster Dulles and Their Family Network*, Dial Press/James Wade, New York, 1978, p 347.
13 Ibid, pp 347–8.
14 David Atlee Phillips, *The Night Watch: 25 Years of Peculiar Service*, Atheneum, New York, 1977, p 51.

### Chapter 6 – **CASTRO**

1 William Manchester, *One Brief Shining Moment: Remembering Kennedy*, Michael Joseph, London, 1983, p 120.
2 Harris Wofford, *Of Kennedys and Kings: Making Sense of the Sixties*, Farrar, Straus & Giroux, New York, 1980, p 358.
3 Interview, Richard M. Bissell, Jr.
4 David Atlee Phillips, op cit, pp 102–3.
5 Interview, Richard Helms.
6 Interview, Richard M. Bissell, Jr.
7 Ibid.
8 Ibid.
9 Robert H. Ferrell (ed), *The Eisenhower Diaries*, W. W. Norton, New York, 1981, pp 386–7.

10 David Halberstam, *The Best and the Brightest*, Fawcett Crest, Greenwich, Connecticut, 1972, pp 96–7.
11 Church Committee, *Alleged Assassination Plots*, p 334.
12 Ibid, p 336.
13 Arthur M. Schlesinger, Jr, *Robert Kennedy and his Times*, Futura Publications, London, 1979, p 701.
14 Felix I. Rodriguez and John Weisman, *Shadow Warrior*, Simon & Schuster, New York, 1989, p 169.

### Chapter 7 – **DOMINOES**

1 Hugh Brogan, *The Pelican History of the United States of America*, Pelican, Harmondsworth, 1967, p 672.
2 Archimedes Patti, *Why Vietnam? Prelude to America's Albatross*, University of California Press, Berkeley, 1980.
3 Dwight D. Eisenhower, *Public Papers of the Presidents*, Government Printing Office, Washington DC, 1960, entry for 25 October 1954, p 949.

### Chapter 8 – **WAR**

1 *Pentagon Papers*, p 313.
2 Peer De Silva, *Sub Rosa: The CIA and the Uses of Intelligence*, Times Books, New York, 1978, p 262.
3 *The Pentagon Papers*, p 340.
4 Cline, *The CIA*, pp 225–6.
5 De Silva, op cit, pp 209–10, 230.
6 Marchetti and Marks, *The CIA and the Cult of Intelligence*, p 245.

### Chapter 9 – **FIGHTING**

1 Interview, William Colby.
2 Interview, R. Jack Smith.

### Chapter 10 – **SPIES**

1 William Hood, *Mole – The True Story of the First Russian Intelligence Officer Recruited by the CIA*, W. W. Norton, New York, 1982, p 13.
2 Deacon, op cit, p 131.
3 Interview, Donald Jameson.
4 Samuel Halpern and Hayden Peake, 'Did Angleton Jail Nosenko', *International Journal of Intelligence and Counterintelligence*, Vol. 3, No. 4, 1989, p 462.

## Chapter 11 – **TARGET**

1 Arthur Krock, *Memoirs: Sixty Years on the Firing Line*, Funk & Wagnalls, New York, 1968, p 428.
2 Richard Helms, speech at Donovan Award Dinner, 24 May 1983.
3 CIA, *Estimates of the Effects of the Soviet Possession of the Atomic Bomb upon the Security of the United States and upon the Probabilities of Direct Soviet Military Action*, 6 April 1950.
4 Donovan Award Dinner, 24 May 1983.
5 Interview, Richard M. Bissell, Jr.
6 Interview, Lawrence Houston.
7 Interview, Richard Helms.
8 Interview, Richard M. Bissell, Jr.

## Chapter 12 – **ESTIMATES**

1 *Newsweek*, 28 November 1983.
2 Ibid.
3 Interview, John Huizenga.
4 United States Senate Intelligence Committee, 'Hearings: National Intelligence Reorganization and Reform Act', 1978, p 21.
5 *CIA: The Pike Report*, Spokesman Books, Nottingham, 1977.

## Chapter 13 – **NIXON**

1 Vernon A. Walters, *Silent Missions*, Doubleday, New York, 1978, p 609.
2 Richard Nixon, *RN: The Memoirs of Richard Nixon*, Grosset & Dunlap, New York, 1978, p 351.
3 Ibid, p 352.
4 Interview, R. Jack Smith.
5 Interview, Elmo Zumwalt.
6 Cline, *The CIA*, p 242.
7 Ibid, p 240.
8 Marchetti and Marks, *The CIA and the Cult of Intelligence*, p 12.
9 Church Committee, *Alleged Assassination Plots*, p 246.
10 *The Watergate Hearings*, Bantam/*New York Times*, New York, 1973, p 603.
11 Walters, op cit, pp 590–4.
12 Ibid, p 604.

## Chapter 14 – **TROUBLE**

1 Colby, *Honorable Men*, p 329.

2 Interview, Walter Pforzheimer.
3 Interview, Victor Marchetti.
4 Interview, David Atlee Phillips.
5 Interview, William Colby.
6 Phillips, op cit, pp 262–4.
7 Interview, William Colby.
8 Gerald R. Ford, *A Time to Heal*, Berkley Books, New York, 1980, pp 223–4.
9 Colby, *Honorable Men*, p 400.

## Chapter 15 – **INVESTIGATION**

1 Colby, *Honorable Men*, p 404.
2 Walters, *Silent Missions*, p 611.
3 Interview, R. Jack Smith.
4 Ford, op cit, pp xxv–xxvi.

## Chapter 16 – **CARTER**

1 Interview, Stansfield Turner.
2 Interview, Thomas Farmer.
3 Interview, Stansfield Turner.
4 Interview, John Huizenga.
5 Gary Sick, *All Fall Down: America's Tragic Encounter with Iran*, Random House, New York, 1985, p 90.
6 Stansfield Turner, *Secrecy and Democracy: The CIA in Transition*, Houghton Mifflin, Boston, 1985, p 113.

## Chapter 17 – **REAGAN**

1 Interview, David Sullivan.
2 Interview, Carleton Swift.
3 *Time*, 22 December 1986.

## Chapter 18 – **PAX AMERICANA?**

1 Testimony to the Senate Select Committee on Intelligence, 1 October 1991; reported in the *New York Times*, 2 October 1991.
2 Ibid.
3 Testimony to the Senate Select Committee on Intelligence, 2 October 1991; reported in the *New York Times*, 3 October 1991.
4 Testimony to the Senate Select Committee, 3 October 1991; reported in the *New York Times*, 4 October 1991.
5, 6, 7, 8, 9, 10 Ibid.
11 *Washington Post*, 4 October 1991.
12 Testimony to Senate Select Committee on Intelligence, 3 October 1991; reported in the *New York Times*, 4 October 1991.

# Index